Madonna King is one of Australia's most accomplished journalists, having won awards for her ABC Radio Brisbane *Mornings* current affairs program. She writes across Nine, *Crikey* and *The New Daily*, and is the author of numerous books, including the bestselling *Being 14* (ABIA shortlisted for non-fiction book of the year), *Fathers and Daughters* and *Ten-ager*. She is also the biographer of Australian of the Year Professor Ian Frazer and former treasurer Joe Hockey. In 2018, Madonna served as chair of the Queensland Government's Anti-Cyberbullying Taskforce, set up in the wake of COAG deliberations. A fellow of the prestigious World Press Institute, she serves on a university-related board, and previously served as a visiting fellow at the Queensland University of Technology and on the Walkley Advisory Board. Her website www. madonnaking.com.au provides further detail. She lives in Brisbane with her husband and two teenage daughters.

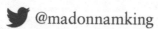 @madonnamking

*Think Smart Run Hard: Lessons in Business
Leadership from Maxine Horne*

Hockey: Not Your Average Joe

Ian Frazer: The Man Who Saved a Million Lives

*A Generous Helping: Treasured Recipes from the
People of Queensland* (with Alison Alexander)

Bali 9: The Untold Story (with Cindy Wockner)

*Catalyst: The Power of the Media and
the Public to Make Change*

*Being 14: Helping Fierce Teens
Become Awesome Women*

*Fathers and Daughters: Helping Girls and
Their Dads Build Unbreakable Bonds*

*Ten-ager: What Your Daughter Needs You to
Know about the Transition from Child to Teen*

MADONNA KING

 **PLATERS**

hachette
AUSTRALIA

Parents in the text are anonymous and the names of children have been changed to protect their privacy.

 hachette
AUSTRALIA

Published in Australia and New Zealand in 2022
by Hachette Australia
(an imprint of Hachette Australia Pty Limited)
Gadigal Country, Level 17, 207 Kent Street, Sydney, NSW 2000
www.hachette.com.au

Hachette Australia acknowledges and pays our respects to the past, present and future Traditional Owners and Custodians of Country throughout Australia and recognises the continuation of cultural, spiritual and educational practices of Aboriginal and Torres Strait Islander peoples. Our head office is located on the lands of the Gadigal people of the Eora Nation.

 A catalogue record for this
book is available from the
National Library of Australia

ISBN: 978 0 7336 4868 7 (paperback)

Cover design by Christabella Designs
Cover photograph courtesy of Roy McMahon / Getty Images
Author photograph by Tyler Alberti
Text design by Bookhouse, Sydney
Typeset in 12.2/18.6 pt Sabon LT Pro by Bookhouse, Sydney
Printed and bound in Australia by McPherson's Printing Group

 The paper this book is printed on is certified against the Forest Stewardship Council® Standards. McPherson's Printing Group holds FSC® chain of custody certification SA-COC-005379. FSC® promotes environmentally responsible, socially beneficial and economically viable management of the world's forests.

To tomorrow's awesome female leaders.
Don't forget to enjoy the journey.

Contents

1   Who am I?   1

2   School rules   20

3   The corona-coaster   41

4   Listen to me   61

5   Friends and family   80

6   Unsocial media   100

7   The anxiety plague   124

8   Please help me: A mental health epidemic   142

9   Growing confidence, growing leaders   164

10   Going places: The bid for independence   182

11   The gender agenda   202

12   Consent and what we all need to learn   220

13   Party scenes   240

14   Finding balance   256

15   Success: A new outlook   275

16   What's next?   291

17   Navigating campus life   309

18   Words of advice   328

Endnotes   343

References   346

Acknowledgements   350

Index   352

1

Who am I?

If life were a smorgasbord, our 16-, 17- and 18-year-old girls would be its grazers. Across arts and culture, careers and passions, friends and social media, they nibble. It won't be Ed Sheeran who draws them in, but the beat or theme of one of his songs, and they'll go looking for more like it – music that makes them feel. 'My music library is random genres and it changes. If the song makes me feel something, it means something,' one 17-year-old says. It's the same with TikTok and the lure of influencers who make them laugh or cry or think. Authors, too, aren't as significant as what they write about. 'It's true even as they think about careers,' social researcher Mark McCrindle says. 'They're the generation of generalists and that's fantastic in a fast-changing world. It gives them options and it means that they can connect and relate to a diverse range of people.'

Diversity has been a stop along that smorgasbord too. 'But they need to know who they are and they need to know what makes their heart beat fast, and they need to start to develop their own particular direction,' he says.

When the smorgasbord is as big as it is, choice is tough. At school, subject options are endless. There is more academic assistance than there has ever been. In downtime, they can choose from a multitude of activities and stream movies from numerous sources. Everything is now. From their bank accounts to their friendship groups, their music library to their meditation apps – they're all packed into the smartphones they cannot do without. They are engaged and global, and wanting to right the world of wrongs. In the schoolyard, these Generation Zs are role models to Generation Alphas in a way schools haven't seen before. They are leaders and shapers and models and protestors and contributors. Ten-year-olds watch them and love it. That mostly makes them good big sisters too. They wear inclusion, as well as their preferred pronoun, as a badge of honour. 'But my question to them is: Inclusive to what?' Mark McCrindle says. They're inclusive and determined and passionate – but often without purpose or direction. Their destination remains elusive.

After 12 months of research, which involved hearing the views of 1000 girls, that's a poignant question. The majority of this cohort can feed on anything from the smorgasbord life has gifted, but making choices is nigh impossible. Too many of them want to be the best – at everything. When principal of Brisbane's Somerville House girls' school Kim Kiepe looks out her office window, she sees girls brimming with aspiration but still deciding who they might be. Comparison is an almighty driver. 'It's like "I have to do what she's doing. I have to aspire to be the best. I want to get that leadership position. I want to be the best at academics. I want to be in the A-grade of netball."' Not every student in Year 11, 12 and 13 (the year given to those in their first year out, irrespective of whether they are at university, TAFE, in the workforce or elsewhere) is like that, but a big chunk are. Still, not all of them can top the class, make the senior debating team or nab the sports leaders' badges. Kiepe, who has worked as a leader in girls' schools in Queensland and Western Australia, draws a comparison with mothers. Any working mother will understand her point. 'We're not super women,' she says. We need to compromise. Her advice to girls is similar: 'Decide what you're going to be good at, and focus on that.' The role of mentors is crucial. Aunts, both real and adopted, surfaced as stellar choices, but so too did parents and teachers and sports coaches. Like their choices in music and careers, these girls see role models in terms of the traits they offer, not the positions they hold. 'Anyone really – as long as they have the attributes I define as a good person,' one girl says. The best lesson a mentor can give these girls is a deep belief that they are 'enough' as they are. It sounds easier than it is.

That push to be 'perfect' became a common thread in my research and it has educators on red alert. Girls who will not hand in an assignment because it's not perfect. Girls recording 92 per cent on a test who focus on how they missed 8 per cent. In their view, they've failed. Comparison is a disease here, delivered 24/7 courtesy of the smartphone they carry in their pocket. It is driving clothes choices and eating habits as much as it is generating anxiety. In some cases, Snapchat surgeries are being sought so a teen can look like the filter on her phone. The irony here is enormous. With infinite possibilities, comparison is funnelling their decisions around looks and activities and dreams. It's narrowing their world. With a thousand viewpoints on offer, they'll mute those they find offensive. With dozens of different pathways forward, for many the ATAR will be the double-digit figure that becomes a single life-determiner. The grass might have been greener on the other side of the fence for their parents but, for this crew, that grass is everywhere, popping up night and day, in their pocket and every time they reach for their device. Off-screen too. 'I aspire to have the qualities of some of my classmates – their popularity, how they study, those little things,' one 17-year-old said. Parenting educator and author Dr Justin Coulson says the almighty girl power they show can vanish in a heartbeat. 'They're incredibly confident in terms of changing the world, saving the planet, having the career of their dreams, but they fall apart at the slightest hint that their body isn't right, or that their boyfriend won't stay with them unless they adopt a more provocative sexual stance,' he says. Linda Douglas, principal of Melbourne's Ruyton Girls' School, raises another irony. Focused on accepting each other as they are, they are brutal in the judgement they mete out to themselves. And the pull of that person with the perfect life on screen is all-encompassing – even though they know the images and videos are doctored.

> *'Being able to see only the filtered versions of others can make me jealous and I don't like feeling that way.'*

> *'It's just natural to compare, even though you know it's not true.'*

Our girls are clever and sassy and thoughtful, and yet that comparison drives everything from the length of eyelashes to active wear focused on their buttocks 'because it's the new look'. 'If it looks good, I'll want to buy it,' says a 16-year-old. 'I don't think anyone else should have an opinion on what others wear. Mum will see someone wearing something I like and say, "Thank God you don't wear that!".' The chasm between generations is just as wide as it might have been for their parents – perhaps wider. This can be difficult for both parent and daughter. 'I see it with my own daughter,' one school principal says. 'She said to me that in relationships I probably never had to look at a boyfriend liking posts of other people.' Her daughter found that confronting. 'It's that comparison thing,' she says. The antidote, no doubt, is a strong sense of self, which many girls find tantalisingly elusive.

So, how do our 16- and 17- and 18-year-old girls see themselves?

> *'I am scared of judgement, or people not caring, or people dismissing my feelings completely.'*
>
> *'I don't know who I am. I don't judge people. It's really, really hard to know someone else and to understand someone else. I don't understand myself often.'*
>
> *'I'm trying to find out. Aren't we all?'*

I feel as though I know these girls well. A couple of years ago, when they were 14, I researched a book called *Being 14*, which showcased that bumpy age for girls. Now those same girls are in senior school and leaving school to take their place in the world. Some of the challenges that popped up in those early teen years are now entrenched. Body image. The search for perfectionism. Their brutal self-judgement. A wonderful ability to accept difference. That acceptance of others stands out to Deborrah Francis, head of senior girls' wellbeing at St Margaret's Berwick Grammar in Melbourne. She is of Indian heritage and remembers crying as a teenager when her peers accused her of not showering because of her darker skin. Her children have never faced that racism. 'They value diversity,' she says of the current generation. 'They don't put labels on things as we do. And that's what I've learnt – they look more to personality, to what you're bringing to the table rather than what you look like.' Francis says her wish for this cohort is to find 'a sense of purpose' not only associated with education. She wants them to discover the joy of finding out who they are, what strengths they harbour and how they can contribute to the world. 'I worry that they will be missed. Parents are busier than I've ever seen, schools are taking on more and more responsibility to nurture, to provide social and emotional (support) for these young minds. And I'm so worried we'll miss one,' she says.

'I would describe myself as someone who is kind yet blunt and honest. I'm humorous and sarcastic. Sometimes that's taken the wrong way. Most of my friends understand that; but some don't.'

'I'm a child. I'm not technically an adult. But I'm expected to be an adult. It's constantly belittling me as a human being – not as a 17-year-old. And it's confusing. You have to know what you want to do but are still treated like a child.'

These teens are fearful of the future and of climate change, and wish their voices were louder. 'We are not being heard,' one says. 'Climate change. Animal rights. Refugees. The education system. We're 16 so our opinion doesn't matter.' They want to be at the decision-making table and, despite not being able to vote, don't understand the enormous influence they wield via social media channels. The ironies are endless. On average, they spend three hours on their smartphone on a school day, but know it is keeping them awake at night and moulding everything from how they dress to how they think. They define success differently from many of their parents, eschewing big jobs and bigger houses. For them, success equals happiness, or simply being content, yet they will worry themselves sick over a maths exam. They understand the importance of their mental health, but will push it back behind a host of other priorities. They are a generation of generalists and they want to find their own space. They eschew traditional categories but are insistent on being categorised. 'That's why these new words keep coming up,' one school counsellor says. 'LGBTQIA+ . . . so everyone has a category. Adults don't understand how important that is. It's a way of describing how they feel. If you define yourself or you identify as this – then you can find people who are like you.'

What's their biggest challenge? The same answers – drawn from 1000 teens – pop up repeatedly. 'Trying to find a position in life where I feel happy, healthy and productive in spite of the pressures I face,' one says. And that view is mirrored by hundreds of others. The pressures of self-doubt. Meeting their own expectations. Anxiety. Anxiety. Anxiety. 'The biggest challenge I face is trying to get up and go to school. Every day I find myself struggling and panicking,' a 17-year-old offers. 'Knowing who I am – I haven't been able to explore that.' Gender identity is raised repeatedly, as is the struggle within school grounds over the use of pronouns, names, unisex toilets and uniforms. 'I just want to feel understood.' Opinions are black and white, and those who don't reflect their views can be ostracised. Yet everything else is 100 shades of grey. 'I really struggle with mental health challenges,' one 16-year-old says. 'I am not diagnosed with anything like depression or anxiety, which makes me feel really confused and left in the dark because I know that I struggle quite badly – but I don't have any real issues, which can mess with me quite a lot.' Time management. External exams. Finding friends who will endure. Imposter syndrome. Living up to others' expectations. ATAR. ATAR. ATAR. Body image. The end of Year 12. The future.

That huge ogre COVID-19 hasn't been a definer as much as the uncertainty it has brought with it. For better or worse, the long drawn-out lockdowns in Melbourne, yo-yo border closures, intermittent lockdowns in many other states, online learning, minimal social interaction, separated families and the unpredictability around it all will colour this generation for years. Lockdown days turning into weeks and then months stole the motivation of many, including ambitious young women who had hoped to study medicine and law and economics. In Melbourne, they told me they just wanted certainty. For others – and not just in Melbourne – lockdowns provided a gift. Sleep-ins. Reduced anxiety. Fewer friendship issues. Some girls felt less on show, and they liked that. 'Being away from the judginess and gossip at school in COVID makes me feel secure and unbothered,' one says. Toni Riordan, principal of St Aidan's Anglican Girls' School in Brisbane, says it struck her that many Year 12s were more 'accepting of disappointment'. She says parents found it difficult, though, because they had mapped out a pre-COVID plan of what they wanted for their teen's education – and COVID took that away. But don't underestimate the influence of this pandemic, either. Experts told me that. So did the girls.

'I'm so lonely. I had no one to talk to during lockdown.'

'I haven't seen my dad in 10 months. He's in Canada.'

'COVID has changed everything. I feel like most people have withdrawn from socialising with friends. I feel isolated. I've lost most motivation with schoolwork despite having always been really on top of [it] until lockdown.'

'I'm a hands-on learner. It was SO hard. I'm social too and I couldn't see people.'

'It feels a bit pointless. I had to do exams online. That was not fun. It was all open book, but we had to keep cameras on. It was so much effort and it didn't feel real in a way. It was like homework.'

'I value my family a lot more. I've got a lot closer to my mum and dad. It's also shown me who my true friends are. They still talk to me. At school, they were only talking to me because they were in front of me.'

'We have been forgotten. It was fair for Year 12 last year to be really helped. But we have missed out on that love. Our Year 11 was kind of ruined and so was our Year 12. They were the test dummies, so everyone was helping them more than us.'

That last comment was common from girls who graduated in November 2021; they believe the 2020 graduates were given bucket-loads of academic assistance and under-standing. They believe ongoing lockdowns prompted teachers and parents to adopt a 'get on with it' approach, despite having graduations and formals, Year 12 trips and 18th birthdays cancelled. This year, many of them will be in their first year of university, navigating new courses and new friendships, on and off campus.

'Over time I have had less online contact with people so now no one ever sends me messages unless I send one first. It basically means I don't talk to anyone but my

family. It has also made uni hard as practical, hands-on experiences and learning are a big part of my degree. It makes me doubt I'll graduate with the skills I need.'

That first year of university, or work, or TAFE – commonly now called Year 13 – has been a tricky one, navigated during a pandemic where jobs were lost and isolation was sometimes overwhelming. University lessons were flipped, and thousands continue to do assignments and tutorials and lectures from their bedrooms. The impetus for this book came from one concerned mother, whose daughter never left her room. Lessons and relationships both moved online. She wondered about the impact of isolation on her daughter. Mark McCrindle says the dismantling of so many structures has made it difficult for this generation to find direction, purpose and belonging. This mother could see that. And so can universities, who are being forced to reassess their models of operation after international student arrivals were stopped and campuses emptied.

Asked to describe 16-, 17- and 18-year-old girls, Brisbane Girls Grammar school associate dean of wellbeing Jody Forbes answers immediately. She lives and breathes this cohort. Curious and anxious, bright, funny, happy, polite, thoughtful, caring and complex. 'Many internalise, ruminate and suppress their emotions. While they like to challenge and question rules, they typically avoid conflict and repel awkwardness.' Many educators say teens can struggle with nuance. 'So when you make a joke, they don't know whether you are serious or not and then there's this awkwardness,' Brisbane's Corinda State High School executive principal Helen Jamieson says. 'They don't know how to take you.' This is a real difference from their parents' generation, where many were raised on humour and sarcasm and banter. 'Are they too delicate?' another educator asks.

Jamieson, who has run schools for 25 years, starting as a principal at the age of 30, sees significant changes in teens' development over that time. 'Society has become more complex. And that is impacting teenagers because of social media. There is no filter anymore. They see it all. They hear it all and their underdeveloped brains are still going through that rapid change. It's very confusing for them,' she says. She sees them as younger now in terms of resilience and self-talk, but more mature socially, because of the adult material they're exposed to. 'And I think that's what throws the whole confusion into the mix,' she says. Certainly, while some are confident others lack assertion and are prone to worry. And as they move through secondary school, they engage in less exercise and sleep less. Rather than misbehave, our girls are more likely to want to do well: they strive to please their parents and teachers, and some strive for perfection. That word again.

Kellie Lyneham is the head of senior school at Carey Baptist Grammar School in Melbourne, responsible for 900 students across Years 10, 11 and 12. What keeps her awake at night? 'I worry about how they are so "on" all the time, and unless they're self-disciplined or their family creates a space for them to switch off, they're constantly engaged with others and therefore constantly concerned about what could and couldn't go wrong,' she says. That brings the conversation back to these girls believing they are 'never quite good enough at anything' – because they are measuring themselves against others and unrealistic online benchmarks. Brisbane's Clayfield College principal Dr Andrew Cousins says he worries how comparison drives 'feelings of inadequacy' because girls are choosing 'the best bit of a whole heap of things to come up with an idealised view of what [they] should be like'. And rather than drawing on their attributes, they move to a 'deficit model'. Teachers say this too. 'It's "Where did I lose these three marks?", not "Oh, I got 17/20",' one says.

Direction. Purpose. Belonging. Those words became increasingly familiar to me over the course of this research. What worries Deborrah Francis from Melbourne's St Margaret's Berwick Grammar? 'The dark cloud that hangs over them, especially in the independent sector, is that sense of purpose of "Where am I heading?", "What's in store for me?", and to have all the answers, yesterday,' she says.

These experts also describe their charges as stronger than they believe, and full of hope. Teen educator and CEO of Enlighten Education Dannielle Miller says this is her favourite cohort. 'What I love about them is they don't give their hearts away too quickly. They have critical thinking skills to be discerning, which I like. But when they're in, they're all in – hearts and minds. I love that passion,' she says. They question everything, including school structures. 'I guess that can be annoying for schools sometimes. But I love it and that's truly what we want – a generation of young people who will think or challenge and question.'

'I think they really are misunderstood,' Melbourne paediatric psychologist Amanda Abel says. 'Whether it's their parents or just the general adults in the world, I don't think that they're a very well understood little cohort.' Geelong psychologist Laura Lee agrees. 'It's just a really formative time in their lives and there's a lot of turmoil around this age,' she says. 'There can be a lot of pain during these years and during their identity formation.' That identity formation is pivotal, and feeds into relationships with their peers, and the relationship they have with themselves. What does she mean by that? 'Do they have the confidence to cope with life's ups and downs – and that's something that really varies in this age group. When I think about relationships with themselves, I also think about the physical.' Lee works with girls who share a difficult relationship with their own bodies, and struggle with food and exercise and appearance and beauty. Their relationship with others can be tricky too. 'High school friendships are evolving or being left behind,' she says. Many are wondering whether they have to tolerate any longer those students they've 'coexisted' with for years, now the end of school is in sight. Others are terrified friendship groups will disband with the final school bell. 'And when friendships are evolving, girls feel like the ground is a little unstable around them.' Gender identity is a new and confusing kid on the block for many parents. Support networks are crucial. 'Parents play such a strong role and something that has really struck me, and seems to have shifted so much from when I was that age, is how much girls want to connect with their parents and are really willing to share with them,' Lee says. 'I can have parents express surprise to me – in a good way – about how much their daughters are willing to share about what's going on in their lives. Whilst I'm sure that's not the case with everyone, that's something that's really struck me.' That's gold to girls feeling wobbly on the journey to who they want to be. But she urges parents not to problem solve or utter the words 'when I was your age . . . and why don't you try . . .' Instead, parents need to 'say something like, "Well, that sounds really difficult".' Josie Tucker, a counsellor with Kids Helpline, agrees. Girls 'need the patience and acceptance of people around them' to sit with the questions raised, and to accept their navigation of them.

Teen girls make up a bigger client base than their male peers at Kids Helpline. On average, 25 to 27 per cent of calls to the counselling service come from 16- to 18-year-old young women. The top five concerns are mental health, emotional wellbeing, suicide-related concerns, child–parent relations and self-injury or self-harm concerns. Invariably, girls call after school, between 4 pm and 8 pm, with the peak occurring just after 6 pm.

Social media continues to play a dominant role with this crew, and many girls describe their own unhealthy obsession with it. Tasmanian psychologist Nicole Young says while staying connected helps, it also feeds that comparison, judgement and fear of missing out. 'Fifteen years ago, you could look at a picture magazine and see one model but today you could go through Instagram and in the space of one minute there might be 50 different photos. That difference is huge and I think that's challenging,' she says. 'I empathise with them.'

The demands of their academic study also jump in the lead-up to Year 11. Melbourne educator Penny Golding says the biggest jump is from Year 10 into Year 11, and that coincides with less flexibility around assignments and exams. Those who have not honed skills such as time management and referencing might find it more difficult. 'Year 11 often is a year where girls feel lost,' she says. Byron Dempsey, founder and host of the popular podcast Driven Young, says that sense of being lost can be seen in the choice of what to study post-school too. 'There's a concept of a paradox of choice,' he says. 'It's kind of like when you sit down to watch a movie, and you spend hours scrolling through Netflix because there's so many options. That's what we have with university degrees.' He compares the career pathways on offer now to those available when his grandfather was a similar age. 'If I look at my granddad, he was basically going to be a builder or a carpenter. And as limiting as that is, there was beauty in the simplicity of it. And so I do think they are crippled with choice, overwhelmed, and obviously have high levels of stress because of the weight they carry with this specific number – the ATAR.'

In the pages that follow, all these issues are canvassed though the voices of our daughters. But even early on, the irony of this smorgasbord stands out. Their opportunities have never been greater. They can see them. Taste them. But that next step, from child to adult, is filtered by indecision. The legal divide between dependence and independence doesn't translate into reality either; it is more nuanced. The adolescent brain remains beyond the legal age. Adulting, as the girls call it, begins later: financial independence, full-time work, starting their own household, coupling up, starting a family, taking on home ownership. All of that is being deferred. Mark McCrindle says, 'Marriage, mortgage, children, and career have traditionally been those life markers that have clearly delineated the transition from young adulthood to adulthood.' This is a generation of DownAgers, because they stay younger for longer. 'All those markers have been kicked way down the road for this generation just because they're in study later, the cost of living is greater and housing affordability is lower.' The average age of giving birth is getting older and young adults are also staying with their families for longer. Mark McCrindle says that means they are, in some ways, younger than their age might suggest. Moreover, COVID-19 has stripped away certain social markers, from school graduations to 18th birthday parties to first dates and early L plates. The impact of that has impaired the growth of many young adults, who remain living at home. So while they might be on the brink of adulthood – in terms of age – they haven't had the experience of 'practicing adult-hood' and making decisions themselves. In large part, that's because they haven't needed to – at home, or at school.

School rules

Four Year 12 students are sitting around a lunch table dissecting their senior experience. Elspeth says she's 'stuffed'. With good report cards in Year 9, she was 'talked into' taking maths and science subjects by her Year 10 science teacher. Maths Methods. Specialist Maths. Biology. Chemistry. Physics. 'I fell for the STEM line, and all I want to do is history,' she says with a frustration that she thinks will linger for life. Shanvika wishes she'd done a science. 'I want to do nursing – midwifery – but I didn't take biology. I'm looking into bridging courses but don't know much about them. Maybe I'll just get a job somewhere.' Ping, sitting at the end of the table, needs to be prompted to speak. She says she's overwhelmed. Year 12 is nothing like she thought it would be. 'I know that the ATAR doesn't matter outside of school but when you are in Year 12, schools make it seem as though it's the biggest thing and crucial to creating a successful future and life,' she says. Some days, she says, she finds it hard to breathe. Hayley nods. She asks whether she looks as tired as she feels. She's been up late studying for English. She hasn't read the prescribed text, she says, and she believes that could smash her ATAR score.

Four students and four letters. ATAR. An acronym for the Australian Tertiary Admissions Rank, a number between 0.00 and 99.95 that provides a student's position relative to all other students in their age group. The average ATAR is about 70, and that means a student is in the top 30 per cent of their age group. The average is higher than 50 because it takes into account some students leaving school, meaning a smaller and presumably more academic group receives an ATAR rank. An equivalence also exists between states – so an ATAR of 92.00 in one state is equivalent to the same ATAR in other states, even though they are calculated differently. About three-quarters of students completing Year 12 receive an ATAR, with the remainder either not completing a sufficient number of ATAR-nominated subjects or not satisfying other conditions. In some schools almost all students receive an ATAR; in others it is fewer than half. Almost 54 per cent of students receiving an ATAR in New South Wales, for example, are female. They have also consistently out-performed male students in the majority of courses and have a higher median ATAR. Of the 54 894 students who received an ATAR in 2020 in New South Wales, almost 79 per cent applied (through the state's Universities Admissions Centre) for a university course.

Universities use the ATAR to offer students a place in tertiary courses. And that means the score has the power to drive tears and fears. It keeps 16-year-olds up at night and has 17-year-olds setting the alarm for 4 am. It's just a number – magical to some and monstrous to others – but it carries a fair degree of mystery for all. It's made up differently in different states, and universities use it in different ways. Some universities even add a few points to it if the student has studied particular subjects, such as a language. A scaling algorithm – which estimates students' marks if all courses were studied by all students – means some subjects are given stronger weighting in determining that final figure, which arrives in the lead-up to Christmas. But it doesn't always carry the promise of a wrapped gift. The ATAR dictates entry into thousands of university courses across the nation. And it has to be the right number. For some students, it's a game of bingo. Some win and some lose. For others, it's a number higher than they need. Or one they don't even require. For many, it's too low. That's when it can be a deal-breaker. A heart-breaker. A life-definer.

Elspeth, Shanvika, Ping and Hayley belong to a big-city all-girls school. But their sentiments enveloping subject selection, anxiety and the mammoth nights of study squeezed in between sport and music lessons mirror those of their peers in public, private and independent schools across the nation.

'I would say I'm a high-achieving student. Certain subjects I think are really difficult and overwhelming. Beyond being mind-numbingly boring, school is difficult because it's just an endless onslaught of work and stress. It's hard to find the motivation to care, and to keep going.'

'There's a massive expectation from family. What ATAR are you going to get? I dread all the text messages asking me what I'm going to get. They expect 95. I won't get that. I hate that anything lower than that is a let-down.'

'Schools have a tendency to only acknowledge the top students, which makes students like me feel they aren't good enough.'

'We are told to study four hours per subject per week in Year 12. You do that and find some balance, and then tell me how to do it.'

I built a storyboard of their answers around my office wall and what popped out, repeatedly, was how too many students in Year 11 and Year 12 are reducing their lives in pursuit of a number. Some have their goal number, in huge letters, on their own bedroom wall. Others have quit sport in the hope that a few more hours here and there will deliver bonus points. In theory, they know this number will not dictate success. In theory. But in practice it's different. It's why they are at school. It's what they hear repeatedly from teachers and guest speakers who tell them stories of how others before them have succeeded.

> 'No matter how hard I try I won't get 90. So why do I have to sit and listen to former students tell me how I can? I know I can't. That just makes me feel bad.'

In addition to the subjects that are required for ATAR assessment, there are non-ATAR subjects and vocational subjects, too, but the focus of many schools and parents lies in that one score. Clayfield College principal Dr Andrew Cousins says many parents believe 'everyone gets an ATAR and then goes to university' and are stunned when they find out many students choose alternative pathways into the workforce and further education, including university, without an ATAR.

The focus on the ATAR is producing a swathe of by-products, including an anxiety epidemic that is stopping girls living life to the fullest, a schoolyard division based on what subjects are chosen in Year 10 and a startling inequality between schools. Add to that a post-COVID-19 lack of ambition – particularly in Melbourne – and a concern by experts about the late diagnosis of ADHD, particularly in 17- and 18-year-old girls.

Some of these factors, such as anxiety, are discussed in other chapters, but suffice to say a tsunami is sweeping our schools, stealing students' smiles and sending some to the toilet to vomit. Others are refusing to attend school, self-harming and fighting eating disorders. Of course, some girls are roller-skating through Years 11 and 12, turning up to class, getting the answers right and then popping off to play soccer and tennis at night. Others love school for the connections it brings. 'I find it pretty easy; it's just a matter of being organised and staying ahead on my assignments,' one girl says. 'I feel accepted, respected and appreciated by my cohort and classmates,' states another. But over-whelmingly, those who felt good, motivated, relaxed or calm were either on holidays or had just finished exams when I interviewed them.

Janet Stewart, who heads Moreton Bay College in Brisbane, says she can see the pressure around ATAR. 'Despite the fact you know that we've got all this data about wellbeing and anxiety, and we know that external exams cause anxiety and issues like not sleeping and not eating well, we ask them to navigate their way through it. And I do think that that extra pressure with external exams has changed the landscape of those senior girls,' she says. Several subjects, she says, are content-heavy and don't reflect the real world, where the emphasis is on finding and using information – not knowing it off by heart. Other senior principals raised concerns about the ATAR – whether it was a fair comparison between states, and the pressure of one-off external exams that count for 50 per cent of the overall score of some subjects. One raised, as an example, a student at her school being ill on the morning of the exam. Should she be expected to do the exam or not? Another gave the example of the external timetable, where some students had evenly spaced days between exams and others had exams packed into fewer days.

The push to ensure girls have the opportunity to advance careers in the maths and science world has had an impact on subject selection in high schools. This has been encouraged by the fact that some maths and science subjects carry a greater weight, or scale higher, than other subjects in determining that ATAR score. Now, masses of girls focus solely on maths and science in order to open doors down the track to career pathways that were not open to their mothers, and perhaps even their big sisters. But there's a flip-side to this that deserves a broader discussion. Girls who focus on the humanities believe they don't receive the same accolades or resources.

'The school is focused on science and engineering and maths. They're really supported. But if someone gets an award for literature, they don't care much.'

'I do really challenging subjects but they are not science and maths. The school and my friends look down on me for that.'

'I definitely think the school pushes STEM. We need women in STEM. But for me, they dismiss my creative ambitions – drama and music and art. I understand the need for women in STEM, but they don't think it's a job option, what I do. It's like something you do on the side.'

'I really get angry about women in STEM. It's not the only pathway.'

'Humanities are dismissed because of the view they don't change the world like science does. We were even told that.'

'Someone actually said to me: "I thought you were bright and then someone told me you didn't do any science."'

'Because of the focus on women in STEM, the humanities are so under-funded.'

Whether real or perceived, this view was repeated over and over, and it is clear that, inside school grounds, the divisions over subject choice are both academic and social. Repeatedly during this project, the perception arose that the humanities were for those who would struggle with science or maths, a suite of subjects some called the Suicide

Six in reference to their level of difficulty. Socially, divisions were apparent between the 'clever girls' and the others. The world needs big scientific discoveries made by women, but it also needs great music and important stories and incredible art created by women. When this was put to educators, most believed that as female representation in STEM fields matched that of their male peers, the pendulum would swing back. Though ANU student Georgette Mouawad, who has served as the National Union of Students women's officer, says the 'feminisation of maths and science meant fewer males were choosing to study it'. Down the track, she wonders, will that mean less funding?

Whatever the subjects, educators and parents universally want girls to reach towards the sky. But an alarming factor popped up during this research, and it pertained almost exclusively to high-achieving girls in Melbourne, where lockdowns had dragged on for more than 250 days. Students who had aimed to become doctors or undertake advanced courses requiring top results lost a big chunk of motivation. And some of them had made the decision not to study post-school.

'There's a total lack of ambition. There is so much negativity. They can say we get compensation, but what is it really going to do? Some of my friends have just tapped out and don't care.'

'I've definitely gone through ups and downs. I'm quite an independent learner. At the start, I was thriving. The longer it got extended and the less help I was getting from teachers and the more disconnected I was from friends, I became less motivated. I saw no purpose.'

'I personally find it very difficult. I used to be a high achiever but my grades have been decreasing over time as I am very burnt out and have lost a lot of motivation.'

'Before COVID lockdown I was studying about four hours a day after school, but now I'm locked down all of my motivation has vanished and I don't do any study after school.'

These girls, and others, are all Melbourne-based, and they mirror a trend where lockdown became so persistent and remote learning such a chore that they altered their Year 13 study plans. Melbourne psychologist Carly Dober has seen that first-hand. 'Some of the girls I work with wanted to go to uni straight after school, and now they're like, "Well, no, I'm not sure I do because I've just done school for the last few years and it's made me miserable",' she says. Some of them felt 'unmoored, adrift' because their experiences – socially and academically – had been hindered. Alcohol and drug expert Paul Dillon says that mirrored some early research out of Europe, but there was a hope also in the research community that these teens would not be impacted in the long term. An overwhelming factor, he says, was how parents responded to the pandemic uncertainty. 'If parents were crumbling, the kid was not going to do well. If the parents were really positive, they [would] go through things quite well,' he says.

Lockdowns also highlighted the enormous inequity in education between schools, and also between city and regional areas and even states. In some junior classes, students had the latest online lessons, with funny hat days and a teacher always at the other end of a video call. In other schools, teachers paid out of their own pocket to photocopy material before dropping it off at individual students' homes. Dr David Mander, a psychologist who has consulted widely with teens in Western Australia, raises the lack of options for students from remote areas, where the 'disengagement rate' during Years 10 to 12 can be between 30 per cent and 60 per cent – depending on the day and time of the year. 'What we know is that when there's young people who are disengaged through schooling, and particularly during the senior school years, it's a life-trajectory changing moment and the likelihood increases over time that wellbeing, particularly mental health, will deteriorate if they don't finish or work towards something in those senior school years.' He says educational 'access and options' drop off about an hour outside Perth – and that presents a problem for policy-makers.

Lockdown and ongoing individual and family quarantines helped hide another inequity – and that is the delayed diagnosis of ADHD in teen girls. Dr Danielle McMullen, a Sydney GP, says ADHD often presents differently in young women who can be quiet and fall under the radar because of the high level of support afforded by some schools. 'There's teachers telling you what you need to do. And yes, there's homework and assignments that require a bit of multitasking, but generally it's a pretty supportive learning environment,' she says. 'Then once you get to university, suddenly it's a lot more self-directed. And people with ADHD, particularly women, will find it hard to keep on task when there's multiple tasks to be completed.' While it was important not to 'over-diagnose' mental health and neuropsychological conditions, Dr McMullen said it was crucial to 'jump on a diagnosis when strategies other than medications could be put in place'. Professor Andrew Martin, from the School of Education at the University of New South Wales, also raised the undiagnosed level of ADHD in young women, saying it was an emerging trend. 'It's something that usually boys [are diagnosed with] during school, and increasingly girls are [diagnosed] after school,' he says. That's because boys present with hyperactivity, while girls might be 'quiet underachievers'. 'Because they don't cause any trouble in the classroom, often they're not diagnosed, and it's often not until high school that parents say, "Look she's bright but for some reason not achieving".' Paediatric psychologist Amanda Abel independently raised the same issue, saying ADHD and learning difficulties occur where 'ability and achievement are not matched up'. Her advice? 'Whenever parents are thinking "my child is not achieving", just go and get them assessed, even if it's just a cognitive assessment – then you can see whether their ability is high or whether it is low and maybe they need support.'

So what needs to be done to smooth the path into Years 11 and 12? No doubt the subject choice, which rears its head in Year 10, is crucial. At that point, students are just 15 and 16 years old. But this year is not afforded the same focus as Year 9, when girls face the tricky 14th and 15th birthdays, or Years 11 and 12, where the focus is squarely on producing the best results.

'Grade 10 to Grade 11 was a huge jump.'

'School become really hard after Grade 10.'

'This year [Year 11] has definitely been the hardest all through high school. I've been a B student until this year, which is a bit upsetting.'

'You think you've nailed it and then you get to Year 11 and it doesn't matter how bright you are unless you have those time management skills and study habits.'

Melbourne educator Penny Golding says that after 27 years of teaching she believes 'the biggest jump in a student's life is from Year 10 into Year 11'. Friendship groups become more defined at the same time as there is a huge shift towards senior assessment. 'There is less flexibility in terms of time, there's less flexibility in the criteria, the way that you are actually marked is really accountable,' she says. Students who had a Year 12 teacher earlier in their schooling might have acquired some of the assessment skills needed, but COVID-19 lockdowns might have meant that other students missed two crucial years of practising a range of different types of important developmental skills. 'Year 11 often is a year where girls feel lost,' Golding says. Her experience suggests mental health issues frequently surface around Year 10, and that's also a year when she sees anecdotal evidence of families separating. Add the increased academic pressure and COVID-19 to that mix and it can present significant challenges. Susan Dalton, principal of Miami State High School on the Gold Coast, agrees that there is a significant jump in the workload expectations between Years 10 and 11. 'We always say to the kids here that your hardest year is Year 11,' she says. And perhaps, she says, Year 10 is where educators might need to focus more of their attention. 'I think it needs work in how we guide them through it, and what messages we give – but without a doubt I feel that Year 10 is that in-between year from junior to senior that needs to have a much stronger focus on preparing them for senior.' It needs to be more of a transition and less of a leap.

Andrew Pierpoint, president of the Australian Secondary Principals' Association, says those conversations in Year 10, between the school, parents and students, are crucial. 'That's the root of all good and all evil two and a half years down the track when they're in Year 12,' he says. Why? 'Because at some point in Year 11 or 12, students will have a realisation that they've got the wrong subjects. They've got the wrong career advice, and they can't go backwards.' That's because subjects are set on teaching lines to cater to timetables, which can often make it difficult to swap. 'And if you chop and change subjects too much, that can also cut you out of being eligible for an ATAR.'

Broadly, the ATAR is considered fairer than previous assessment methods, and allows a comparison between students in different states. But the pressure it puts on students and the use of external exams have educators and psychologists calling for a rethink. There needs to be a different way, according to Janet Stewart from Moreton Bay College. She says other countries have navigated paths from school to university that are seamless, and have been able to pinpoint those students worthy of acceptance without the burden of external exams. Some universities and courses in Australia require auditions or statements or interviews, but the ATAR stands as the central point for university admission. Other educators noted what they labelled the 'unfairness' of ATAR. It's a roll-of-the-dice in some subjects where 50 per cent is assessed in one exam; some subjects focus on recall and don't measure a student's understanding; it doesn't reflect how you seek and assess information in real life; and it doesn't judge the 'suitability' of a student for particular university courses. Others raised the chasm between the academic ability assessed and the 'soft skills' such as teamwork and empathy and the ability to listen, which are so vital in the workforce and leadership, but are not assessed in any way.

Byron Dempsey, founder and host of the Driven Young podcast, believes Australia's education system is failing the next generation because it ignores the practical life skills that are needed. And he might be right, given that he has more than 650000 followers and 500000 podcast downloads – a huge chunk of them in this age bracket. 'A lot of people think I hated school when I was younger. I really didn't. I enjoyed school,' he says. But after graduating, he wanted to be a filmmaker and couldn't see any value in going to university. He nabbed part-time work making films and learnt by osmosis. 'I got to meet all these clients and build these relationships, learn the skills of how to pitch to businesses, how to build your brand, marketing, etc. And I went, "Oh my God, in one year, I've learnt more relevant skills that will be applicable in the real world than I feel I ever did in high school."' And that was the start of a podcast that now focuses teens' attention on everything from financial literacy to consent. It begs the question of whether school is equipping girls for life and the workplace – or just meeting the entry needs of universities.

Some students are studying for enormous numbers of hours, giving up extra-curricular activities, often without a purpose.

'My experience with school is the reason I do not want to go to university. I don't want to feel that kind of never-ending stress, always worrying about when things are due and not being able to truly relax.'

'I try extremely hard but it is not reflected in my marks. I'm a bit above average, which doesn't sound bad but I have put in so much work to be at this place. It's hard seeing some cruise through school with excellent marks when they don't care about education.'

'The workload is what takes the biggest toll on everyone, mainly the blind-eye towards how fragile we all become mentally because of it.'

When asked how much they studied, answers varied widely, as you would expect. But two to three hours each day was standard. And often that was on top of homework and other activities. Teachers sympathised with workloads, and most girls believed teachers tried to understand them as much as they could.

> *'My English teacher is an angel. She understands my internal battles.'*

> *'I know I can reach out and they will help.'*

> *'I feel as though the teachers [who] care about me as a person are the best teachers because they understand what works for me.'*

'Across the board, I think kids are over-scheduled,' psychologist Amanda Abel says. 'They've grown up with that in the younger years, and it becomes their expectation as teenagers. They think "I need to do this. I need to do that. I need to be the best at this and that."' She says that makes it difficult for them to both make decisions and prioritise activities. How much time should be dedicated to rowing versus homework? Andrew Pierpoint says the teen years are more complex than they were a decade ago, and a big swag of students are balancing part-time jobs with sporting commitments, separated families, and even caring for elderly family members. 'They're all things that the average student does much more now.' Pierpoint says the conversations between parents and students and the school need to be three-way: the school providing the rules and guidelines, parents delivering 'the commonsense stuff around the kitchen table that schools aren't privy to' and the student providing their own perspective on what they want to do. Gold Coast principal Susan Dalton says she advises Year 11 students to focus on time management. 'Make sure you only take on what you need to take on,' she says. In the mix of school and sport and other activities, this is also the time when students become more independent and social. 'Choose wisely what you take on.' Certainly students should seize opportunities, but they shouldn't overload themselves 'because sometimes there are too many opportunities placed in front of them. And they really need to find the balance.' Many schools are trying to respond to this, and Susan Dalton's Miami High is an example. 'I'm seeing a much bigger trend in students going into part-time work,' she says. That can provide them with wonderful skills they need for life, but add to an already-packed workload. 'Knowing that, what we have done here at Miami High for the last two years now is we've changed the timetable for seniors and so they only have a half day on a Monday and a Friday and they can go home early.' That allows students to take up part-time work opportunities, and to also have scheduled time to catch up on study.

Seven hours at school each day, at 16 and 17 years, throws up more challenges than the classroom lessons. Friendships and fitting in. Finding their tribe. Finding their stride. Confidence. Dealing with what might be happening at home too. Feeling like a square peg in a round hole. Finding out who they are crammed between physics and modern history lessons. Wondering why they are being told to run their own race, and then being put in a uniform that matches everyone else in the class. For some, the challenges are outside the classroom. So how do the girls in this cohort describe their school life?

> *'I come to school and I love learning. But the friendship and people side is hard.'*

> *'School is a super toxic environment just full of judgement and status. Exclusivity, judgement and borderline bullying.'*

> *'I feel like I have little opportunity to express my individuality and creativity.'*

> *'There's definitely some comfort in the routine it provides, but I don't have any close friends at school so it becomes tiring sometimes, especially with the workload of Grade 12.'*

> *'I feel like every movement I make is put under a microscope by everyone and they always have something to say.'*

> *'LGBTQIA+ students feel scared or like they need to hide. Male students with high sporting accomplishments are the only ones celebrated and promoted.'*

> *'Students feel unsupported and gaslighted.'*

'A rollercoaster. Sometimes it's fun, motivating and fulfilling; and sometimes it's stressful, draining and mundane.'

'Good teachers. Too much drama. Bad rumours. Mental health issues. Some bullying and drugs.'

'A lot of girls talk about self-comparison with physical features – but I find a lot of us get jealous of mental states – that girl who always has it together, happy and bubbly.'

'I enjoy learning and love my friends and teachers but I've often felt school wasn't a good fit for me.'

And how do they feel today, in the moment?

'Numb. Stressed. Overwhelmed. Tired. Tired. Tired. Flat.'

'2022 captaincies were announced two days ago and I didn't get a position so I feel pretty downgraded with a low moral value.'

'Mentally, emotionally and physically exhausted. Right now I need a break from everything.'

And that's before we have a closer look at the legacy left by a pandemic that has upended all of our worlds.

3

The corona-coaster

'What kind of world is it where we were not fearful of COVID? We feared not being able to do our exams.'

One comment, by one 17-year-old, but it speaks volumes about how this pandemic might impact our girls as they move forward. Millions of people have lost their lives globally, as these girls have moved from Year 10 into Year 11, or Year 11 into Year 12 or from Year 12 into Year 13 – university, TAFE or the workplace. Thousands of lives have been stolen. Each day, the news broadcasts begin with the latest endless tallies that dictate whether they can play sport on the weekend, attend their formal, graduate in person or travel. 'This is the generation that has been most impaired through COVID,' social researcher Mark McCrindle says. The focus might have been on the older generation, who were more vulnerable from a health perspective, but this cohort – girls aged 16, 17 and 18 – has copped the COVID-19 lashings from every other perspective. Their social lives have been stymied. They've been isolated from friends and classmates, and in many cases family members. Their mental health has been challenged, over and over again. The sense of belonging and purpose has faded. Connection has been challenged. 'That hasn't got the headlines but in Australia, where actually the biggest impact has been economic and social, this is the generation that has really felt the pain of that,' McCrindle says.

We know they've missed out on formals and graduations, 18th birthday parties and blossoming relationships, on-campus university and Year 12 rites of passage. Melbourne educator Penny Golding gives the example of the cancellation of annual muck-up days, which usually happen in the final days of Year 12 in most schools across the nation. Muck-up day traditionally provides a sense of freedom and joyfulness and a sense of occasion, she says, a bond driven by the energy of planning and doing something together. It might be hard for others to understand the impact of losing such an event, considered trivial by some. 'The only thing I can liken it to is that you can't understand what it's like to be in a lockdown for this long just as you can't understand about being a parent until you are a parent.'

In life, you only turn 18 once. You graduate from school once. These are important milestones, which are built up over their school journey. Many of these students have seen older school sisters pick the dress of their dreams for formal night. They've dreamt of the day they'll sign their names on uniforms, or throw their school hat high into the air, with all their classmates, for a final time. That's the picture they want captured. That hat had been lost and found more times than they can remember. Some were forced to pay for their own, after not looking after the first one. Some were stuck together, by Year 12, with equal doses of glue and good luck. And they could see themselves, some of them, in that old, tattered hat. Exhausted. Worn. And set to be freed. In the absence of that picture is the telltale sign of a pandemic that has been robbing families and friends of loved ones. One million. Two million. Three million. Four million. Five million. They lost count. But the impacts of it were there, daily, in how their final years of school were being reduced and recorded in history.

Many of the impacts were less visible. Casual jobs were cancelled, particularly in exposed industries such as hospitality. Those in Year 13 and starting work missed out on in-office experience, filled with the chatter of those who might become mentors. Mark McCrindle is from their parents' generation. 'In our generation, we loved it,' he says. 'The younger generation actually need that interaction in the workplace because in those early years that's how they learn.' Yet, despite all that, outside their families and school communities there has been little whingeing. They've accepted this pothole in our history, and all the hurt that comes with it. McCrindle says they also missed both the pity and support given to others during lockdown. 'That's to their credit,' he says. 'Maybe it's a little sign of resilience or maybe it's a sign of the generation – perhaps even like their parents' generation – they just get on and get it done.' He hopes and thinks so. But, like their parents and teachers and health professionals, he knows this pandemic has thrown up a mental health challenge that is difficult to meet.

Author Rebecca Sparrow says it's impossible to measure the impact of COVID on teens. 'I think it's all coming home to roost in a way,' she says. 'They've got all this brilliant energy and ideas and enthusiasm and opinions. And I think a lot of them are terrified.' Many lacked the confidence to navigate a path forward, and perhaps we – parents and educators – have failed to equip them with that. They have lost the ability to interact because they have been isolated. 'They don't want to pick up the phone and answer a phone call, that's my concern,' Sparrow says. 'The fear of answering the door or ringing a shop. They've got all this magic inside and they don't know when they walk out the gate how to apply it.'

When it comes to COVID-19, girls report a mixed bag of emotions and impacts. Bullying, away from school, plummeted. Family issues, including domestic violence, turned up just as sharply. Early entry into some universities was delivered as a pre-Christmas gift. More time with the family, especially fathers who were home for the second year in a row for dinner and happy to break mid-morning to fly a kite in the local park. Kids Helpline counsellor Josie Tucker says an increase in calls from teen girls tracked directly with lockdowns. Distress. Suicidal thoughts. Self-harm. Concern for family. She says while the number of calls relating to bullying fell, calls concerning mental health and emotional coping increased. 'They tend to be a very perceptive group; they will notice the stress of their peers or the stress of family members. And that will often be a prompt for them to contact – so they might notice Mum or Dad or whoever they're living with is stressed at this time because of finances or whatever,' she says. Some days in lockdown were joyful, slow and simple, and then at other points, lockdown hit students like a tsunami. Almost everyone reported experiencing a paralysing day where they couldn't move from the couch, overwhelmed by everything around them. 'I think the kids are really going through that, and they're at such a young age and this is for such a prolonged period of time,' Penny Golding says. Brisbane principal Toni Riordan says she fears COVID-19 and the media wall around it have also driven a 'disconnect' in the three-way engagement between parents, teachers and students, and a 'mistrust of authority'. Girls say connections, especially to friends, folded. 'I stopped contacting people, and then they stopped contacting me,' one Melbourne student says. Motivation dipped. Anxiety crept up to new levels. If COVID-19 was a paint, you could throw it at the wall and see the impact running down everywhere. And in 2022 and 2023 and beyond, it will colour most of the lives of those students who were at the centre of it.

'COVID has caused a lot of strain on my dad. He lost his job. Normally he is an angry person but during the pandemic he got angrier and meaner. I have two jobs and he knows how much I make and constantly makes me feel bad that I'm earning more than him and that I should start paying for things for them. He has also made more degrading comments to me and my sisters, like that I'm on the spectrum, ungrateful, selfish and rigid. My mum deals with things by going silent, so there's not the best communication with my parents. Because of this, I don't feel comfortable at home.'

'When you are in lockdown, you can take things less seriously. The school environment puts everything in a more serious setting. So I don't know where I should be or not. Teachers aren't saying you should be at this level or not. And my friends and I are not taking it seriously. In Geography, my teacher just talks and talks and no one cares. That would not happen in a regular class because

we are right in front of her. We just turn off our camera and play a game.'

'*COVID has made it lonely. I'm not big on social media. I have a hard time keeping in contact with people over text. I just don't get in touch and they don't and then I just isolate by myself. I know it's not good.'*

'*I felt so isolated.'*

'*Do they understand Year 12 has changed? It's changed. And we are struggling with that. We're trying to accept it, but give us a bit of support.'*

'*But our school just focused on Year 12. How hard it is. How it was ruined. And then we went into lockdown at the end of Year 11 and it was like "get on with it".'*

'*I know all the content but staying motivated is really hard. If we were at school, I'd still have days when I wasn't motivated, but doing it all online and not having face-to-face is certainly reducing motivation.'*

'*Due to lockdown, I have gotten way closer and open to my parents and my brother.'*

'*The best thing about schooling is socialisation. Take that away, and what do you have?'*

'*Some teachers have given up. If you are in person, they'll have a discussion. But no one is as comfortable doing that online. There's no real discussion. I just turn the volume down and let them think I'm listening.'*

'Every day is the same. Same. Same. Same. We have exams coming up. I have no idea how my revision is going.'

'It's an annoyance. I'm not scared of it. I'm missing out on a lot of stuff. My life is on hold. I've never been scared of the disease itself. I just want to move on. I'm missing out on so much.'

'I'm more careful of the people I associate with. I'm not meeting any new people.'

Almost unanimously, COVID-19 – the disease – was not the ogre. It was how it upended their school and social lives, and drove levels of uncertainty that played with friendships and exam timetables, along with almost every other routine they'd grown to trust. And just as routines would go back to what we might have known, a new strain would turn lives upside down again. Different variants, with different symptoms and different impacts on different cohorts of people. Melbourne school principal Linda Douglas sums it up: 'The problem we're finding here is the level of uncertainty,' she says. 'That event scheduled for December – is it going to happen or isn't it going to happen? We've gone through that for nearly two years. And of course everyone this year thought it was going to be better and effectively it's been worse.'

No doubt Melbourne was both the epicentre of the pandemic and of how it impacted students. But the effects were felt states away, including in Queensland and South Australia, where lockdowns were limited. Dr Nicole Archard, principal of Loreto College Marryatville in Adelaide, says the latter period of adolescence brought together a stack of pressures as students considered the next phase of their lives. 'I certainly think the pandemic has had an impact on all children's mental health,' she says. Dr Archard says she asked herself why she was seeing high levels of anxiety and stress in students in her state, with limited lockdowns. And she found the answer: regardless of where we live, many of the impacts had been the same. Constant disappointment over not being able to travel. Not being able to organise family get-togethers interstate. Last minute cancellations. Families separated by borders. 'My family have been stuck in a caravan parked on the border,' one girl said. Another hadn't seen her father for almost a year. Both those girls were from Queensland, where lockdowns were limited. Job losses and business closures. Casual jobs drying up. Parents out of work. 'In South Australia our girls have been wearing masks to school all of term three so there's this constant awareness that there's something that is changing in the world,' Dr Archard says. 'The world isn't as they knew it previously.'

Melbourne educator Deborrah Francis raises something that underpins many of the girls' responses. The constant media hype around numbers and statistics, and a whole new library of words: flattening the curve, epidemic, pandemic, quarantine, isolation, respirators, ventilators, locally acquired, internationally acquired, herd immunity, corona coaster and coronacation. Alpha, beta, gamma, delta and omicron drowning in numbers. 'I'm a lot more cautious about particular things when case numbers go up,' one student says. 'I find myself finding excuses not to go out. It really has created a social anxiety I didn't have before.' Children saw a number that just kept climbing. Explanation was limited. The discussion needed to dissect it couldn't happen in closed classrooms. 'Normally we would do that at school,' Francis says. That worried her, because educators like being proactive, in front of the curve. But this pandemic swept everyone off their feet, and those conversations in the school setting didn't happen. Melbourne Girls Grammar School principal Dr Toni Meath says she noticed even young children talking about the daily tallies. 'Then . . . we've got the whole climate change debate and then, on top of that, we had the consent and sexual assault issues [brought up] by female warriors like

Brittany Higgins and Grace Tame. These all fed into a kind of a hotbed of pressures for these girls.'

No doubt education is where COVID-19 had the biggest impact. Remote learning. Changes to assessment. Sharing the kitchen table with siblings. Inequalities that saw students from some schools sit in an air-conditioned home office, with a new you-beaut computer while students from other schools chased notes, sometimes photocopied and delivered to them, and might have access to one computer shared with siblings or parents. Patchy internet access could disrupt a day. Some schools rebuilt entire technology hubs in less than a week. Many girls struggled with the motivation to listen all day, then turn around and study at night. And many extroverts struggled without the energy of friends, just as many introverts blossomed online. Teachers also recorded advancements in those girls on the autism spectrum, and others who sat in the middle of the class. Perhaps they were given time and space, without the class competition, to develop at their own pace. There was a lack of motivation and a sombre tone in many responses from girls in Melbourne – but not all. This pandemic wrote different chapters for different girls.

'My grades have gone down and I am constantly stressed and worried.'

'School has become my entire life. It feels as though it is all day until I go to sleep.'

'Made me lazy with schoolwork, addicted to my phone and sleeping.'

'I've become a more independent learner.'

'I am way less motivated and my school life declined.'

'I'm doing more schoolwork but don't talk to anyone. I go days without talking to anyone outside my family.'

'Because school is at home, I felt I was always at school.'

'I have become so demotivated and I hate feeling like that.'

'I used to be really, really good at snowboarding and I wanted to pursue a career in it – but I haven't been able to do it for two years. It was kind of the only thing I wanted to do for myself in my life and now it's pretty much out of the picture. I'm lost.'

'I love it, being at home. I smash through my work so much more effectively. If you're on a roll you're not interrupted.'

School leaders rarely get the kudos they deserve, and this pandemic should deliver them national respect. Wellbeing departments tracked individual students in many instances, and teachers used their own money to fund resources. Some called every student in their class, personally, during lockdown. Others disbanded school times and were available when they were needed. And without doubt, COVID-19 delivered a lesson in individual or personalised learning that will influence school lessons going forward.

Paulina Skerman, principal of Sydney's Santa Sabina College, says she's seen students grow a capacity for independent learning that will benefit them post-school. On Zoom, she told them how she had to bury her father-in-law, and that loss and grief was something they could share. They talked about lost birthdays and not being able to see grandparents, how they weren't allowed a last day of Year 12. They were sad and cried and some took it out on a punching bag. But then she told them to think of the shiny bits. She had an extra coffee with her husband each morning. Found new walks around Sydney. Did they learn to cook? Have lunch with Mum and Dad? And the school got a new dog. 'There's no way I could have actually had this joy in my life if COVID-19 hadn't given me the opportunity to do that,' Skerman says.

Melbourne educator Linda Douglas says the school gathered data during the long periods of distance learning. 'And one of the most interesting things that came out of it was the sense of independence girls gained during distance learning,' she says. The student voice and student agency grew too because girls were being consulted about how their learning could improve. And they spoke up, in a way they might not have in a packed classroom, and that voice was proactive in discussions including diversity and inclusivity, gratitude and kindness, and reconciliation. It's been a hard slog, but she feels it's gifted them a toolkit of accepting each other, valuing other people's roles, showcasing kindness and 'a healthy dose of grit and resilience'. Toni Riordan says students who were well supported, connected to their communities and prepared to ask for help shone over the past couple of years – those who would admit that 'I'm a bit messy, I'm a bit wobbly, I need help' showed a resilience and an ability to work with adults during this time. This is an important point – because asking for help is awkward and difficult for this cohort. Dr Toni Meath says the lessons learnt through COVID-19 need to be remembered. 'The very fact of living the lives they have . . . they've learnt to appreciate different things. That's not a defect,' she says. She can see how students have learnt, over two years, to appreciate these small things, the quiet times and each other. 'And that's an important learning that often we don't get until we're experienced women,' she says. 'So let's turn that into a positive and a talent for them.' She bought every Year 12 student a copy of Charlie Mackesy's *The Boy, the Mole, the Fox and the Horse* and posted it out to them during lockdown. It was a small gesture, heavy on meaning. On one page the mole comments on how small he is, to which the boy replies, 'But you make a huge difference.' On another, the boy asks, 'What is the bravest thing you've ever said?' 'Help,' replies the horse.[1] The words and images were also plucked out to use in emails to students.

The ways education was disrupted during COVID-19 will deliver better lessons going forward, and it has taken a pandemic to teach educators, parents and students that. In one school, a partnership is being set up with a global online academy, which has meant girls are able to study extra subjects like financial literacy and climate change. Many girls have also, according to one principal, 'completely pivoted in what they want to do'. That might be the time spent reflecting at home, or the opportunity provided by lockdown to develop other passions. 'But I think there'll be more varied careers that will come out of this,' the principal said. Susan Dalton, principal of Miami State High School, began a co-teaching model, where contract teachers sat in classrooms, with regular teachers in their lounge-rooms over the border. That's because one hard closure meant she lost 24 staff. That helped the mental wellbeing of teachers, who were isolated in their homes, as well as the students, who then had two teachers. 'COVID taught me that there are so many possibilities out there to improve conditions and outcomes for students that we're not tapped into early – and that we definitely need to really adapt that positive mindset,' she said. Going forward, time-table changes will allow for part-time work, and students with heavy workloads will do some classes at home. That way, they won't lose valuable time travelling to and from school and will be able to fit in other commitments. At Brisbane's St Aidan's Anglican Girls' School, Toni Riordan said students' creativity was inspiring. They worked around it, she says, giving the example of a school talent show. Auditions were online, which encouraged shy students to join in, and the whole production was staged online. 'It had people at the heart of it as well,' she says. They 'imagined and adapted and pivoted' to connect with each other and instil a sense of belonging. Other schools are embarking on different innovations – all a product of the disruption delivered by COVID-19.

COVID-19 also provided parents with a look inside their children's school lessons. In some states, lessons were overseen by parents. In others, parents played a bigger role than in previous years, particularly if their child needed help. Sally Marcroft coordinated a seminar for the Wimmera Development Association in Melbourne. The online session had 1500 people attend live online with more than 4000 people viewing a recording. Parents were given a chance to ask questions prior to the webinar and several themes stood out, including the management of emotions such as anxiety, fear, sadness, anger and loneliness, boundaries around screen time, how to keep children motivated and the difficulty around distance learning. That reflected the questions being asked of schools too, although several principals believe the pressure around Year 12 meant many parents wanted to find an easier path for their child. In one school, a parent campaigned to have practice exams stopped because she didn't want her daughter to complete them. The principal said, 'I remember ringing these parents on a Sunday morning to say, "Now I can appreciate your panic, and I can see that you are distressed about this but the girls are going to go ahead and do this." They wanted me to cancel for everybody because of their daughter.' She said COVID-19 taught her that some 'parents need to back off and let the children find their way because the kids want to find their way, and it's been these parents who have wanted to rescue them, which has caused much of the stress'. Other educators reported parents who wanted exams marked by outside professionals; who argued over part marks; and who sent individual teachers 'rude' emails, demanding that they change lessons, be available at other times and so on.

Much of that concern was motivated by a loss of connection. Families were split, but so were friends and classmates, sporting teams and theatre groups. When that stopped, in many cases the friendships suffered. School and class, as a glue, came unstuck.

'It's made me stop talking to the smaller characters in my life. I'm stuck with my own thoughts now.'

'I don't really talk to anyone anymore. I miss being able to hug my friends and have a laugh in class.'

'I haven't seen my family for months. I feel like we are strangers now.'

'I have withdrawn from all my peers.'

'I've found out that if I don't attend school with people every day, I don't interact with them at all.'

'It's had an extremely harsh effect on my mental health.'

'I'm now socially anxious and I didn't even know what that was before.'

'Having to wear masks has really affected my body image as the masks make me have huge break-outs.'

'My mental health is fragile.'

'I lost touch with many of my friends.'

Many educators say they believe COVID-19 simply magnified existing feelings of loneliness, isolation and anxiety, but for some students, the loss of connection gave them the space they needed for themselves.

'I have stopped being friends with toxic people and grown in confidence.'

'How has it changed me? I spend more time alone. I think about myself more, not caring for others. I'm not saying others aren't important.'

'COVID let me know that it's okay to work on myself and that at the end of the day it's only me who matters. It's also let me isolate from people I don't want to be around.'

'It's given me time, and I value that.'

Melbourne educator Penny Golding says the students who thrived were 'typically the ones who are going to work without anybody watching. They're the ones who will do that hard effort whether somebody is watching or not. They're self-motivated. The self-motivated student can still have that connection online with their friends or go and do a bit of exercise with a one-on-one walk, or that sort of thing, or has a lot of online connection with a small group of friends that they're very confident with.' Falling through the loopholes, she fears, were those 'students who need the energy of others, who need to look over their shoulder to check in with their work' and who learn better in groups. But she believes the corona coaster ride delivered by this pandemic will provide girls with a greater respect for connection, making time for others and balancing their work and home lives. That will be COVID-19's legacy. They won't work from 7 am to 7 pm and compromise time with their family. This generation will value time and prioritise. 'They'll know themselves more,' Golding says. Their emotional regulation skills will be higher. And the adversity of the pandemic will show them how to bounce back.

That positive message is reflected strongly across school leadership teams. It's a belief and a hope, all wrapped up in one. 'What they need from me is positivity,' Deborrah Francis says. 'What I've been saying to my girls at school is that it is like riding a bike. You hopped on last year. And you fell off a bit and you hopped on and we did lots of work at school. What worked for you? What didn't? What did you learn about yourself? What did you like about what you learnt? How could you change?' She tells them they have a second shot. 'And it's like riding a bike. You're going to get faster and you're going to get more skilled.' Paulina Skerman delivers a similar message. 'If you go through something difficult and get through, then you know next time you're faced with something terrible, you're going to get through.' That's the basis of neuroplasticity. 'I'm sounding like a pollyanna, but I don't think there's any other way to look at it.'

4

Listen to me

'We talk about representative government in Legal Studies; this government is not representative in any way – particularly over climate change.'

'I'm worried about First Nations justice. I want to change things but not in a "white saviour" type of way.'

'We are not being listened to – give me an example of where we are.'

'The whole "collecting crystals" thing. It's not cultural appropriation but it's just not right. I have a friend who is Indian and is confronted by it. It's become something that white teens do now. But when teens from diverse backgrounds did it, they were laughed at.'

Sassy, opinionated and socially aware. Articulate, black and white in their views, often with a reliance on funnelled sources of information. Our daughters want to change their classroom and their school and their world. They want to support their peers and lend their words to those who are silenced. In the process, they butt up against their parents, and often their teachers and schools. But it's their voice, and they want to use it.

This cohort of girls has been raised on a diet of research and analysis and classroom presentations. They have been assessed on their ability to critically analyse statements. They've joined debating teams to argue a case with conviction and clarity. And parents have applauded that. Often, they've paid money to enhance their daughter's ability to find and use her voice. Speech and drama lessons. Presentation training. Public speaking workshops. Debating trials. So it should not surprise any of us that teens want to use their voice and be heard.

> 'Governments and big companies aren't doing enough for climate change. [Soon] it will be utterly irreversible.'

> 'Even though we're young, we shouldn't be treated like we don't know anything. We have more knowledge than adults think. We might interpret it a different way, [but] it doesn't mean we're wrong.'

'Climate anxiety is real. We see it. The media tell us that. We see the protests. We feel hopeless. We can go to rallies but nothing is changing. There is a lot of climate anxiety in Gen Z.'

'We have so many different perspectives on things. We want to make a difference, be heard and acknowledged.'

'Why do we still celebrate female achievement? It should be normalised. There should be an equal amount.'

'[I worry about] my rights as a woman as they're being taken away, what the world will look like with climate change, and the lack of action.'

'Politicians should start taking student voices more seriously. In two years, we all vote.'

Consent, climate change and housing affordability – or a future where they believe they will not own their own homes – top the list of concerns for this clever cohort. And we've heard their voice on all those issues. Encouraged by Grace Tame and Chanel Contos and Brittany Higgins, they are willing to take on the bad behaviour of some of their male peers and speak up about wrongdoing. They are willing to cut class and give up their weekends to attend climate change rallies. They will make posters, and march and hold sit-ins. But mostly they are using their voice in the schoolyard and on social media to elevate their concerns. They have courage in spades.

Toni Riordan, principal of St Aidan's Anglican Girls' School in Brisbane, says their desire is to 'make a difference, and be the difference'. 'I'm in this game for hope,' she says. 'The words and the attitudes that come out of young people just give me hope that life will be okay because these young kids try so hard to understand the world they're in. They're not really anti anything. They're prepared to challenge it, and work it out,' she says. 'These girls impress me every day,' says Victorian school psychologist Carly Dober. 'I wish I had their kind of courage when I was their age, but I think they've also been forced to be like that.' In an age of information, they can see good from bad, how countries and policy-makers act differently, and how some are given social support and others are refused it. While they have different views, the need for action around climate change unites them. 'They can see governments act in their own self-interest and they feel ripped off,' Dober says. 'They feel anxious. They feel angry. They're confused. And they can't understand how Australia, the so-called lucky country, would do this to them.' They might not all label what they believe in as 'ethical investment', but pouring money into coal is offensive. 'They just want renewable energy, clean jobs, a just transition. They want the government to act in their interest, strong policies that safeguard a future.'

Social researcher Mark McCrindle says that, despite how they feel, they are empowered. 'They really do have a voice,' he says. It's not a voice that delivers in a voting booth, but it is a voice that leverages and influences markets daily. 'They are the 16- to 25-year-olds who are the popular culture leaders, the social media consumers and contributors, and they drive the future of brands and products.' They don't just consume; they create and influence. That leverage is something this cohort doesn't recognise. This is the generation that has been moulded to understand the importance of climate change and sustainability, including financial sustainability. 'They've seen a disposable society, a throwaway culture, and are taking action,' McCrindle says. This is the case from recyclable fashion to where they work and how they eat. 'They – more than the older generations – actually walk the talk in this space, and I think that's very admirable.' Queensland Investment Corporation (QIC) chief economist Matthew Peter says, 'They believe they have the right to success. They see it as their right to learn, their right for you to help them and their right to be successful. They want it all and I think that's a good thing.' Their parents wore 12-hour days as a badge of honour, forgoing holidays at the boss's request and working at weekends. 'Young people don't want that – and good on them because that wasn't sustainable.' At work, their voice is united – and it has upended the workforce. Their parents believed they had to earn recognition by proving themselves to their bosses and doing that unquestionably. 'That's not the case now. They feel entitled to ask questions – and that's changing the nature of the workforce.'

What excites you most about this cohort? My question is to Dr Nicole Archard, who has worked as a school leader in New South Wales and South Australia. She doesn't skip a beat. Her answer is immediate. 'Their power and their voice,' she says. 'I think it's incredible. I'm totally blown away.' She gives the example of a consent video students made in conjunction with their male peers from another school. 'I've watched that video probably 500 times because I'm so proud of their voice . . . it brings tears to my eyes. I'm so proud of their ability to actually stand up and be strong women. And that's the important thing regarding education – to have a voice.' McCrindle says the reality is that these girls are 'shaping democracy, perhaps even more than they would at the ballot box'. The national discussion about consent might be a stellar example of this. 'They understand the role of social media more intuitively than the rest of us, and through those trending hashtags, through magnifying those social media campaigns, they're bringing about policy change, government backflips on key issues.'

Just as a toddler goes through milestones in finding their voice, it's understandable that teen girls need to find the right tone – a voice that encourages action. Kim Kiepe, the principal of Brisbane's Somerville House, admits to being intimidated by some of the young women she meets. They are feisty and passionate and determined. She loves that, but emphasises that the art of communication – of being articulate and strategic and able to tell a story or deliver a message – is often the deal-clincher in changing views and inspiring action. While senior students are shut out of voting, she agrees with Mark McCrindle that different channels can provide the answer. She says groups such as Amnesty International provide a forum for students to be heard, and they present opportunities that were not open to this generation's parents.

Of course, some of the teen campaigns where students' voices are loud are confronting. Mandated vaccines, for example. Right to Die or Right to Choose campaigns in Catholic schools. Gender-fluidity in the schoolyard. 'I really struggle with that one,' one principal says. She gives the example of girls who wanted to address an assembly about gender-fluidity and sexuality and the need for the schoolyard to embrace that – but the same attention wasn't afforded to other girls talking about their relationships. Gender issues are discussed later in this book, but this principal wonders what issues need to be loud and voiced, and what issues are private individual matters. Other principals raise the difference between genuine activism among teens and those who just felt they needed to join in. 'You can tell the difference,' one says. 'I could look out my window and watch a girl pick up papers and think she's the real deal because she's showing she cares for the environment [when no one is looking].'

Despite their influence and the empowerment delivered to them by social media, almost universally the girls believe they are not being heard. 'I want to be taken seriously. A lot of the time when I express an opinion I am passionate about, I am dismissed as I am too young and "don't know how the world works", and although that may be true, I still think my opinions are just as valid as the next person, because they know what they know and I know what I know. What's the difference?' This 17-year-old says she will make 'countless mistakes' in giving her public views, but that was an important part of learning to be an adult. 'So it's all rather confusing, because I want to be taken seriously, but I also want to have the benefits of being a kid. It doesn't really make sense and it isn't really fair, but it's how I feel.' That insight is offered by many. I asked around 1000 teens aged 16, 17 and 18 whether they believed they were listened to by others.

'I'm made to feel my opinions are less valid because I'm young.'

'I feel very listened to and validated by some of my closest friends, but definitely not my mother.'

'When I have spoken up, I have been told it's my fault or I'm being overdramatic. After this, you stop speaking up at all.'

'It is just being my age – that some adults don't hear you on any opinions politically or on social issues because they think you aren't mature enough or old enough to understand.'

'I think when it comes to my opinions in class, no one listens to me because I am a girl; they think it's me being a stupid feminist.'

'In high school I felt very insignificant but I've grown up and matured a lot since then.'

'I often feel like I could stop talking and no one would notice.'

'I feel like people may not value my opinion as much because I am a child and also a female.'

'I don't think my parents really understand why our generation is so focused on environmental issues.'

Ellen Fanning, the host of ABC's *The Drum*, says schools, particularly all-female schools, encourage women to have and express views. They deliberately engineer settings that provoke them 'to think, to ponder difficult societal issues and to formulate views about the world'. It is outside school that they find their opinions carry less value and are often marginalised. 'The challenge we have set for ourselves on *The Drum* is to expand the range of voices in the public square by very simply broadening the notion of what constitutes expertise,' she says. She points out that a valuable voice in the public debate could come from lived experience, knowledge of a geographic place or gender, ethnicity, and culture.

Carly Dober says that feeling they are being excluded from public debate or not being heard can prompt stress and anxiety in these girls. 'They're quite angry and despondent that adults who can vote aren't really voting for the protection of young people,' she says. 'They certainly are the most switched-on cohort of people I've ever worked with.' A despondency over housing affordability popped up repeatedly in girls' responses to their concerns for the future. 'They're the first of the generations where [home ownership] might not be an option for them,' Dober says. That often-quoted Australian dream will be a nightmare for many of them, without strong government intervention. Options available to their parents will not be available to them. 'So they think, "Well, what's the point of having a good job because I'm still not going to be able to afford something?"' That means the goal posts that were available to their parents, don't seem as attainable to them. Perhaps that's why so many aspire to leadership: they're drawn to wanting to change that trajectory. 'They're all incredibly switched on. They really want to see a positive difference in the world,' says Dober. The girls view not being listened to politically as equating to them not being seen as important. They hear, 'You're not paying tax so you're not really important, you're not 18, so you're not really important. We'll see you later, later, later, later ... kick the can down the road. So they've got all these ideas, all this energy and see nowhere really to channel it,' Dober says. Josie Tucker, a Kids Helpline counsellor, says she also wonders about the impact of this cohort feeling as though they are not being taken seriously. She says their views 'can really easily be dismissed as teenage girl behaviour, when in reality they are passionate about them and should be celebrated more'. Ignoring their views on the future, housing affordability and climate change is 'short-changing their ability to participate in that conversation and be active in changing anything.' Tucker's view, which is drawn from conversations with those who have called Kids Helpline, is so important here. We want our teens engaged. We want them to be thoughtful and considered and articulate. But they believe – and perhaps it is not relevant whether it's true or not – that they are being shut down. 'When we dismiss their interest in things because we think it's silly or because we think it's childish, we're not allowing them to develop that sense of self or their pride or their interests and passions,' Tucker says. 'And that's a real shame when you think about how central connection can be or how peer groups can just have fun connecting over something that they're excited or passionate about.'

'I hide behind the girls who are loud. I don't feel comfort-able speaking up.'

So how does a teen girl find her voice? Kim Kiepe, who has spent decades in senior leadership roles in all-girls schools, believes the power of role models is often under-estimated. Aunts feature highly, she says, and they can be 'real or adopted'. Neighbours. Godmothers. Women who want to mentor other younger women. 'Girls get drawn to the power of those mentors. There's an incredible power in that.' Kiepe is a good example. She is quietly spoken. But she can close her eyes and see a visual line-up of women who helped her back herself, grow her confidence and gift her a strong voice. A neighbour was the first. An aunt was second. And then there was a more senior teacher at a low socio-economic school where she taught as a 19-year-old. Watching another teacher in action at that school showed her what she didn't want to do. 'I didn't want to be like her,' she says. Perhaps picking apples off a tree might be an apt analogy. Girls look around and decide which apple they want, and they pick it off. And later, when they want another, they'll search for the one that best suits their taste. Role-modelling is no different. And perhaps that puts the onus on us – educators and parents – to have our daughters tripping over good role models. Of course, a girl's voice will change as she travels through young adulthood. Many say their opinions are formed because of a personal experience or the experience of a friend. The consent debate, for example, has many women taking up that issue, and demanding action and education for younger students at school.

Social justice experiences have also delivered impetus for girls to use their voice for the homeless, the aged and many other groups. Most of these experiences are delivered through schools. Kiepe says that in previous years some of her Year 12 students have played basketball with inmates at a juvenile detention centre. In other schools, girls pack lunches and deliver them to the homeless, visit aged care homes, tutor primary school students and raise funds for domestic and international causes. All of that is to be applauded, and their views will be massaged further on leaving the safety net provided by school and navigating the world on their own. Whether it is at university, in the workforce, at TAFE or in volunteer jobs, they will meet other young adults unlike them. That's when they will be challenged more to consider what they think and how they should use their voice. Several educators raised travel and seeing the world as an important influence on how girls see big-picture issues. Since 2020, those school-organised trips to Vietnam and other countries to help build toilet blocks and school demountables have ceased. They're not travelling with their parents to see how other teenagers live. That, according to some educators, might change how they give back to the community; their charity and views and voice might be given to more domestic causes, which run parallel to their jobs – whether they are a doctor, a lawyer, a carpenter, a teacher, a retail or office worker or a nurse.

Along with debating and public speaking and critical thinking skills, some schools have also poured resources into teaching girls to have a voice to encourage change. For example, Canberra Girls Grammar School runs a Women in Politics and Government program called The House, which is designed specifically to empower girls with the skills to follow a career in politics or government. The program, which began in 2019, is inclusive of students from Years 6 to 12 and includes signature courses, studies in humanities, debating and public speaking skills, leadership training, guest speakers and workshops. Anna Owen, who served as principal there before moving to Queensland's Sunshine Coast Grammar School in 2022, had an office only 100 metres away from Parliament House in Canberra. A part of the program looks at self-judgement, self-acceptance and finding one's voice. 'What we needed was to make them realise that if you go into a position of power, you are going to be divisive, and if you do nothing, not many people push back on you,' she says. 'If you do something significant, you're going to get the equivalent of an internet pile-on. And so we have been using this program to talk to them really overtly about shame and resilience.' The non-compulsory program is co-created with students, and grows in content each year. So what skills does a graduate of The House have? 'They have a voice, they know how to make a choice. They've got ownership, empowerment, and they have leadership,' she says. It's about having a voice, but also knowing when and how to use it most effectively.

That co-creation by students, or using the student voice to build the school community, has been increasing slowly over recent years in a number of schools. It shows that the pupils have a stake in the school community, it provides engagement and it also delivers a community that matches the needs of its students. That has allowed more students to take on leadership roles, despite the fact that they might not wear a badge. 'A decade ago we had a student council and a prefect body and they would be the voices to bring problems forward,' one school leader says. Now, routinely, we have groups of students meet with the leadership team, sometimes formally and sometimes informally, to provide feedback and make suggestions. It allows all students the opportunity to speak, even if they choose not to. Kim Kiepe makes a point of telling her Year 11s that she never wore any sort of badge. 'I always say you're talking to a woman who never ever had a formal leadership position at school. I was that shy person who wouldn't have had the voice at the table and would have relied on the louder girls to speak up,' she says.

No discussion on speaking up is complete without a discussion around 'cancel culture' – a term bandied around easily, but not always understood and often misused. Repeatedly, girls describe it as a virtuous activity in which they engage to shut down racism or misogyny or other bad behaviour. 'If an influencer is saying something that means they don't believe Black Lives Matter, I don't want to follow them. Cancelled.' It's hard to argue with that. But the flip-side is brought up by others, including educators, who worry that it inhibits girls from hearing arguments different from their own, and doesn't have a clearly definite beginning and end. Beth Blackwood, CEO at the Association of Heads of Independent Schools of Australia, raises research done by McCrindle Research to look at it from another standpoint. Just under 70 per cent of those surveyed agreed they would like charities they supported to make their views clear on current social issues, even if they were outside their area of focus. This includes issues like #BlackLivesMatter and climate change. And it was Gen Z, at 84 per cent, leading that charge. Ninety per cent reported that they stopped supporting a charity or not-for-profit because of its behaviour or a stance it took. Again, Gen Z led the pack there too, at 63 per cent. Blackwood says a feature of 'cancel culture', which at its extreme is essentially a modern form of ostracism, was that an 'organisation can be judged by its failure to speak out on social issues as much as by the position it adopts in relation to them'. 'McCrindle Research found that 65 per cent of those surveyed reported they self-censor when sharing their opinions, while 54 per cent said they hide their perspective on topical issues because they are afraid of how people will respond,' she says. While we might wish that all social media users hesitated a moment or two for some brief self-censorship before choosing 'send', the notion that cancel culture can potentially silence half of the community is deeply concerning. 'Will inclusion and diversity be its victims, too? And what of truth and justice?' So how might that play out with sexual assault and consent?

Anna Owen says girls can feel shame when they 'put themselves out there and it sounds like the majority disagree with them'. But it doesn't mean that every time somebody disagrees with you, you are right and they are ignorant. Those girls who debated sometimes understood this better, because they were accustomed to hearing polar opposite cases, and having to argue in support of views they did not hold. Listening to opposing arguments provided them with ammunition to debate against them. Owen also raises the 'the principle of charity' – that before you offer an opinion, you should seek to deeply understand the opinions of others. Teen educator Dannielle Miller also provides clarity here. She says that often when we have one extreme set of behaviours, there tends to be a backlash that cultivates an equally extreme set of behaviours. 'And then somewhere in the middle is probably where we will eventually sit,' she says. 'I think there's much more awareness now that people are more than their less proud moment.' And that redemption is possible. 'But I do think social media definitely feeds almost a gratuitous sense of pleasure in joining a pile-on and feeling that you are on the right side of history by publicly shouting someone down if you don't agree with them,' she says. Miller wonders whether lip-service is often paid to wanting to 'create assertive, world-changing girls'. 'But the reality is that having a person like that can sometimes be a little tricky, which I would argue is a great thing. I loved it when my daughter would challenge me. It's exhausting. But you think, "Oh, wow, she's really becoming someone here!" It's cool that she's questioning – but not everyone likes that.'

The hard line between listening and not listening to other views spills over to friendship groups, discussed in Chapter 5. But author Rebecca Sparrow wonders whether 'we're at a time in society where we're nearly weaponising belonging. And it's that idea of "if you're not with me and not for me, you're the enemy".' Perhaps that has bled out from the inability of our politicians and public figures to listen to each other? 'I don't know,' she says. 'But we used to be a lot more tolerant, even politically, of different views on a whole lot of topics.' Or did we simply not voice them so publicly? Victorian principal Linda Douglas says debate around 'cancel culture' will always be tricky. The more we empower young women, the more views might differ. 'And at times, they do want to – as we all do – shut down those who we don't necessarily agree with. So how can you keep those channels open when one group thinks the other isn't being respectful? It's challenging.' She says the problem lives in what we see modelled. 'Where do we actually see it modelled well? That is the problem. It is very difficult for our young people when I'm not sure that, as adults, what we say is what we do.'

Let me end here with Grace Tame. The 2021 Australian of the Year has taught all of us – teens, their parents and policy-makers – how much change can be forged through speaking out. But she's also shown how using your voice can come at an incontestable cost. In Tame's case, speaking truth to power brought ferocious criticism from those who simply didn't like her message. That delivers a mixed message to those wanting to be heard. Even speaking up, over little things, can draw the ire of others. But to take their place in a society shrill with opinion, we need to teach our girls that their voice is worth it. We need to hear them. And, if we do, they, just like Grace Tame, will make the world a better place.

5

Friends and family

This is the generation raised on choice: of music and media, what they read and what they wear, what extracurricular activities they choose and what they eschew, what they eat and what they don't. Smaller families and bigger homes, particularly in middle-class Australia, mean some will get to choose their own bedroom. And these young women own their choices. Perhaps television entertainment is the window into the rest of their lives. For their parents, it was a choice of this channel or that, and each movie was punctuated by advertisements and censorship laws and viewing habits. That's gone. The choice now is as seamless as it is endless. Watch whatever, whenever, wherever. On a smartphone or a big screen. In bed or on the bus. Choice. It's a remarkable gift for this strong, sassy and introspective generation of girls. But it catches other parts of their lives too. Like friendship.

By ages 16 and 17, girls have had a long history in friendships. Different groups, shoe-horned by passions and popularity, sporting associations and family connections. It starts early, as they begin to crawl and walk at parents' groups, and then into the sandpits and toddler classrooms of pre-schools and kindergartens. At school, even early on, drama can kill off friendships before they reach any sort of maturity. Groups develop. She's in my group. I'm not in her group. I can't invite her – she's not in my group! What parents of tween girls have not heard those dramatic declarations? Time is spent cajoling daughters not invited to a party, or even uninvited. Of worrying about the influence of the smartphone, even before they're allowed to access social media. Few parents – especially mothers – have not lain awake at night staring at the ceiling, hoping their daughter finds her 'tribe', hoping like hell that they will be sitting next to someone tomorrow at lunchtime. In high school, it gets even harder because many girls choose not to articulate their lunchtime heartache. Bullying. Exclusion. Whispered comments. Choice is harder too. This group, or that group. The group wanting to vape, or the group that thinks it's immature. We want to help our girls make good choices along the friendship smorgasbord, but many girls continue to graze, creating transactional bonds that feed their immediate needs.

But then, in Year 12, according to so many girls I have talked to for this project, something else happens. Perhaps it's a friendship maturity. Perhaps it's the result of the introspection that marks this cohort. Perhaps they are simply pragmatic. But those hard friendships are often let go. They turn into a nod on the way to class, or a passing acknowledgement at the school gates or the party they're both attending. That choice brings enormous clarity, and they're able to hone in on those friendships that build them up, not those that tear them down. In many cases, that leads to beautiful bonds that will be seen, no doubt, in bridesmaids' photos and Uber-sharing to school reunions. But in other cases – many, many cases – the end of school marks the end of the need to fit in to someone else's story; it provides a freedom to reimagine friendships and networks and relationships. With the end in sight, even by the close of Year 11, many girls are more confident about their own values and how they see the world. That allows them access again to that choice that has coloured their lives. They'll walk away from some groupings. 'True belonging doesn't require you to change who you are,' Brené Brown says in *Atlas of the Heart*, 'it requires you to be who you are.'[1] They'll choose to be part of the drinking crew, or not. They'll judge the views of their peers – on everything from racism to vaccination roll-outs – and make sharp decisions about where they belong in this big class thrown together years earlier.

For much of this task, I found this heartbreaking. Girls throwing away bonds built over years. Students walking away from friendships that filled smartphone albums. The social challenges faced by those on the autism spectrum or with learning difficulties that could lead to misunderstandings or misinterpretation. Friendships that demanded a down-payment on the traditional end-of-Year 12 schoolies week imploding. Transactional friendships fill the buffet of choice for many of these maturing teens.

'I've stopped being friends with people who don't make me happy and create negative energy.'

'By this age you pick friends and don't mind putting people offside.'

'Friendship should be sorted by 16. At least, that's what I thought. But it's not.'

'Some friends I had didn't care about keeping in contact during lockdown, so I don't make an effort to try to talk to them.'

'I had a group of 11. We split in two now because we have different values and ideas of fun. One half likes to go clubbing, drinking, get with guys, vaping and drugs and don't care. The other half are more anxious and concerned about being safe.'

'Our school is interesting – a broad range of people with money and without. I know people who have two jobs and some who got a car for their birthday. For our friendship group, it all clashed. There were a few girls who thought they were entitled, and would put other people down.'

'We'd call them out over racism and sexist things. That's when we went our separate ways.'

'The differences were always there, but we kept the peace. But in Year 12, you decide to take them on.'

'I feel as though I've given so much more than I got. It doesn't bother me now because they're not my tribe. The system of groups in schools is something that we all struggle with. When you get out of school there are no groups. At school they are the most important thing in the world.'

'You form your own ideas and values and if your friends don't align with them, you don't want to put up with stuff you don't necessarily enjoy or like.'

'I have been able to detach myself from toxic friend-ship groups and find somewhere I'm happier to finish off Year 12.'

'I put less pressure on myself to be close to people at school now because I have found friends outside school.'

'I've drifted back to an old friendship group who better share my values.'

'This year you can afford not to be friendly to people who are toxic. In a few months I don't even have to talk to them.'

'At school you are friends for friends' sake. Also to keep the peace. In COVID you don't have to do that.'

'My friends are anti-vax and it has basically changed my whole opinion of them.'

'As we've moved into Year 12, people start to focus and people's values become clearer – friends drift together when they have the same interests.'

'We are just coexisting until graduation.'

'Some want to go to uni and some don't. We know the friendship will end so no one is trying really hard anymore.'

But this is good, experts say, and their reasoning is forensic. Girls are making their own choices after enormous rumination. They are nutting out their values and beliefs and how they see themselves, and choosing to – or choosing not to – continue bonds with those they've shared classes with for years. That means it's inevitable that groups fracture. Some bonds will remain, but others will be removed from the smorgasbord of choice.

'I'm so excited to branch out and not be pigeon-holed . . . for that opportunity to reach out and meet new friends.'

'I think groups are really big in Years 7 to 10. The cool group. The better group. I want to make friends all over the place, not just from here. I want people with different ideas and [who] think differently.'

Those 'groups' girls talk about are part of their identity development. And they continue into Year 12, often facilitated by schools that grant senior students privileged seating areas. There, on their assigned seats, groups are locked in, one teacher explains. School counsellor Jody Forbes says Year 12 friendship changes can be dictated by changing values, but also an eye to Year 13. 'So they might get less invested in friends who they know are going away or going interstate or if they themselves are going interstate, so they just bide their time,' she says. That changes the energy levels of friendships. Some girls will spend their time in the library, focused on the external exam six months away, while others will remain in groups, waiting it out. Others, knowing their friends will be part of their post-school life, cling to their group. According to Forbes, 'Girls are sort of analysing friendships to see how it suits them. What sort of purpose it's going to serve. They're also thinking of the consequences. "I don't like this group." "I don't like this girl, but the alternative is X,

Y and Z and then that won't work out because of this. So I'm better off staying here. I'm only going to have to spend the next four months with her."' Psychologist Laura Lee says discerning friendship can be a feature of Year 12. 'There's kind of a sense of "I know this friendship has served a purpose for me in high school but I won't take it any further into my life".'

But isn't that transactional? 'I think this is how they do it. Friendship will be like this for them,' Forbes says. Social media influences friendship in many ways, but here it allows girls to maintain contact into the future, whether they are friends or not. Most will walk out of the school gates for the last time with the whole 200-strong cohort following each other on Instagram. Educator Dannielle Miller says this age also brings a level of purity about themselves, and that's something to be celebrated. 'We have this notion that everyone should all be friends and we preach that to them from quite a young age in schools,' she says. 'And I think we do them a disservice by saying that because the truth is that we're not always going to be friends with everyone – but we can be friendly.' She's right, of course. Look around our own workplaces. Not everyone is friends. 'We want this to be a utopian world where no matter how annoying someone might be to us, they're supposed to put up with that, and I think by the senior years, they just don't buy into it as much.' Author Rebecca Sparrow says it was a myth that friendship should be easy. While it shouldn't be a rollercoaster, it requires real work. '[Friendships] do require work like any other relationship, and I think friendships get dismissed and we think that the only relationships that need a lot of work are romantic relationships.' You don't meet old friends today. And hard work means showing up and having difficult conversations. 'It means having an ability to self-reflect and say "I'm sorry".' Every authentic friendship will hit bumps and require forgiveness when the friendship is bigger than the argument, she says.

The way friendship is unfolding in these senior years almost mirrors the networks that have helped young men nab good jobs for decades. Bonds with benefits. Friendships in the here and now, not forever. Women are often attributed with better friendship skills – an ability to listen, empathy, loyalty. Just imagine if this modern friendship fell over into networking. It might pave the career path with gold. Brisbane principal Dr Andrew Cousins says that for some senior students there is almost an 'escape', where they determine they can be who they want, follow the path of their own dreams and reimagine themselves post-school. That leads to less comparison with peers and more focus on their own journey. Sometimes those who were happy to 'dive feet first into university' knew they'd have an opportunity to connect with peers in smaller class sizes. Those in classes with 1000 others might be more challenged in the friendship stakes. 'I don't really have contact with anyone from high school anymore but I really quickly became friends with some of the other girls at my college which was super surprising,' says one girl, in a view echoed by others. University colleges offer that friendship opportunity. So do big share houses, whether girls are studying, working or training. But those taking on study from home found it harder. Educator Deborrah Francis, from Melbourne, says she worries about the impact of COVID-19 on girls' friendship circles. First-year university, for the past two years, has been off campus, something many girls considered both lonely and isolating. She says those girls who were never bound to one group, or who found themselves sitting outside groups, almost never warranted concern. 'They've demonstrated the ability to get along with a lot of different people without feeling the need to have someone, you know, as a best friend,' she says.

Rebecca Sparrow says our teens need to genuinely understand that nothing beats 'hanging out with our friends in person'. 'I know we're seeing a spike in anxiety and loneliness amongst school leavers. Contributing to that, I think, is a lack of social connection,' she says. 'Texting and messaging cannot replace in-person catch-ups. We are hardwired for connection as human beings and we need to be around each other.' Brisbane principal Janet Stewart says the social media landscape adds enormous complexity and pressure to friendships. Everything is in the now. Instant gratification dictates decisions for all of us. Friends are made and lost with haste. And everything is public. 'When it's good, it's collaborative, and when it's bad, it's collaborative as well,' she says.

When our daughters are in their early teens, we know the tug-of-war between their friends and families will very often favour friends. They become overriding influences in their lives, from primary school on. But here's another nugget of gold when looking at older teens and their relationship with friends and families. Many are talking more to their parents than in previous generations, and perhaps even more than a few years ago. That appears to be driven by two factors. Girls are confronting teen challenges such as body image and eating disorders and self-harm, along with tricky friendship issues, earlier and earlier. School counsellors are now seeing in Years 7 and 8 and 9 what five or six years ago they saw in Years 11 and 12. The early teen years are fraught for many teens, who are searching for a sense of belonging. That involves distancing themselves from their parents. But by the senior years, many girls – irrespective of the challenges they face – are no longer dismissing everything about their parents, and particularly their mothers. And they're happy to confide in and talk and speak openly to her. That's the first factor. The second factor is that parents, faced with raising a teen in a tricky world, are encouraging those conversations in a way our own parents might not have bothered or might have struggled to do. 'I think we have done a much better job than our generation of parents in terms of having open communication and respect and engaging their opinions and listening to them,' Sparrow says. A school leader echoes that: 'My daughters tell me all sorts of things I would never have told my mother.' And this from a school counsellor: 'I'm told more than I want to know!' Parents are trying to act as a sherpa as their teens make decisions. This is what girls say:

> 'We eat dinner together every night and have good conversations.'

> 'They're good to me and we get along most of the time.'

> 'I wouldn't say we are close but we do talk every night at dinner about our day and our problems. However, closeness with my family stops there.'

> 'It's been a little rocky lately but I feel lucky to have them.'

> 'Strong and supportive.'

> 'We have our bad moments but there is more good than bad.'

> 'My family are at the end of the day the people who I know will always have my back. I've had a few downs

this year and situations that have knocked me back and they always support me.'

Now, at 17 and 18 especially, many girls describe their relationship with their parents in more glowing terms than might have been the case two years earlier. Michelle Mitchell, author of *Everyday Resilience*, says that from about 16 up, girls are 'so open to mentors in their lives' and no longer always buck authority just for the sake of it. 'They have this "understand me, hear me and help me do life" and "I think it's such a beautiful time in life" [attitude],' she says. But there is no doubt that the relationship is still developing and can be fraught – with trust, independence, academic pressure and financial control being the chief factors.

'My family is like a box of chocolates. When I come home, I never know what it's going to be like.'

'There are differences of opinions between me and my parents about education and how to succeed in life.'

'My parents are experts at gaslighting. They twist everything.'

'My dad and I never got along and my mum is always on my back about schoolwork. I wish it was better but I don't think there's anything I can do about it.'

'They put pressure on me. When I do try and take a break from my almost constant work, I become the worst child known to humankind.'

'Stop putting pressure on me to receive perfect results on externals.'

'I'm an only child so I feel a bit controlled by them and we argue a lot.'

'I keep my family life and friend life separate so [my] family doesn't know much about me outside of the home.'

'I'm so excited to move out away from my family.'

Those last two comments, and others like them, were singled out by one counsellor who made the point that at this age, some girls might 'detach' rather than have loud emotional arguments with their parents. Some were even just 'coexisting' – like they do with school friendships – until they could move on. Another says, 'We have some girls who will simply be estranged from parents – but there won't be those awful sort of relationships that can happen when they are a bit younger.' Divorce and acrimonious parental relationships also colour many girls' bonds with one or both parents.

'My parents got divorced when I was little and I have a very difficult relationship with each side of my family. My

*mum and I are really close. But when Dad got remarried
to my step-mum we lost our relationship because she
wasn't a very nice person.'*

*'Me and my dad's relationship can be very difficult. It's
because of my parents' divorce.'*

*'I am very close with my mum and get along with my
siblings. I don't talk to my dad.'*

*'Good relationship with Dad. Mum is a bit off and on
over whether she likes me or not.'*

By this age, sometimes separated families have learnt
how to operate; in some cases, that will mean they work
together with common rules, where teens spend time with
both parents. But in others, or often in new separations,
hostilities remain. This was the only time where the
girls I spoke to showed divorce to be an issue – when
parents didn't get on. In amicable relationships, girls
complained about being shunted between homes, but their
relationships with both parents didn't differ from those of
friends spending every night under the same roof. In some,
relationships with step-fathers were especially treasured.
Family relationships came under the microscope for many
during pandemic lockdowns, even if those lockdowns were
brief. Kids Helpline received a spike in calls on the issue.
Domestic abuse calls to police escalated. Some girls saw

their parents' relationship up close, and came to the verdict that it was unhealthy. But in other cases, teen girls say they spent more time talking with their parents, particularly their father, who, because in 'normal' times so much parenting still falls on mothers, might have been travelling less and around the house more. In other cases, that led to big tensions because families had tended to function well without Dad present. His daily involvement 'upended the harmony'. Some schools reported increased engagement by fathers. You could see that. Fathers in the park with younger daughters, flying kites. Going for walks with their daughter and the family dog. But older girls, not keen on kites or father–daughter walks, sat and argued and even 'reacquainted'. My point here is that every family is different and a separated family can work much better than one where antagonism umbrellas the relationship. It only becomes an issue when children are not considered first – and even then, by this age, that is often sorted.

Being a parent is a high-wire act. Engagement not involvement. Listening without judgement. Encouragement not pressure. Advice not homilies. School leaders are unanimous in believing that mothers in particular can be 'over-invested' in their children's lives and, while it ebbs and flows, Year 10 is when both parents can push the 'involvement needle'. That's often around subject selection for Year 11. Then academic involvement occurs again, around exams and pressures and results, in Year 12. Several educators say the range of parent–teacher interviews through that time was aimed at tempering that. In some families, parents struggle to let go. In one example, a mother organised a semi-formal partner for her daughter but did not tell her. She found out when a classmate, whose parents knew her parents, told her. 'I broke down in tears and ran out of the classroom. I felt embarrassed and so disregarded by my parents. I just know a similar thing is going to happen for the formal.' In another case, a mother offered to pay a boy to take her daughter to the formal – but on the condition that he also ask her to his formal.

Some of the stories around involvement feed the view, discussed in Chapter 17, that once school and the structures it offers are disbanded, teens can languish. Schools prop up many students, allowing repeat exams, special consideration, numerous drafts, wellbeing check-ins and a host of other services. That stops at graduation. It's easier for parents to intervene while their students are at school. Parents calling teachers on the weekend to question homework. Parents demanding that schools 'retract' detention because their daughter's rudeness is a sign of her standing up for herself. Parents who get a 'lawyer friend' to re-mark a legal affairs assignment before demanding changes to results. Parents even filling in university course applications with the preferences they have chosen for their daughter. One relays the story of a student who did the course their parents wanted, and 'on their graduation, handed them the certificate and said, "Now I'm going to go and do what I want."' Principals say that girls routinely change course in the second or third year if their parents have chosen what they are studying. They develop the confidence – albeit a bit later than others – to pursue their own dream.

So what are the parental attributes of those students who flourish in Years 12 and 13? 'Rather than it being all about the result at the end of the term, it's about how they're living as a person,' says Brisbane principal Dr Andrew Cousins. That comment is repeated by his peers over and over. Providing support. Granting staged independence. Being engaged, not overly involved, in their school lives. A guide, not a best friend. Role-modelling forgiveness. Showing vulnerability. Open communication. Sharing their own experiences. Eschewing micro-management. Principal Helen Jamieson worries that parental confidence is waning. Parents wanted a good relationship with their teen but some struggled to find 'that separation between being the parent and being their friend'. She suggests taking your teen on a date. 'It's about breaking bread with them too. Have a meal. The best conversations we have are either at the dinner table or in the car.' Author of *Miss-connection* Dr Justin Coulson says many parents will be challenged at some point when their daughters are aged between 15 and 19. 'There's going to be a 12- to 24-month period when many parents wonder if they've lost their daughter,' he says. Often that's because of a romantic interest. But open lines of communication need to be maintained. It is also important for parents to find a window into their adolescent's world. 'When our kids are little, we spend a lot of time with them. We connect with them. We roll around with them. We engage in what psychologists call "serve and return" interaction,' Dr Coulson says. We give back the coos and gurgles we hear. As they grow, we join them in colouring in and other activities. 'Then something happens,' he says. They seek independence and their parents enjoy a Sunday sleep-in. 'We don't have the same level of connectedness that we used to. As all that's happening, they lean more towards friends. Our relationship is becoming more sidelined and other relationships become primary.' We've lost influence. 'We discover the romantic interest in their life might impact their decision-making or they're experimenting with substances that we're uncomfortable with or they're just not coming home and we don't want them to be having sleepovers at their new friend's house or whatever it might be.' At that point, it will rarely work to pull them back and demand changes. 'We've got to do what we did when our relationship was good, and they did want us in their lives,' he says. The metaphorical toddler tickles and pre-tween pool jumps. 'We need to be back in their world to find ways we can reconnect.' But it can take time, not a 40-minute chat over a cuppa. 'You've got to work through things,' Dr Coulson says.

Rebecca Sparrow says it's never too late, but when your teen wants to talk, 'drop what you are doing' within reason. 'Stop cutting the carrots. Stop looking at your phone. Give them your attention.' Attention is the currency of this time. 'Go into their world.' Once upon a time we might have been expected to take an interest in what our parents wanted us to be interested in. That's flipped. 'Watch whatever TV series your daughter is into. Put the effort into going into their world. That will pay off.' School counsellor Jody Forbes encourages parents to 'contain their own feelings'. 'If parents are scared, then they'll be over-protective. If a parent is worried about the future, they can put a lot of pressure on their daughters,' she says. She's a parent, so she understands how difficult that can be. 'It takes a lot to feel it and contain it, but I talk to parents about responding rather than reacting.'

6

Unsocial media

At schools across the nation, in rural and city areas, social media pages are set up to showcase semi-formal and formal dresses. The aim is to post photos of the dress once it has been bought so others don't purchase the same one. Girls do it with enormous pride. Many of them have saved for months to call an outfit their own. Others have been bought by parents who believe this gala is the social pinnacle of their daughter's school life. The prices are as varied as the dresses, and in this project some girls had spent as little as $40. Others had spent $1900. And while it goes off without a hitch in many instances, psychologists and school counsellors have found alarming trends in recent years. Some girls get hundreds of likes on their dress while others get a handful. Some dresses are held up as belonging to stars; others sit there with messages that are passively unkind. Some girls post their dress being worn by a model. Others post their own selfie, from the change-room where they found it. But it's the comparison that spreads concern. Tasmanian school psychologist Nicole Young says she's seen a 'culture' develop around dresses and prices and how people look. 'And it's pressure before they even get to the formal of "What am I wearing and how does that compare to everyone else?".' In the few days before our interview, she was contacted by two girls, sending screenshots of comments made in one group. And it was the brutal self-judgement that worried her. Comments like, 'I can't find a dress', 'I hate my body', 'I'm not comfortable'. In these cases, others tried to build them up. 'I think the fundamental concern is they're not happy with their own self-image. And this is exacerbating it because it's kind of putting it on a platform where they feel as though they have to compare themselves to others.' And it particularly hits those who are already prone to anxiety or insecurity. It worries cyber safety expert and author Susan McLean too. 'I've seen it descend into a whole lot of nastiness very quickly. I've even seen formal pages from boys' schools where it's basically, rate the date. So you've got to put a picture of (your date) up, the dates are then rated, and unless they're rated eight, nine or ten, you can't bring them.' Confident girls are not going to be held to ransom by boys or other groups of girls. But many girls don't fall into that category. 'Have you found a principal brave enough to cancel the traditional formal?' one principal asks. And it's clear she would be happy to follow suit.

The formal dress upload is just one way social media plays a role. There are others. Despite cyberbullying peaking earlier, girls in Years 11 and 12 are not immune. But at 16 and 17, McLean, a former Victorian police officer who now educates students about social media, says it can switch to using their bodies – from nude photos to highly sexualised snaps, to having accounts on subscription porn sites to make money. What? 'Yes. One girl said to me, "It's my body. I'm proud of it. Why shouldn't I make money from it?" So why flip burgers at McDonald's when you can make a few hundred or a few thousand by sending out these sexy snaps?' That goes to the heart of the 'body image' issues that strangle so many in this cohort. How girls see themselves. How they see others. 'Too many times it's linked to porn,' McLean says. 'And the porn star look – I need to be svelte, carefree, compliant. I need to have big boobs.' Medicos also report girls coming in with sustained injuries from trying to copy what they have seen in porn movies. McLean says some teenage girls are now asking for vaginal surgery because they think they look 'different' from what they are seeing online. More common are the filtered photographs brought into the surgeons, with requests for them to look like the fake snap in front of them. 'That picture might be "Mary Smith" but it's a doctored photo of Mary Smith, or it's a photoshop of Mary Smith. They want to believe in the story, the fairytale. It's "I don't want you to tell me that this photo is photoshopped because I just want to believe it's real",' McLean says. Victorian psychologist Carly Dober says girls are looking at those filtered snaps and thinking, 'Oh my God, look how ugly I look when the filter is removed!' And that can be the impetus for Snapchat surgery.

Snapchat surgery? 'Wanting to get surgery based on those filters,' Dober says. 'And that's quite disturbing to me because you know the majority of girls I work with may have had better self-confidence, but the online world – especially for the past few years – had been all they have been able to experience.' And so girls are visiting plastic surgeons, with 'Snapchat dysmorphia', requesting fuller lips, bigger eyes, more symmetrical noses. Whiter teeth. Eyes like a cat. 'There's been an increase in requests for Snapchat filter surgeries.' Doctors label the phenomenon, which has also been trending up in other countries over recent years, 'alarming' because the filtered selfies are an unattainable look and blur the line between reality and fantasy.[1]

But it is not just the experts who acknowledge the distortions that online interactions can bring. At 16 and 17 and 18, students are honest about their use of social media and how it impacts them. Few say their relationship with their smartphone is healthy, and many would love to be able to put it down more often, or to voluntarily embark on a technology detox. About 1000 surveyed 16-, 17- and 18-year-olds responded to questions about how often they used social media, their preferred platforms and how they saw their use of those platforms. Many were surprised when they focused on how many hours a day they spent screen scrolling.

'I use it three hours a day.'

'Wow! I just checked and I'm scared. Two hours a day on average and 12 hours a week.'

'Not too much during the week but on the weekends definitely more than five hours a day.'

'Each day between two and five hours.'

'I know it's bad but in lockdown, up to six hours a day.'

'I spend around four hours on social media on a school day because that's how I communicate with my friends.'

Two themes popped up across the nation: students were surprised by how much they used social media, once they were asked to calculate their usage, and lockdowns – even short ones – led to a significant increase in their post-lockdown use. 'With this age range in particular, social media is so ingrained in their life,' digital wellbeing expert and author Dr Kristy Goodwin says. She suggests the focus, at 16 and 17, needs to be on encouraging teens to have a 'healthy relationship' with social media and that 'banning it or cancelling' is outdated and unhelpful.

Social media platforms varied, but without doubt Instagram, TikTok, YouTube and Snapchat topped the list.

'I love Instagram because of the amazing creators I follow (body positive creators, environmentalists, music artists, ethical brands, people questioning the world, and critical thinking). I also love Tik Tok for a similar reason – as well as the humour it brings.'

'My favourite social media app is Snapchat because it allows me to communicate with friends easily, while seeing their faces.'

'Snapchat. It's more raw and I only have to talk to the people I want to and can filter what I see from other people. I also find that it is the least toxic social media platform.'

'TikTok. People are relatable and funny on there. I know I'm not the only one going through things.'

'TikTok because there are teens out there who have exactly the same understanding as all of us and [it] is a place where you can easily express yourself with minimum judgement.'

'YouTube is my distraction.'

Of course, there were others too. Twitter to express opinions, DeviantArt, WhatsApp, Tumblr, Discord. And gaming also rated highly. Psychologist Amanda Abel says the proportion of girls playing video games has increased, perhaps as a result of COVID-19. And while younger teens were more likely to game, she says research by The Insights Family showed that about 65 per cent of teen girls aged 16 to 18 played video games.[2] However, something to celebrate here was the recognition that their use of social media might be unhealthy; there was also a determination to use it less. This was my question: 'How would you describe your relationship with social media?'

'I deleted social media in the lead-up to the externals so I can focus on study. I've found I don't miss it that much.'

'It's made me a more insecure person and made me compare my life to everyone else. I tried to take a break but when I went back on occasionally, I would just feel like shit every time.'

'It doesn't affect me negatively because I only follow things that I enjoy seeing and I am interested in. It makes me laugh, I get to see what my friends and distant relatives are up to. I also see many opportunities for school, jobs and career pathways.'

'It's my escape from the world.'

'Toxic – but I really enjoy it. I get all my news and information from social media. I love being able to have access to all my friends at the click of a button.'

'I've developed an almost co-dependency [with] Discord and TikTok at times.'

'Social media makes me feel like I'm not doing what I am meant to be doing at my age.'

'I am addicted and it's bad.'

'It stresses me out when I have a bunch of messages, especially when I want to go to bed.'

'I wish I had more self-control.'

'I think of it like a toxic friend who needs to be kicked out of my life. It creates so many dramas.'

'Social media terrifies me. The way that algorithms work to cater to each and every consumer is scary. But in saying that I actively use and am willing to be a consumer for entertainment and communication purposes.'

Despite its undoubted influence, research around social media use is limited. For example, some research says social media has a negative impact on young people, particularly in relation to body image, self-esteem, anxiety and depression. But much of that is self-reported and involves non-clinical diagnosis of the issues. Dr Goodwin says that makes it difficult to determine how positive – or negative – social media use can be. But the wasted hours frustrate some parents, as well as the teens themselves. So does the blue screen that hinders sleep. But perhaps the algorithms used by social media provide the invisible danger – and they're not easy to understand, even for those who are experts in this area.

Dr Emily van der Nagel, a lecturer in social media at Monash University, says every time we log onto a social media platform or our internet browser, we create 'digital traces', which can be tracked. 'The internet companies, especially big social media companies and platforms like Facebook and Instagram and Twitter, are always really interested in what people are doing on the internet because they want to serve people ads. This is how they make their money,' she says. The way we use and move through those digital spaces influences the type of advertising we are personally fed – from targeted advertisements for clothes to trending topic information. 'If you're searching for something, if you befriend somebody, if you click on something, if you like something – these are all digital traces that give platforms an indication of what you're interested in.' In practical terms, it might work like this: with the formal only three months away, Mason, 17, is looking for a dress. She searches on Instagram, and looks up her favourite styles on Google. Next, she'll see photos of those dresses pop up as advertisements in the platform feeds where she has an account. Her advertisements will be different from those lobbing into the feeds of her best friend Adrina, who is looking at different styles. These 'dark ads' are only visible to those who receive them. That means the content – pictures and text – are not available for public inspection. Research has also shown that the pattern of distribution is unclear. They tend to exist only for a short time and change regularly – making them difficult to track. 'That is such a really powerful part of how algorithmic advertising operates. It's not the same as if you pick up a magazine and everybody's getting the same ads. Everyone's driving past the same billboard. You can see that billboard and you can talk about it in class; you can say, "Why do you think this company is showing you a skinny woman? Because it's trying to sell you something? Because it's trying to convince you that this sort of body is right?"' Dr van der Nagel says. Dr Goodwin says algorithms are clever in how they are fed each time we click on a post, even if our search relates to healthy eating or good nutrition. 'When you share those insights with young people, they are flabbergasted with the way they've been manipulated,' she says.

The influence is perhaps most worrying when it comes to advertisements about diet and body shape – an area of concern raised by school counsellors and teen psychologists. It's not new; for decades now, television advertisements and magazines and billboards have delivered us messages about different body types and what is perceived as 'attractive'. But it's different when the advertisements are so personal, and appear on a device that we carry around in our pockets, school bags and handbags. They become impossible to avoid. Sponsored accounts pop up with each screen scroll, a paid influencer's message slips in between others, almost as though it belongs there. 'We know it's not as simple as saying, "Well, if you see an ad that you don't like that means it's time to log off from all your social media and never use it again",' Dr van der Nagel says. But at the age of 16, girls should be prompted to think 'What do these ads mean?', 'Where do they come from?', 'Who's serving them to me?' A starting point, in terms of girls critically analysing what they see, is a recognition that those influencer posts and sponsored feeds are advertisements. 'It's important to know why a person is holding up a product or why they are talking about how fantastic their new diet is,' she says. This is particularly crucial given how important this cohort is to advertisers. They are seen as future customers, even if their spending habits are confined now. But they are a social mob, making new friends and new connections, spreading their wings at universities and in workplaces. 'And they are turning into the kinds of customers they're going to be for the rest of their lives. That's a really important cohort for advertisers,' Dr van der Nagel says.

Big social media companies regularly announce changes in this space, in an attempt to convey that they are trying to protect young people. For example, Instagram – which has more than one billion users – moved in 2019 to regulate the selling and promotion of weight-loss products and cosmetic procedures. That meant users under 18 years of age were prohibited from viewing posts relating to detox pills, diet pills and cosmetic procedures. But whether there has been any impact is harder to determine. Dr van der Nagel says if she had a 16-year-old daughter, she'd be most worried that they do not understand how complicated these power dynamics are: platforms have enormous power and deep pockets, and their users are their targets. 'But I would also want a 16-year-old girl to know that they have power too. And it's really important that they know where their power in this relationship they have with social media lies and how to exercise it. So, for example, they don't have to follow celebrities just because their friends do. They can follow all kinds of wonderful body positive and really diverse representations of women.' That's perhaps easier said than done, though.

'[Social media] makes me so insecure about my pale skin and my acne or how my hair looks disgusting or how wide and round my face is.'

'I enjoy connecting with friends and see tons of funny and entertaining content; however, it has a negative impact on my relationship with my body as I can't help but compare myself to the beautiful girls I see.'

'I find it can be really overwhelming and toxic in the nature of comparing yourself [against] unattainable beauty standards. It has stunted my self-confidence a huge amount.'

'I find myself hating how I look more and more.'

'Please cover body image. I suffer because of social media. A lot of my friends are the same. It's a big issue that hinders me going about my life normally. Going to school each day, I get stressed because I don't have my legs shaved. In society in general; why can't they accept us all as different.'

'Social media. We know models have been touched up. It still gets under our skin.'

Those comments, from six teens aged either 16 or 17, don't surprise psychologist Laura Lee. 'Rather than just comparing themselves to the girls in their class, or in their neighbourhood, they can now compare [themselves] to girls all over the world who are presenting a really curated version of their lives,' she says. That means it doesn't take much for them to find someone they compare less favourably with.

Educator and counsellor at The Modern Parent, Martine Oglethorpe, says social media models are often programmed as 'the girl next door'. 'It's as if they've woken up and they look like that, with their hair down, wearing their latest active wear and drinking a green smoothie. And they're marketed as you and me – they're not marketed as models.' Shouldn't girls be able to distinguish that at 16 and 17? 'If you were to ask, they would likely know – but it doesn't change the fact that when you're scrolling, what you're seeing is that end product and it's still a comparison.' It is just human nature to compare when your whole world is being fed by aesthetic images. The girls acknowledge this. They know what they are seeing is fake, but it still gets under their skin. The possibility of looking like that. The comparison. 'I know people who really are stunning and amazing and they still struggle. No matter what you look like you're always going to find something that's wrong because you are not a supermodel,' a 17-year-old explains.

Carly Dober says strong media literacy programs in schools have tried to address critical thinking skills, so girls can discern the real from the fake. 'But it's not enough if you get a media literacy program to critically assess that once or twice a year. [They're] using these apps every single day.' They are fed by the dopamine hits that come with likes and interactions, and their online worlds can become unreal; highlight reels of 'incredible people and these influencers who live incredible lives' are more potent than the programs created to combat these issues. Another group of thinkers showed up in this research: 17- and 18-year-olds, predominantly, who knew they were being fed fake photographs – but they wanted to mirror them anyway. One gave the example of a crop top. 'When we dress up, it's not for ourselves,' one student says. 'We understand marketing. It's just marketing. We understand that social media is made for us. It makes us feel as though we want to fit in. We recognise that.' And they still follow it anyway. Brisbane educator and psychologist Jody Forbes studied body image for her PhD and says, 'How much comparison a girl embarks on is central here.' The key is not the amount of time they spent on social media, but rather the amount of comparison they make between themselves and what they are seeing. 'So it's not about necessarily reducing the social media. It's about helping your child not to compare themselves to others,' she says. Females also use social media to compare themselves with others more than any other form of media, and feel worse after doing it. 'Females also engage in more upward comparison where they compare [themselves] against somebody who is better, richer smarter, thinner – [which] usually results in poorer mood, less appearance satisfaction and more thoughts of dieting and exercise,' Forbes says.

'I think social media is the scourge of our world,' Sydney principal Paulina Skerman says. 'I think it's one of the most destructive forces. And while we can't censor the world, I think the way social media works and the way it reinforces, and the way that those algorithms work is incredibly destructive.' COVID-19 has intervened to exacerbate things here. It has meant teachers haven't been able to talk to girls and 'challenge some of the stuff that you would usually challenge'. It had left many students 'at the mercy of what was going on in social media', according to Skerman. 'For me, social media is in every way the most destructive thing – the whole dopamine hit, the likes, the whole self-worth tied up in that … as educators we've never had a challenge like we do now to make these kids understand that they are who they are inside, and not this superficial …' Her voice trails off but her frustration remains. 'Even the TV shows they watch. Oh my God – *Married at First Sight* and *The Bachelorette*? It's showing them a way of living that is destructive and toxic and artificial.'

A cyber safety expert, Susan McLean says she is concerned about girls' 'willingness to tolerate harassing behaviour by others'. 'They'll say to me: "What can I do about my friend?" My reply? "Well, first of all, that person is not your friend because friends don't harass. Friends don't put you down. Friends don't have unrealistic expectations of you. That's not a friend."' At the heart of girls wanting to be liked and wanting to have friends is a willingness by some to 'turn a blind eye' to bad behaviour, to cop harassing demands for nude snaps. 'If you want to prove that you like me, you need to send the photo to me . . . There's not a week goes by that I'm not dealing with a scenario like that in the upper end of the school,' she says. So what can we do? 'All we can do is try to empower them [to understand] that they're worth more than that. Their self-esteem shouldn't be based on the sum of a naked body photo. You're worth more than the number of likes. You are more than a number. You are not a number of likes, comments, shares and followers. Try to make them understand that they do have self-worth and it should not be led by other people's perceptions.' The power of influencers is also hard to fathom here. The influencer marketing industry in 2022 is expected to be a $16.4 billion industry.[3] Girls hanging off every word of someone, somewhere, who can get hundreds of thousands of likes for a photo of a single handbag.

When parents contact Martine Oglethorpe about their daughter's use of social media, it usually starts with a concern that she is 'obsessed with her phone'. But as they talk, it's what the phone delivers that becomes more apparent as the problem. Drama. Emotional energy that takes up too much time. Small misunderstandings magnified to a big audience, where the ramifications are wide and it hangs around, for people to see, forever. 'When little niggles and things happen online, the amount of emotional energy that gets invested in these dramas can really take over their lives,' she says. It's made worse because a girl's brain, at this age, is still developing, and their relationships are emotion-focused. The most popular platforms – such as Snapchat, TikTok and Instagram – are also visual mediums. Oglethorpe continues, 'So it's about the photos, the videos, the dance moves and all of those things. It has an aesthetic base.' Paulina Skerman says the number of online untruths means educators need to teach children to be critical of what they read and what they see. She's also had parents believe what they are told online. 'I've had parents ring me to say they've seen something on Facebook, and they know that next week I'm going to line the children up and vaccinate them all. And I said, "But that would be illegal. Where are you getting this information?" The answer was "online". I think it's so insidious. I don't think we've ever had to work so hard in our lives to do that work, and I don't think we're even anywhere close to doing it well.' And lockdown, when parents were coping with several children, has probably made smartphones even more omnipresent.

Oglethorpe says girls this age – and younger if possible – need to 'put boundaries around themselves for themselves'. Failure to do that leads them to check their phones relentlessly, in case they are missing something, and to still be using it at midnight. 'I think it's really important that we teach them to put boundaries around their relationships. And good friends will respect that,' she says. That means girls wouldn't have the need to respond to requests immediately or join a group chat when they shouldn't. 'I say to girls, I've got friends who I send a text message to and it might be six hours before they respond. I've got others [who] respond in five seconds.' She knows what friends respond when and no offence is taken. A by-product of this, perhaps, is instant gratification, where many young people (and perhaps us, their parents) expect everything right now. The smartphone has enabled that. We can book holidays online and pay off mortgages. We can check the weather interstate and have the groceries delivered. We rarely have to wait for anything anymore. A few years ago, I wrote the biography of Professor Ian Frazer, who with Jian Zhou developed and patented the technology behind the HPV vaccine to prevent cervical cancer – a vaccine that is now eradicating this deadly disease around the globe. But what struck me, even then, was how they had to persevere. Nothing came quickly. Indeed, the experiments continued for days and months and weeks and years before a vaccine was even seen as probable. When you tell that to a teenager, many are incredulous. Imagine if Professor Frazer had given up after a year. Or even ten years! Oglethorpe says she and her children were laughing recently because they were waiting for their favourite song to start on the radio. 'There's nothing for young people today that they can't literally get their hands on within moments,' she says.

Oglethorpe's advice is to encourage 'mindful moments', where technology is put away and we encourage simple reflection, to provide balance in their lives. 'I guess a bit of a fear of mine is that we're not learning to let our minds go enough to be able to ruminate on things because we're constantly filling our brains with information and trying to process everything that's in front of us.' As Oglethorpe points out, we need to create those moments. Bounce on the trampoline. Look up at the clouds. 'We know, as adults, that nobody stands in line in the supermarket without pulling out their phone. We're afraid of wasting time.' Psychologist Amanda Abel agrees with that idea of encouraging teens to consider a better 'balance'. And she adds that reflecting how social media makes them feel might also encourage them to reconsider its use. And that's certainly the case among many girls. 'This is the main thing that impacts my mental health. I've spent so much time hunched over my phone, and locking out the rest of the world. It's been an escape into another world. It's made my life so much worse. It's not just what you see online, it's the time you spend constructing a fake world to live in. It's all perfect, and then the real world never lives up [to it]. It makes me forget the life I have. You come out of the phone, look up and really think "Oh this is my life."' That 17-year-old had closed her accounts two months earlier.

This approach to discuss, rather than dictate, is sage advice because at 16 and 17 and 18, it might be virtually impossible to remove a phone or demand that it be used less. That horse has probably bolted. 'You certainly don't want to be lecturing them about the dos and don'ts so much, because that's not going to go down so well anymore,' Oglethorpe says. 'It's more about having conversations, and I often talk about this idea of mindfully scrolling.' When they scroll through their feed, how do they feel? What are the images that make them feel good? What are the images that make them feel a bit antsy? What are the ones that make them feel a bit down on themselves? Perhaps, if their love is photography, it's worth encouraging them to follow talented and surprising photographers. That advice is not lost on our teens. 'As much as adults try to understand, they are missing the boat,' Eliza says. 'They just see it as a negative and don't see the positives. How it connects us. How it opens conversations.' Eliza uses social media to follow body positivity influencers and rail against racial injustice. 'You just have to follow the right people,' she says. And certainly social media can be a force for good: communication, knowledge, entertainment. 'I follow Taylor Swift, Olivia Rodrigo and some politicians like Jacinda Ardern and Julia Gillard. I like Abbie Chatfield too – she was on *The Bachelor* and has an online platform where she talks about the vaccine.'

At this age, a phone in the room is still a bad idea, but probably more difficult to police and in some instances even impossible. However, Oglethorpe warns, 'late at night is when a lot of the crappier stuff happens, because that's when our emotional brain is switched on, and our rational thinking brain is going to bed. And so we don't want young people having those conversations that are sensitive, and all of those chats that are awkward and ugly and all of those sorts of things then. Everything feels worse at night and we react more emotionally usually.' No longer is it about rules and regulations, but conversations and encouraging balance. 'By now we really want to be focusing on the connection that we're having with them so that we know if things do go wrong, that they come to us,' Oglethorpe says. But if the phone is in the room, putting it in flight mode or turning it off at night is a good idea, no matter what age we are. 'Often I say social media is like footballers; nothing good happens after midnight,' says Dr Kristy Goodwin, who also happens to be married to a footballer. She suggests another strategy too: encouraging our daughters to have conversations with their peers, where they 'almost collectively bargain'. For example, they might make a pact with each other not to message after midnight. Or to pledge against posting something that might be unhelpful or hurtful. 'This is empowering young people to actually have these transparent conversations because lots of them are saying they are struggling with this.'

This age is tricky because, while some parents will still have influence, many won't. It might be impossible for an 18-year-old, living away from home, to have her smartphone out of her bedroom at night, and it's unlikely that she will – even if she agrees to do so. 'But one of the things I've found with this age range, in particular, is saying to them, "Look, you've got to, as an independent person, make smart choices around you using it,"' Dr Goodwin says. So, for example, late at night when we're tired, our 'emotional brain' is turned on. That's when we're more likely to click on upsetting posts or respond to something. 'We're much more reactive then,' Dr Goodwin says. The message is to encourage thoughtful use of social media. A ten-minute buffer at the beginning and the end of the day is a suggestion many teens are more likely to take on. It's doable. 'But I think if the strategy is about keeping it out of your bedroom by that age – you're fighting a losing battle,' Dr Goodwin says. These girls are smart; they're young adults making their own decisions and that needs to be encouraged. A parent's role is to help them make good decisions. Science can work there, because it's factual. It's not Mum and Dad saying what's good or bad for them. That raises the spectre of the displacement effect for adolescents in phone use. Dr Goodwin nominates three big physical and psychological needs that are being displaced by screens. The first one is sleep, which is dealt with in Chapter 14. But experts say that, without any doubt, a lack of sleep impacts our mental wellbeing. 'It's not just the volume of sleep, it's the quality of sleep,' Dr Goodwin says. Research found young people were 'wired and tired' when they were not only having insufficient amounts of sleep but, due to the displacement effect, the sleep they were experiencing was not good-quality restorative sleep. The second need displaced by screens was the connection with real people, which could not be replicated by direct messages (DMs). And the third was physical movement. 'They're increasingly more sedentary. We know a whole lot of neuro chemicals that make you feel good are produced when we're active.'

This is an interesting time, because many of our daughters might be mothers in a decade, and in less than that time parenting has been tossed into the digital age. There are myriad examples, but one is 'brexting', where mothers text and scroll while breastfeeding.[4] Perhaps, it is multi-skilling? But research would suggest something more sinister. Half a century ago, an experiment was held where mothers sat across from their babies and were told to remain expressionless and unresponsive. The babies became distressed. Another 'still-face'[5] experiment, in the 1980s, suggested infants were more upset by their mother's emotional unavailability than their physical absence. Now experts believe brexting might have a similar effect. That's just one example. The international phenomenon of 'sharenting', or parents over-sharing content about their children on social media platforms, is another shift where social media plays a bigger part in parenting. So what will things be like in another decade?

7

The anxiety plague

When a 16- or 17-year-old girl makes an appointment to see West Australian psychologist Majella Dennis, that girl is often already highly anxious. 'About everything,' Dennis says. 'The dam is too full.' Dennis's dam analogy explains how anxiety can creep up and steal the smiles of our daughters. Imagine a dam, she says. If it's at a low water level and it rains, there isn't a problem. 'If you have a moderate level of water and it storms, you can absorb that.' The dam is able to hold the water, just as our daughters can absorb a level of stress. 'But if the dam is already really full, a tiny raindrop or a storm can cause a flood. The trigger then doesn't matter so much as what you are holding already.'

Anxiety is robbing our teen girls of the ability to live full lives. It's there in the pit of their stomach when they wake each morning, and it follows them around all day, like an unwelcome visitor. They see it in their friends. Others don't turn up at school because they can't get out of the car. 'Anxiety is now normalised,' one 17-year-old explains. 'We are all anxious. And we don't talk about it until it builds up and overflows,' another says. 'People don't want to get out of bed because of what will happen throughout the day. It's a domino effect,' says another. About two-thirds of the students I talked to say they feel more stressed than they did two years previously. This is understandable. Lockdowns in Melbourne and Sydney particularly, but also in other states, along with the establishment of a new university entrance system in Queensland, stood out in the reasons given. But the list ran to pages.

'In the last two years my anxiety has increased exponentially. I'm a completely different person [to who] I was in middle school. I always wanted to do well at school and get good grades, but I always liked coming to school. Now I hate it.'

'The unpredictability has contributed to my anxiety.'

'I stress over education and friendship and my own life so much more than I used to.'

'I'm so much more anxious. I graduate in a year and have no idea what I want to do.'

'I'm scared of the real world. There is greater expectation to be at a certain standard.'

'I'm definitely more anxious. I feel as though in Year 12 we have a lot of pressure. Everyone's expecting us to succeed, which is great, but it sometimes feels like we can't express that we aren't okay and instead get told we should be grateful it's our last year.'

'I get horrible anxiety about schoolwork. I'll be lying in bed and if I even think about a task at school my heart rate speeds up and I can't breathe.'

'Everything's been pulled out from under me. It constantly feels like something bad's going to happen.'

'Anxiety is a complex issue for girls,' South Australian principal Dr Nicole Archard explains. 'We know from research that girls have a higher level of anxiety than boys. I think anxiety is also linked to that drop of confidence that happens in adolescence and the whole impact of all the pressures on girls in particular through adolescence,' she says. Anxiety carries a genetic component in about 30 per cent of cases, experts say, and some say their clinical assessment would also suggest that children who are shy or sensitive might be more prone to it. And while 50 per cent of mental illness comes on by the age of 14, anxiety can raise its head at any age. COVID-19 might have flipped much of that research on its head too, with one global study reporting a doubling of anxiety in children and adolescents.

> *'For a long time I didn't know how anxious I was. How it accumulates with me is that it starts small and then grows to the point where I can't focus. I fidget, I start to make irrational decisions.'*

> *'I try to breathe and I can't and then I panic. It's so scary. It looks like I'm having a heart attack.'*

> *'I just feel so sick in my stomach, like I want to vomit.'*

Dr Jodi Richardson, an anxiety and wellbeing educator, remembers experiencing anxiety as a child. 'I would struggle to breathe. That was one of my great symptoms,' she says. 'I had a lot of difficulty breathing and in fact I was diagnosed with asthma – which was not my problem. My problem was anxiety.' Listening to Dr Richardson, many will see their own child. 'I had a lot of worry, and very high expectations of myself, and a lot of perfectionistic traits as well.' Dr Richardson, who has a Bachelor of Education, an honours degree in exercise science and a PhD in physiology, says she sees herself in so many students but knows that social media, with its unbridled ability to encourage comparison, has made this a more complex issue for today's teens. 'We are wired to compare ourselves ... And the pressure to keep up makes it a lot harder for young ladies than it was when I was growing up.'

So what happens when we feel anxious? We know we might be thinking irrationally, but what physiological changes take place? 'The anxiety response is the physiological change that occurs when a threat has been detected. And so the brain detects the threat and there's almost an instantaneous response by the body as it is being prepared for fight or flight,' Dr Richardson says. Our hearts can beat faster to deliver more oxygenated blood to the large muscle groups. Our breathing can become more rapid because we're trying to maximise the amount of oxygen that we can bring into the body. 'Often when we're experiencing low levels of anxiety, we breathe in a sort of a shallow way quite quickly for a period of time, then we can end up with an imbalance in oxygen and carbon dioxide. We're looking for that big, deep, satisfying breath that will help to kind of balance our gas levels, and that can be difficult when we've been struggling with our breathing for a while,' she says. The blood from the digestive system can also be diverted away to the major muscle groups, in preparation for fight or flight, which is why many people might feel sick in the stomach. That was Dr Richardson's first symptom – when she was just four. 'When we become anxious, because digestion is not needed in a life-threatening situation, blood from the digestive system is moved elsewhere. It's moved to major muscle groups like the large muscles of the legs to help us to run. And that's why a common symptom of anxiety is feeling sick in the stomach. Everything from butterflies to a nauseous feeling to vomiting – that's why that symptom comes about.'

Symptoms do vary. And panic attacks can occur with anxiety about the anxiety. 'So what happens is when people can't recognise the signs of anxiety – the heart rate building up and the changed breathing, and they're getting all sweaty and their tummy is sick – and don't have the tools to start to shift the dial on all of those symptoms, then they can become quite anxious about what's happening.' Why is my body reacting like this? Why am I having a heart attack? What's going on? What's wrong with me? 'That anxiety about these anxious symptoms builds and it becomes a cycle that amplifies all of these symptoms and creates that sense of panic.'

Psychologist Amanda Abel says in teens the brain is still developing, and they are learning impulse control and reason, so it is sometimes more difficult for them to see perspective and be rational about their worries. It could become all-consuming, and they begin to feel as if they're 'drowning in that one worry'. It might not be logical, and they know that. 'School causes so much anxiety because of the workloads and whether I'm doing well enough. I feel anxious that my friends secretly hate me, but the logical part of me knows that isn't true,' one teen said. Several educators also raised the prospect that

COVID-19 disruption had stunted their ability to deal with this because it had limited exposure to different experiences and adventures, and even decision-making. Certainly the past couple of years, and the uncertainty around health, public policy decisions, travel, and schooling have created increased levels of anxiety. 'I think it's a state of being, actually, for some of our girls,' says Melbourne educator Kellie Lyneham. 'And I think that this state of being has been exacerbated by the pandemic.' Lyneham is the head of senior school at Carey Baptist Grammar School in Melbourne, and her passion for her students can be heard in her voice. 'They're screaming out in some instances for schools and other structures in their life to provide them [with] more support with managing it and understanding it.' These mental health challenges for our students are real. 'Some students feel there's a disconnect between what they're experiencing and what we expect of them.' She gives the example of flipping between offline and online learning. While, as a community, we applaud the ability to do that, many students found it hard to return to school and take on face-to-face assessment after even two weeks at home. She saw social anxiety grip many of them. She also saw the loss of experience have an ongoing impact on those aged 15 and 16. While some girls were struggling to 'be everything to everybody', others continued to 'feel a bit lost'. Her observations match, almost identically, what the girls say. 'Everything's changed. It's like someone pulling a

THE ANXIETY PLAGUE

rug out from under you,' one said. 'We've missed so much. SO MUCH. And I just feel as though I'm treading water. I've lost all enthusiasm for everything. Thanks COVID!'

The future surfaced repeatedly as a concern for students. 'We know as adults that whatever choices you make at this age, you can change your mind, you can start one degree and then change. You can end one degree and do another. You can go and work and come back, but we know there's more fluid opportunities for young ladies to take the path that ultimately is the right one for them,' Dr Jodi Richardson says. 'But the mindset I think that they're growing up with is "I've got to get this right. I've got to make the right decisions about my Year 11 and Year 12 subjects. I've got to do well, to get into the course I want, to have the life I want." And so there's a lot of weight being put on these decisions that they're making in this age group.'

The word 'worry' comes up as much as 'anxiety'. Worry is a hallmark sign of anxiety. The good news is that there is a toolbox of skills to recognise that and change it. Some strategies assist girls in settling the physical symptoms, which can be overwhelming. But what can you do if your daughter is worried about something? Can you address that specifically? The answer is a resounding 'yes'. Dr Richardson has a three-point strategy. Let's say Emily is worried about her VCE results not being high enough for entry into the course she wants. The first step is for her to notice she is worrying. The second is to ask herself a simple question: 'Is this helpful?' Some worries will be based in fiction and some in fact – so saying 'Don't worry' doesn't work. If they can ask that question, then the next step is 'What is helpful?' – and that should be engaging in life in the here and now. In this research, girls were worried about myriad issues. ATAR. Failing school. Friendships. Being a disappointment. Identity. 'My future' was the most common answer. ATAR was a strong second-placer.

> *'I worry I won't get a good ATAR and Dad will feel as though he has wasted his money.'*

> *'Who am I supposed to be? I still don't know. I feel some days that I'm acting.'*

> *'What my parents think of me.'*

> *'Life outside school. I'm not ready.'*

> *'Whether I can afford to live in Sydney and send my children to good schools.'*

> *'Disappointing my parents.'*

> *'Getting fat.'*

> *'I'm worried that I will disappoint those around me and most often myself.'*

> *'Getting into uni.'*

> *'Not being perfect.'*

That last answer, while not the most common, is a phenomenon that is concerning educators and health experts.
Perfectionism. In years past, it's been seen as a positive
trait, a goal that leads to more work and better performance. The way it is described by girls is the polar opposite.

*'It's hard if you get 23 out of 25 and you are disappointed.
It's the pressure you put on yourself. You set expectations
high and then you are always sad.'*

*'I've got to learn that it's okay to not get perfect scores all
the time. I've been constantly thinking about my ATAR
next year and putting all this stress on myself. My parents
aren't putting it on me.'*

*'I think I need to prove to myself I'm smart. In middle
school, I was popular and I think I had a persona of
being dumb. I'm not as popular now and I want to prove
I'm not dumb.'*

*'Some parents are so disappointed if their daughter is
not a captain because they say that will show on their
résumé. You have to be perfect now to have a good life.'*

*'If I work at something, I need to be an exemplar, or I
won't do anything at all. I'd rather fail for not participating
than get an average score for working. People see me as
the smart one; it's often an achievement to do better than*

me. If I lost my academic status, I would feel like I'd lost a part of my identity.'

The problem with perfectionism is that it is largely unattainable. An assignment is not going to be perfect. It is likely that some marks will be deducted for analysis or interpretation or presentation or spelling and grammar, or for lack of context. And if a 'perfect' mark is given, it's unlikely to be repeated in every subject, every time. But that's the rabbit-hole many girls are going down. 'Please girls,' one Year 12 male teacher says, 'look at the marks you got; not the marks that have been deducted.' That chase for perfectionism, academically, is seeing students put off doing an assignment because they don't want to start it. Or spending days on the first paragraph because they don't want to move on to the second one until the first is right. Or handing it in late so they could check it 'one more time'. Or not handing it in at all. This phenomenon was raised with me by educators in my last book, *Ten-ager*. They could see the beginning of it in Years 5 and 6. 'I wish they saw themselves as "enough" just the way they are,' one Year 11 teacher says. And that wish was offered up by school leaders across the nation. The push for perfectionism is not just academic; school counsellors are seeing it in sport and in music lessons, and there is no doubt social media demands it physically. The perfect body. The perfect hair. The perfect lashes and eyebrows.

So what's the relevance of perfectionism to anxiety? 'It's a risk factor,' Dr Jodi Richardson says. 'It's avoidance. Procrastination is a symptom of anxiety; they want to put things off and the perfectionism is an avoidance technique because there's so much anxiety about "Will this be good enough?" It's a big problem.' The A word – avoidance – is raised as a partner to anxiety constantly. 'Anxiety and avoidance go hand in hand,' one expert says. 'Avoidance is a big problem when it comes to anxiety,' maintains another. 'That's where school refusal comes from,' a third says. School refusal is the term given to students who simply will not go to school. Some might get to the school gates and no further. Others won't leave the house. Anecdotally, it's increased phenomenally over the past two years. Psychologist Nicole Young says that anxiety might have intensified for those students who were already anxious before COVID-19 visited our shores. Lockdowns meant they were able to 'avoid' many activities that might have caused anxiety. 'Coming back from that has been really hard,' she says.

'I often try and hide it from my parents. They make you think it is a thing.'

'My parent thinks mental health is an excuse or a label.'

'I tell Mum people have social anxiety and she says it's just made up.'

'Lots of parents and teachers undermine our stress. A lot of people say, "You're not stressed; I was so much more stressed". We are juggling a lot of things. That just makes me feel bad. It makes you feel as though you are not worth it.'

So what can educators and parents do to ease the anxiety load, to stop our daughters' and students' dam from filling and overflowing? Sydney GP Dr Danielle McMullen says she believes everyone suffers anxiety symptoms at some point in their life. 'We've all had worried days and particularly in this Year 12 group. It's normal to feel anxious, with big exams and school being high pressure. The world is about to open up. It's a scary time.' She says 'feeling anxious' doesn't always mean a diagnosis of anxiety. 'But it might – and we certainly don't want to mis-diagnose when people need support.' She says support comes from us 'all gathering together as a group to look after each other'. That is echoed by others who say that, as parents, we need to understand this phenomenon and not dismiss it. 'I think the difficulty with some parents is they feel ill-equipped to help. One of the great things that you can do with somebody experiencing anxiety is to validate how they feel and show empathy,' one expert says. Another says parents could be challenged by the fact that teens can become anxious 'about irrational ideas, worries that on the outside looking in, a parent can see are ridiculous, never going to happen or impossible'. But for the person experiencing it, it feels very real.

The girls offer those activities that help them. Breathing, meditation, reading, music, crocheting. Talking to people. Making lists. Planning. Singing. Netflix. Dogs. Drawing. Talking to a psychologist. Seeing my horses. Swimming. Writing in a journal. Social media. Sleep. Exercise. The power of sleep, diet and exercise should not be underplayed, and is discussed in Chapter 14. Dr Richardson says one of the immediate responses that helps to settle anxiety is to 'name it and tame it', a phrase coined by author and psychiatrist Dr Daniel Siegel. Recognise it. The second point is to provide 'validation'. Perhaps you might say, 'Tests are really hard. I understand why you are feeling anxious. I used to get anxious about tests too.' 'That validation is a really beautiful way to let the child know they've been seen and heard, that somebody can relate to what they're going through,' Dr Richardson says. Psychologists say this age group is 'renowned for not feeling understood by adults', so this is particularly important. And a third part of Dr Richardson's strategy is to then help your child 'get out of their head and into their body'. This might be done by movement, or taking breaths to calm down, or using their senses to smell something, or listen to music. 'Bring their attention away from the future and back to the moment,' she says. We don't need to fix it; we need to give our children the skills to manage it. Adelaide principal

Dr Nicole Archard echoes these sentiments, saying practising mindfulness needs to be part of a girl's toolkit. They
need to learn to stop, centre themselves and breathe, rather
than being caught up in a 'spinning wheel' that perpetuates
anxiety which builds and builds, until it pops. 'We've got
to teach them the skills to be able to bring those feelings
back down within their control,' she says.

And while anxiety can pop up at any time and in any
place, most girls pointed the finger at school – whether it
was friendships or pressures or workloads. Many schools
have restructured with a bigger focus on wellbeing, or
increased their counselling staff in response to the anxiety
epidemic in classrooms. Melbourne principal Linda Douglas
says her school has focused on 'academic buoyancy' in a
bid to ensure students are aware of the signs of anxiety and
have the strategies needed to deal with it early. Professor
Andrew Martin from the University of New South Wales
has been helping the school. He says the biggest difference
between boys and girls in his research is in relation to
'academic anxiety'. 'Girls are significantly more anxious
academically than boys,' he says. 'Girls worry about how
they're going to perform and what marks they [will] get
and what sort of test is coming up.' The irony is that girls
are further ahead of boys in a bunch of measures that
should help them – such as motivation, planning, self-
management – but they are behind on two areas: anxiety
and what Professor Martin terms 'uncertain control'. 'That

is where you have a sense you are not quite on top of things . . . that you're not in the driver's seat; you have a sense that a lot of external forces or pressures play a big part in how things are going to turn out for you,' he says. The risk in 'uncertain control' in a pandemic era – to which he has been alerting schools – is that girls can start to abandon their efforts because they feel so much is out of their control. 'Because if you genuinely start thinking things are beyond your control, you start losing ambition,' he says. This is reinforced by girls, as explained earlier. But Professor Martin says that while girls report more uncertain control, they are actually more in control – whereas boys are more likely to believe they are on top of things when they might not be. It comes down to a sense of self-belief. 'The reality is different from the perception. So girls generally are more on top; they are ahead of the curve in terms of the assignment that's coming up and all that sort of stuff, but they often have the sense that they're not.' Later in life, this might be why they take longer than their male counterparts to apply for a promotion or a pay rise.

So where does the term 'academic buoyancy' fit in? 'It's where students are able to deal with everyday challenges or everyday setbacks,' Professor Martin says. Resilience is what is needed for the tough stuff, and to deal with chronic or acute setbacks or major adversity. 'We proposed a construct called buoyancy and buoyancy refers to everyday setbacks, low-level adversity, getting a mark that you don't like, having a run-in with the teacher, significant deadlines that are colliding,' he says. It isn't aimed at the big stuff, but rather the smaller hurdles faced by girls each day. 'Every student will get a mark they are disappointed in, but only a relative minority will experience major adversity. So when we started researching buoyancy, we found that girls are significantly lower in academic buoyancy than the boys. For boys, a bad mark could be water off a duck's back, whereas the girls really did feel it.' A run-in with a teacher might prompt a significant setback for a girl; a boy might have forgotten it by the next lesson.

How does this tie in with anxiety? 'When we did our research to look at the things that underpin a lack of buoyancy, what we found were high levels of anxiety, and high levels of uncertain control. And that was starting to explain why girls were lower in buoyancy because they are high in anxiety and high in uncertain control,' Professor Martin says. Pointing out the reality – that girls were often more in control of things than they thought – was a start. 'They are actually in control so that's a nice starting point . . . looking for very concrete evidence to point to girls to say, "You know what, you're on top of that" and basically go through the parts of their academic life where it is obvious that they are on top of it, that they do have things sorted. That's the first step.' The second step was to clarify the three things that were in their control. The first was effort – how hard they tried. The second was strategy – the way they tried. 'That's in their control. How they write a topic sentence, how they present their PowerPoint. That's in their control,' he explains. And the third step was attitude. 'What they think of themselves, their schoolwork, and the teacher – that's in their control. And really being clear to them that the more they focus on good luck, bad luck, nice teacher, nasty teacher, easy marker, stingy marker – all of those are beyond their control.' Professor Martin's advice to girls is to focus on those things that they are on top of, and that they are in control of – and then back themselves. 'And if you back yourself, you will go a long way. You will realise your potential.'

So a final word on anxiety: where did all this start? 'Anxiety is a normal human emotion. It's protective,' says Dr Jodi Richardson. 'And we want our young ladies to tune into anxiety if they think they're being followed. Or if something feels off about a person that they've met. We want them to be able to tune into that anxiety and know that it's there to keep them safe and that it can be quite motivating in terms of helping them prepare for exams. It is only an issue when they get stuck and when it gets in the way of daily life.'

Helping our girls learn how to manage anxiety will pay off for them throughout their whole life. Parents should look out for the signs, try to keep open dialogue and help their girls find professional help before the dam breaks.

8

Please help me: A mental health epidemic

Imagine 1000 students packed into one room. They're all 16 and 17 and 18, and you have one question for them: 'What's the biggest challenge you face?' They all scribble down an answer, and you ask those who nominated a mental health issue to move to one side of the room. Those who wrote those two words 'mental health' move first, and then those who nominated anxiety and then eating disorders and then depression and isolation, body image, stress and panic attacks all shuffle to one side. Soon one side of the room is not big enough, and they spill back to where they were. About 700 of them.

That's how many respondents – about seven in ten – tagged mental health, or something that broadly fitted that description, when answering that question. Seven out of ten! While 'time management', 'passing maths', 'motivation', 'balancing everything', 'the future' and 'external exams' popped up many times, most girls saw their key challenge as relating to how they viewed their mental health. Answers like: My mental health. Anxiety. My perfectionist tendencies. Body image. Getting up every day and dealing with everything going on. Managing my anxiety and learning to not let my intuitive thoughts overwhelm me and impact my life. Thinking about things too much. Living with depression. Anorexia. Attention deficit disorder. My inner anorexia demons. Many haven't been diagnosed, and that means that how they feel doesn't fit into any neat little box. 'I would say I really struggle with mental health challenges,' one girl explained. 'I am not diagnosed with anything like depression or anxiety, which makes me feel really confused and left in the dark because I know that I struggle quite badly but I don't have any "real" issues that can mess with me.'

Just as telling as the number of girls feeling challenged by their mental health is the response by health experts. None of them is surprised by those high numbers. Sydney GP Dr Danielle McMullen served as president of the NSW division of the Australian Medical Association (AMA) until 2022. 'My waiting room is full of everyone struggling with their mental health,' she says. 'And I think at least 80 per cent of my GP consultations across all age groups have a mental health aspect at the moment. So I'd say that doesn't surprise me.' In addition to specific diagnosable mental illness, a level of stress has been sitting over the whole community, and the impact of that should not be underestimated, she says. 'It can have physical and mental consequences. It can be really debilitating. And whole communities can feel anxious, feel worried, feel stress.' That can impact teens, who are also feeling the stress around the pandemic and worrying about the climate and their futures. 'At the moment, they're worried about those big issues and the acute stress of financial strain and how to get through the COVID crisis the same way the rest of us are,' says Dr McMullen. Outside waiting rooms and inside classrooms, educators see the insidious and widespread impact of the mental health challenge being faced by their students. It keeps Australian Secondary Principals' Association president Andrew Pierpoint awake at night. 'I think mental health has been on a very, very slippery slope for many, many years . . . long before we ever knew what the word COVID meant,' he says. It's been fertilised by heavy workloads, how society sees itself, and the pervasive nature of social media. 'The workload at school now is crazy; it's absolutely out of control,' he says. Add teens' busy schedules, including part-time jobs, and there is no downtime. No balance. In 2021, Brittany Higgins and Grace Tame also threw a light on the struggle of many female students, and the pressures they could face. 'A girl in any Year 12 classroom will be thinking of a whole lot of stuff that you and I would not have thought about [while] sitting in class,' Pierpoint says.

This can be a tough road for parents, and for daughters. Not all girls tell their parents about their struggles: how they feel they can't breathe as they walk into the school grounds, or how each morning the small spot of sickness in their stomach overpowers their appetite and everything around them. Not all girls understand how or why they might be feeling the way they are. Their marks are good. Their friendship groups are strong. So what's wrong with them? And not all families have the resources to seek a diagnosis or access psychologists, whose waiting lists are growing longer and longer. The moniker 'mental health' is a tricky one too. 'It's very broad,' psychologist Amanda Abel says. 'All the mental health challenges are lumped . . . under the banner of mental health.' Josie Tucker, a Kids Helpline counsellor, says the breadth of 'mental health' is much larger than the specific diagnoses or pathologies that might be used for the term. 'Particularly [at the ages of] about 15 to 16, you see a lot of emerging mental health issues from a diagnostic lens. But larger than that, what you're also seeing is just mental ill-health emerging. You see patterns and ways of thinking. You see, particularly with the development of self-esteem and sense of self, that mental health and mental wellness really rise to the forefront,' Tucker says. 'For this group in particular, they move a bit faster than their male counterparts so they are thinking often in a lot more depth about who they are and how they exist in the world and who they want to be within that. And if they are struggling with their self-esteem or with their peer group or with the pressures that they're experiencing in their lives, it certainly has an impact on their mental wellbeing.' Tucker says mental health is a strong focus for Kids Helpline counsellors dealing with teenagers. 'But the interesting thing about that is, often from a counsellor lens, we understand that their conversation is about mental health or mental wellbeing – but it might actually be attributed in their storytelling to something else.' What does she mean by that? Teens will call to talk about the stress they are feeling around study or a friendship fallout, and how that is impacting them. 'Various areas of their lives sort of rise up to cause that mental health distress,' she says.

With teen girls, issues work together. Social media, body image and eating disorders all get mixed up. With mental health, it's the same. Causes are complex and multi-factorial. But certainly experts point one finger at social media. 'Mental health and social media – you can't talk about one without the other,' Abel says. She paints a picture where social media can be the source and impact girls though misinterpreting communications, bullying, placing high expectations on themselves, eating disorders and body image problems, isolation and disconnection. What's happening online – from friendship issues to a fear of judgement – can then cause offline responses, like refusing to go to school. Tucker also raises anecdotally 'how strong their sense of themselves is', the strength of their connections and their own expectations. 'It comes back to "Who am I?" and "How do I exist in the world?",' she says. What keeps her awake at night are the nation's suicide rates and the suicidal thoughts of our teens. 'It is very common that people will encounter thoughts of worthlessness and being a burden, not wanting to be alive anymore. We have a real privilege ... being able to be there to participate in those conversations and to be able to safely talk about something. What keeps me awake is the thought that someone would be navigating that alone.'

The mental health challenges nominated by girls, and backed strongly by experts, are not being met. Whether it is year-long waiting lists for psychologists, or intervention systems, or rural services or school wellbeing programs, they are falling well short of what is needed. Psychologist Laura Lee works in Geelong, only a short distance from Melbourne, where a number of young people have taken their lives over recent years. 'What I would say about suicidality in regional areas is ... that it's chronically under-resourced. We're certainly not a rural area by any stretch. But it's still really hard for people in regional areas to get the support they need when they need it.' It is a double-whammy too, because a suicide in a regional area ricochets around the school and broader community. How school communities deal with mental health issues across the spectrum is crucial. That's for a few reasons: teens spend most of their waking hours at school; many of the signs someone is struggling might surface during that time; and schools are filled with students who might be struggling. That impacts their friendship groups and their classes. The mental health presentation might vary. But the need to address it is universal.

When asked what issues, if any, girls believed were mishandled by their school or parents, again mental health starred as the answer, particularly among those girls in Years 11 and 12. Here are the responses in relation to schools.

'Even though they think they are doing so much, it is nowhere near enough – nor is it the right support needed by students.'

'Their priorities have things wrong – like they care more about uniform, hair, makeup and things like that, rather than more important issues like bullying, mental health and general wellbeing.'

'Schools just deal with it in superficial ways. They don't care about it. They want you in class. I don't think they listen to the students. They just say, "Go for a walk, have a drink and you'll feel better".'

'The school cares more about reputation than the wellbeing of students.'

'My school is very bad at dealing with and managing people's mental health – there is a massive lack of understanding. The way the school deals with important issues like LGBTQIA+ consent, mental health – I think they need to be talked about more so more people understand and accept the issues.'

'I think my school mishandles mental health a little. I know it's very tricky and you can't expect teachers to also be therapists. One thing is that there is very little confidentiality with the school counsellor. One of my friends struggles with mental health and [the counsellor] has told her teachers and parents things [my friend] said to her in confidence.'

'My school likes to think it handles student wellbeing well, but no one who's actually struggling thinks it does.'

'The school focuses on how to avoid mental health issues, not how to deal with them.'

'Saying you have a great wellbeing program doesn't mean you have a great wellbeing program.'

Many girls pointed out that there is a wide acceptance among peers that they are struggling, and that acceptance has destroyed the stigma attached to mental health challenges. But the girls say that, despite that, and even with schools accepting it is a big issue, they are not changing structures in a way that eases the problems. Andrew Pierpoint says it is 'as plain as the nose on your face' that more needs to be done. He is unapologetically strident regarding this issue, saying you can't just have a guest speaker in Period 1 on a Wednesday in the last week of school and believe that addresses students' mental health. 'It's got to be sustained, it's got to be consistent and it needs to be embedded in the school's practice,' he says. Teen expert and author Michelle Mitchell mirrors that sentiment, along with many others. 'I feel like sometimes when we're just bringing speakers into schools or doing the band-aid approach, we're actually just tapping the bruise,' she says. The impact of COVID-19 has also made it more difficult for some students, as expressed articulately by one girl. Extroverted students' support systems were typically their friends, who they didn't see during lockdown. She saw it in her younger sisters – 'extroverts to the core' – and how their personalities changed during lockdown. But a second factor, she explained, was the loss of any distinction between work and home during lockdown, particularly in Melbourne. Home was no longer a sanctuary away from school: it was school work in the lounge room and the kitchen and their bedrooms. At home, too, some girls believe they are hitting up against unsympathetic parents when it comes to mental health challenges.

'I told my parents I'm not okay and they never did anything about it. Going to see someone would have helped a lot but they didn't really ask if I wanted to go see someone.'

'I'm really struggling with my mental health and I know my mum knows but she won't take me to a psychiatrist.'

'I did not get the help I needed for years because of how my emotions were dismissed by adult family members.'

'The "toughen up" thing really pisses me off, probably because I'm friends with people who are really impacted by it.'

'I wish my mum and dad would understand that I'm not coping. I'm not.'

'How do you tell them that you are suffering with a mental health problem? I don't want to get out of bed, and then they yell at me.'

'I wish I felt comfortable enough to ask them to take me to a therapist but I just can't.'

Despite that last answer, many girls have sought professional assistance.

'I see a psychologist for severe panic attacks.'

'I needed help during my last year of schooling to get me through.'

'*I saw her for sexual assault.*'

'*I do see a psychologist. That was prompted by me feeling that I had no confidence and that I was often in a negative state of mind.*'

'*I was referred by my doctor.*'

'*It was prompted by anxiety and depression as well as the beginning of an eating disorder.*'

Others were prevented by long waiting lists, the expense and their parents 'not believing in that sort of thing'. 'I wish I could talk to someone about eating. I know I have a problem,' one girl said. And that one answer points to a frightening epidemic unfolding among our teens.

At one inner-city school, girls are unpacking their lunch. They're sitting in a circle. The formal is nearing, so the focus is on dresses and partners and nails and hair. But it's the food they're about to consume that perhaps points more to how they see beauty, and the body image issue confronting educators and parents and health professionals. A lettuce leaf, wrapped around grated carrot. Three pieces of lettuce and a few slices of cucumber. Carrot and the tiniest bit of hummus. One girl's lunch is bigger than those of her peers. She has olives and tomatoes, as well. And that's the subject of the chat. 'That is common,' a student, from another school, says. 'It's not talked about. It's the big issue that no one talks about. It's such a mental thing. No one understands it.'

Mental health challenges envelop anxiety and depression, school refusal and suicide ideation, along with several other conditions. But two stood out in the research for this book, partly because of their frequency and partly because they are areas of concern where parents might be confused. Let's address eating disorders first. Most parents will be familiar with some of those, such as anorexia nervosa and bulimia. But two other disordered eating behaviours popped up in this research. The first is chewing and spitting, and it describes what those words suggest. Food is chewed so the girls elicit the taste, but it is then removed from their mouths. Dr Gemma Sharp is a National Health and Medical Research Council (NHMRC) Early Career Senior Research Fellow in the Monash Alfred Psychiatry Research Centre, where she leads the body image research group. She understands that most parents might not have heard of this behaviour. 'We never used to ask about it,' she says. 'But now we ask routinely and people go, "Oh, I didn't realise that was a harmful thing to do." The second is orthorexia nervosa, which comes from the Greek words ortho, meaning 'correct' and orexis, meaning 'appetite'. A person with orthorexia is focused on quality rather than quantity of food, to a magnified degree. It can often start with 'clean' eating or a desire to be healthy, and then progress to the point, according to experts, where teens will eliminate whole food groups, such as dairy or grains. Then they might move to avoid foods with fat or sugar or salt, for example, and then those with artificial additives, in a bid to only consume what they see as pure and healthy. Danni Rowlands is the prevention services national manager at the Butterfly Foundation, a respected national organisation that provides support, treatment, resources and early intervention programs to address eating disorders and body image issues. She says those with orthorexia might be 'really fearful of putting anything into their body that isn't absolutely pure'. Orthorexia is not currently recognised as a clinical eating disorder, like bulimia and anorexia, but is instead a 'sub-clinical eating disorder' or a form of disordered eating. Changes to eating behaviours and patterns such as being obsessed with healthy eating or chewing and spitting need to be taken seriously by parents.

About one million Australians are believed to have an eating disorder. While the number of those aged 16, 17 and 18 (both female and male) is unknown, Rowlands says this a 'key time of transition and that's a high-risk time for the development of eating disorders'. That transition is around forming their identity, performing at school and moving from secondary school into further study or the workplace. The first onset may be younger, around 12 or 13, with some eating disorders being diagnosed even earlier. The cause of eating disorders is complex and can be as tricky as their diagnosis and treatment. Body dissatisfaction can increase the risk of developing 'disordered eating', which is a significant risk factor for developing an eating disorder. There are many biological, psychological and environmental factors, such as bullying or teasing, along with trauma, family history and other mental illnesses such as anxiety and depression that can also place a person at greater risk.

Dr Danielle McMullen says that eating disorders can affect people of all body shapes and sizes. 'Sometimes with people who have big bodies, their eating disorders go undiagnosed for longer because people expect (those) who suffer from anorexia to be underweight. And that's not necessarily the case,' Dr McMullen says. It's about the behaviours and the relationship with food. Eating disorders are also seen as a form of self-harm, an attempt by girls to increase the sense of control over their lives, and those experiencing them often had other mental health challenges such as anxiety, addiction and obsessive compulsive disorder (OCD). 'We know that eating disorders are a way to manage intense emotional pain,' Rowlands says. A clinical psychologist in the field of eating disorders, Dr Gemma Sharp, says that eating disorders can often re-emerge at certain points through big life transitions – the move into adulthood, or pregnancy or even menopause. This cohort of 16-, 17- and 18-year-olds sits inside a big transition square. What makes it more difficult is that entire peer groups can engage in disordered eating, which then becomes 'normalised'; it isn't seen as an issue, and has the potential to become quite contagious. COVID-19 also saw a spike in reported cases, along with other behaviours. For example, food shortages in some lockdowns had a significant impact. That's because people with an eating disorder often want specific foods. Some clinicians had clients who drove to four or five supermarkets to get the staple items they felt comfortable eating.

Rowlands appeals to schools to foster a positive body image environment and look at it from a whole-of-school 'prevention perspective'. Wellbeing needs to be the focus, rather than weight or body size. Staff also need to be educated and empowered in how to do that, as well as being able to identity and intervene when more serious issues develop. 'With so many schools reporting an increase in students with eating disorders, post the various and enduring lockdowns and restrictions, staff can learn how to support students in their recovery,' Rowlands says. The Butterfly Foundation has a range of programs that help school communities to address risk factors and develop protective attributes in children from primary to secondary school. And parents? It is important to role-model healthy and balanced relationships with eating and exercise. And that might mean seeking help themselves. 'An important message we share is it's never too late to seek support if they are struggling. Just because you're a parent doesn't mean that any issue that you've had around eating or exercise or body image just disappears,' Rowlands says. She says it is also important for parents – including fathers, who play such an important role in the development of girls' self-esteem – to value and respect their child for who they are regardless of their body; not doing that can be 'incredibly harmful when it [comes] to children and adolescents'. Dr Gemma Sharp says she feels for parents because they have been exposed to the same detrimental beauty culture. While commenting on body size negatively is not intended maliciously, it is unhelpful, particularly given how important parents are to how young people view their own bodies and their place in the world. She preaches 'function over form' – the body's job, not what it looks like. 'View your child as a whole person and do the same yourself,' she says. 'You are not just an outer shell; you're not an appearance. You have talents and personality and characteristics and abilities.' She also led the team that created KIT, a positive body image chatbot. It allows anonymous and confidential discussions between a teen and the chatbot, which provide information and education. KIT provides 'in-the-moment' support, including information and resources and evidence-based strategies, among them cognitive behavioural therapy skills and mindfulness. In less than 12 months after commencing, it had 20 000 users. 'We were never expecting that many,' she says.

So what are the warning signs parents need to consider? Christie Arbuckle, a clinical psychologist with an interest in eating disorders, puts them into behavioural, physical and psychological groupings. Is there a change in the person's behaviour? Is there a change in their eating habits? Are they calorie counting or fasting? Is there any evidence of vomiting or laxative misuse? Are they avoiding food or avoiding social situations that might involve food? Are there physical warning signs, such as changes in weight? Arbuckle also says sensitivity to things like feeling the cold, or changes in menstrual cycles, fainting and dizziness can be red flags. Sydney GP Dr Danielle McMullen says parents should be alert and aware – not fearful their child is developing an eating disorder but, if they are concerned, willing to seek support. 'It might be nothing, but it doesn't hurt to have a conversation.' Dr McMullen has that conversation with teens regularly. The day before our interview, she says, she had a teen girl who wanted to be 'skinny' and asked how many calories she should consume. The answer? 'She shouldn't need to worry about calorie counts. Instead she should be focusing on having a broad range of foods and being active and all those types of healthy life habits, not focusing on the number on the scales,' Dr McMullen says. Seeking support. Open conversations where words are important. And even eating together around the table can help. Arbuckle says a communal responsibility also exists. 'Are we promoting body acceptance? Are we promoting acceptance, inclusivity and diversity? Are we allowing people to actually feel that they can accept who they are and not need to fit a mould?' They are good questions, which we all have a stake in answering.

Self-harm also needs to be addressed specifically here. While an eating disorder can be a form of self-harm, educators report a growing number of girls cutting themselves. It can be hard for parents to understand the motivation for this. 'Self-harm is about easing the pain,' educator Penny Golding says. 'It's a different sort of pain and physical pain is easier than the emotional pain. I hate to say it, but that's what those kids think. The emotional pain is such a soul-ripping ache that a physical pain numbs the emotional pain, gives them a different focus.' Author Michelle Mitchell describes self-harm as 'deliberately intentional behaviour to hurt yourself in an attempt to express, cope or control emotional pain'. It's the intention that defines self-harm. 'So girls can binge drink to have fun or they can binge drink to self-harm,' Mitchell says. So why are they embarking on the behaviour? 'They do it because it works and it releases a huge amount of endorphins into their body and those endorphins are like happiness triggers,' she says. When talking to parents, she compares it to climbing a mountain. It is strenuous on your body and hurts – but your body releases endorphins. 'By the time you get to the top of that mountain and you stop, you've got this knock-on effect,' she says. Girls describe the knock-on effect too: the emotional experience of cutting and actually seeing the blood is almost like it's a distraction. 'But it's the endorphins that are changing the chemistry of their body,' Mitchell says.

Often it starts younger than this cohort, in middle school, but like other mental health presentations can revisit during transition periods – such as their senior year, or starting university or work. They might be swimming in opportunity but still feel overwhelmed with self-doubt. 'And so they are revisiting their coping strategies, I guess with a different level of maturity,' Mitchell says. Self-harm has different presentations too. At 14, it might be cutting their arm. At 18, it might be staying up all night 'when they know that it's not good for their health, but they're doing it deliberately to punish themselves because they haven't got on top of their uni work'. Mitchell says that what worries her most here is that our girls 'have not grasped the idea of developing success from the inside out yet'. She's not even sure if many of them know what that looks like. 'They're so motivated by the externals, including their appearance and having a look online, and external validation that I feel like sometimes they want a round of applause for eating a smoothie for breakfast. Everything is so public. They don't understand that little tiny voice inside of them is the one that needs nurturing and that's the one that talks to them all day.'

Schools also report a sharp increase in self-harm, often spotted by a sports coach or teacher. 'They don't really care about self-harm,' one student told me. 'They will pretend. They say, "I'll call your Mum."' Another said, 'Therapy should be compulsory. Personally, I've been seeing [a psychologist] since I was 12 and not only has it helped me with my personal stuff, it has just made me a better friend and person in general.' Schools know the problem, but dealing with it can be difficult. Limited resources. Limited expertise. A parent community that is struggling with this too. But the trajectory is good. Educator Penny Golding says she's been looking at what needs to be in a girls' toolkit to meet mental health challenges. 'The key things are looking for that meaning and purpose in life,' she says. Along with emotional regulation skills and a sense of self. Josie Tucker from Kids Helpline says she has seen greater discussion, education and awareness over the past five years, and that it was being driven by senior students. 'They are constantly preaching and telling us that this is a core part of their life. And I think, similarly, that feeds to young people being, in increasing numbers, much more comfortable and much more vocal about identity, gender, their sense of self, how they view the world and how they would like the world to view them. And I think even just in the last five years, I've seen much more maturity in that conversation and it's being driven by young people telling us what they want.'

Olympic gold medallist and world record-holder Libby Trickett, OAM, has a message for teen girls, born of a lived experience. She remembers being 16 and not yet having discovered elite swimming. 'I was probably in the process of getting better, but I hadn't 100 per cent committed to swimming in my mind.' She'd seen her older brother drinking and partying, and decided that was the way to find friends. 'I was drinking and going to different parties, and that continued until the end of Grade 12,' she says. Just after drinking too much at Schoolies, she raced in the World Cup – and recorded personal best times. 'That was the moment that I needed. I then wanted to commit to that. I'd seen the path my family – my brother specifically – had gone down and I didn't want that.' She didn't understand the grip anxiety and depression had on her back then, but as a mother she now sees that the drinking and partying was an attempt to fit in, to make boys like her, and she found her value in that. 'If a boy liked me, then it meant I must be okay,' she says. That's what she thought. So she understands how 16- and 17-year-olds haven't figured everything out. Life is a marathon though, she wants girls to know.

Trickett also wants them to know that she's now studying, at 36. She started off with a Bachelor of Arts, and then a Bachelor of Communication and is now doing a Bachelor of Counselling. 'It takes time. You might start with one thing and then realise your passion lies elsewhere and that's okay. Kids need to understand that. Young women need to understand that – but also the parents need to understand that.' It's wise advice; life is not run in a straight line. We all need to be adaptable and understand that experiences will change expectations and that resetting goals can be valuable both personally and professionally.

9

Growing confidence, growing leaders

This could have been a book about the tales of teens in casual work. Young mothers who allow their children to throw food at 16-year-old assistants and then laugh. Older women who will let out an expletive rant as they exit the drive-through. Young men who suggest they meet up after work. Older men, who think it's appropriate to put their hand on the small of a 17-year-old student's back, or squeeze their hand, or invade their personal space to the point where they feel strong discomfort.

'Oh, the stories I could tell,' says Kassie, 17, who has worked at a big retail store every week for two years. 'I seem to get older men wanting to get too close to me all the time. I used to get so nervous and call over one of the boys and say, "My colleague will help you", but now I just ask if they wouldn't mind giving me my own space.' Or middle-aged women who it seems have all been unfairly labelled 'Karen', the name made famous in Australia during the COVID-19 pandemic by the outburst of a woman at Bunnings. 'Just last week this woman started complaining that I was too slow. And then she raised her voice, demanding to know how to lodge a complaint and how disgraceful it was that the register wasn't working. The more she did that, the more I panicked.'

Aanya and Lottie. Padma and Hayley. Ines and Mollie. They all have stories, drawn from a few hours a week when they work at fast food outlets, or retail chains, in local restaurants or grocery stores. All have customer-facing roles. 'This man came in not too long ago and he asked if we had $5 headphones. So I turned around to the headphones on the wall behind me and said, "Sorry, we only have $12 headphones",' Mollie says. Antagonised, he started speaking louder. And louder. '"I asked if you had $5 headphones, not $12 headphones. Listen to people, girl, when they talk to you." And then he started yelling at me, calling me a stupid idiot woman, and then he stormed out.' She was shaking, tears threatening to spill out and race down her face. Being attacked on a personal level is really upsetting. But the next person in line – a young mother – fixed it. 'You're doing an absolutely wonderful job. Ignore him,' she told Mollie.

Casual jobs. They provide a big dose of independence, which is discussed in Chapter 10. But learning how to deal with rude or difficult customers is also a way of building capacity, and that is a big, wide road to building confidence. Particularly in Year 11, before the workload of Year 12 takes over, casual jobs are popular. Routinely in the research for this project, girls told me they worked between five and 30 hours outside school each week. While fast-food chains such as McDonalds and KFC feature strongly, so do local cafés and Spotlight, as well as jobs tutoring, sports instructing, delivery driving and babysitting. Many girls offered reflections on how they had grown in confidence through dealing with the unpredictable. 'My job has helped me develop as a person. I'm more confident at talking to people,' one said. 'I did it until Year 12 and then I had to buckle down. I learnt so much doing it.'

Dr Terry Fitzsimmons is the managing director of the Australian Gender Equality Council (AGEC), an organisation whose members are drawn from national bodies representing women across industry sectors. He's also an associate professor at the University of Queensland Business School, and his PhD focused on the successful attributes of CEOs and differing pathways to CEO roles for men and women. He says most high school students don't have a job, and boys and girls hold them in the same proportions. 'However, those who did have a part-time job showed significantly greater levels of self-confidence than those without,' he says. One of his many studies has looked at the key ingredients of self-confidence, by examining 20 separate activities that engage adolescents. Three activities stood out in terms of generating self-confidence. Travel – particularly local and interstate travel – topped the list. 'Local travel on holidays, for example, is likely to allow for children to spend more unsupervised time away from adults, relative to trips either interstate or overseas,' he found. Team sport came a solid second. 'When you pull apart the elements of team sport, what you're seeing is getting to understand others, getting to work collaboratively with others, working towards a goal,' he says. 'Team sport is also highly structured, and those are the key elements – the better you know people, the better you know yourself, and how you interact with other people.' Are those skills also acquired playing in a music ensemble or performing in a ballet production? 'No. Music didn't rate,' he says. 'There's something about team sport and the actual interaction. If you think about a music ensemble, even though you collaborate, you're not physically interacting and moving around.' Crucially, he also found a drop in confidence levels when girls drop a team sport, as they frequently do in senior years. 'I think there's a very strong connection between the two. So if girls are dropping team sport earlier than boys, then that's one of the major contributors to confidence collapsing.' The third activity was participation in leadership roles and leadership development. And just as they were the main components of confidence – along with casual work and household chores – other activities were shown to steal self-confidence from teens. 'Overall, computer gaming and social media usage were identified as the greatest detractors from the development of self-confidence,' Dr Fitzsimmons' study found.

I'll come back to leadership in a moment, but those components of confidence perfectly match the anecdotal evidence of educators. School leaders have a valuable 'fly on the wall' perspective here. They see students grow through primary school and into high school. They see some teen girls blossom in confidence and others retreat into a shell. They see the schoolyard knocks, usually delivered by a smartphone, and see how some move forward with strength and determination while others are swallowed by it to varying degrees.

Dr Nicole Archard has been principal of Loreto College in Marryatville in Adelaide since 2016, having also been dean of academic studies and dean of students at large Sydney schools. What worries her most about this cohort? 'I think everything comes back to the self-concept and understanding of self. We have to be able to get girls to look at themselves and say, "I'm enough. I'm happy as I am, I'm enough",' she says. A girl needs to learn not to measure herself against 'everything society is telling her to measure herself against'. 'It's very easy for me to say that as an adult with life experience, but that's a very hard thing for a teenage girl to say.' Her next words are so crucial, but remain hidden in the public debate about graduating students. 'It's not about an ATAR. An ATAR will get you into a university course; it will not make you successful at life,' she says. 'If we can focus on those skills regarding how you feel about yourself, your identity, your self-concept, your self-efficacy, that you're a good person, that you care for others – they're actually life-building skills that are going to get you through life a lot better, more successfully, a lot more happily than, "I'm just going to work as hard as I can, and work myself into the ground to get the highest ATAR that I can."'

Tasmanian psychologist Nicole Young says we also need to work at creating a 'culture that validates differences and allows people to be confident with who they are'. That flies in the face of the stereotypical culture around popularity that still swamps school grounds. She also sees the heavy structures around young people, which prevent many from solving problems themselves. 'So they're not learning lessons. And we know that when we try things and we make a mistake then we learn from it and then we succeed – that is building our reinforcements. It's reinforcing and building resilience and it's building up confidence. We've got to let people make mistakes.' Repeatedly, in my research, experts provided a formula, even if they didn't use these exact words: experience = confidence. Young says that when young people are asked about their interests, Netflix and even video games can top the list. 'There's not the young people who seem to be out in the garden or drawing or knitting or cooking or catching up with friends, hiking or fishing or things that there used to be.' Academic pressures don't allow the development of skills and confidence in other areas. Melbourne educator Deborrah Francis wears the passion she has for senior girls as a badge. She teaches anyone who will listen about the elastic band theory. 'We've all got these elastic bands in our brain. And what we do is tend to only stretch ones where our interests lie. For example if I like music and my parents were interested in music, I keep pulling on those elastic bands, and they end up being lengthened and they become my strengths.' But she wants girls to know that they have elastic bands for almost everything. 'And it's what you tend to, what you pay attention to – that's what you learn. If you want to learn the piano, you can, but you need to tend to that; you need to say I'm going to stretch that elastic band. And then that becomes one of your character strengths.' Psychologist Laura Lee says self-assuredness, and a girl's place in the world, can also grow if she knows she has a support network and a safety net. That allows them to explore the world, make mistakes, take safe risks, talk about that and learn from it.

Repeatedly during the project, the idea surfaced of girls wanting to be perfect, as mentioned previously. Perfect with marks. To have the body Instagram labels as perfect.

To have that winning personality. Often, they put that expectation on themselves, but as Dr Archard says, 'No one puts expectations on themselves, unless it's a cultural and social expectation of them. So we've built that world. We give them *Love Island* and say, you know that's what relationships look like. We give them the Kardashians, and say that's what beauty looks like. We tell them to be successful is to look at high-performing women who are working 60 or 70 hours a week in order to achieve that goal. We're showing them that's what they need to do in order to have a pathway to this perfect life, and they're trying to be perfect in every aspect of their life, and there's a difference between being perfect and just being good at something and accepting that it's actually okay to get a B result or a C result. You don't have to be the A person all the time.' And we need them to understand that, as a big buffer to the anxiety that grips many of them. 'If they fail at something, or if they perceive that they're not as good at something or they don't look as beautiful as they would like to, they internalise that and that's where the anxiety comes from – the internalisation of that doubt, the perception that they are not good enough.'

So how do 16- and 17-year-olds see their confidence?

'It's easy to put on a happy cheery face. Inside I'm not like that.'

'I fake it until I make it.'

'Sometimes I really care what people think. And sometimes I really don't care.'

'I wasn't confident in early senior school. I wasn't prepared to put myself out there. The experience [of] seeing confident people made me want it. And then my life changed that.'

'I was at a low point and then doing exams, I realised I could do that.'

They don't use the words either, but building capacity – whether it is in exams or another skill – and wanting to be confident can help teach them how to be confident.

'I think the school has done well to help foster confidence. You can try different things. Everyone is trying new things. I came in on the first day and did a musical audition in front of a bunch of high school students.'

'I became more confident I think when I decided it was okay to try things and not be the best at them.'

'When I first came here, I don't think I talked to anyone because I was just really shy and lacked confidence in myself. This year, I've actually challenged myself to not worry if I'm not good at something. So I've tried all different things that I'm definitely probably not the

*best at – badminton, water polo, throwing in athletics
and cross country. I don't do those for competition or
anything. Just for myself.'*

*'I think I'm fairly confident but it's definitely been an
evolution. When I was younger, I wasn't very confident
in myself. It was that fear of being judged. But then once
I got over that, I could just be me and have a laugh
at myself.'*

And it waxes and wanes, depending on the challenges. Dr
Terry Fitzsimmons says confidence can be that ability to
meet a challenge. 'You've got to understand yourself and
what you're capable of, and have a realistic assessment
of that. And you've also got to be able to look at whatever the task is and be able to break it down and see the
similarity between what you've got, perhaps, and what
you don't have. To get that, in my view, is confidence.'
These girls also nominated trying new adventures, and
often failing, as a step on the ladder to the confidence
they now feel. 'I don't want to sound cocky, but I was
sort of that, like, naturally clever kid who didn't have to
put in a lot of effort and could, like, cruise by. By Year 9,
you can't just rely on natural ability anymore. And so my
grades took a hit,' Alison says. Her confidence plummeted.
'But I learnt you can get it back too.' Author of *Everyday
Resilience* Michelle Mitchell says that between the ages of

eight and 14, girls are 'unhinging from their parents', but by this older age they are often moving away from their friends to 'stand on their own two feet'. 'When you really sit down and talk to young adults, they're moving through another transition where they can be quite critical of their friends' choices,' she says. And they're beginning to analyse the world from where they stand, not from where their group of friends stands. Our discussion on confidence keeps coming back to what Mitchell calls a 'genetic blueprint that kids have to understand, embrace and work with – not fight against'. The external pressure often encourages them to be someone they're not. She encourages the 'tiny voice' they might be hearing and the genetic blueprint each of them owns. She explains the blueprint this way: 'It's often a time where they're recognising what their genetic drives are – what they're good at, what they've inherited, what their personality leans towards. Instead of fighting it, and trying to be like the person they're following on YouTube, it's a perfect opportunity for them to dig into that.' This makes so much sense. It's only natural for teens to try on different hats and different labels, and to buck against their mother in particular. But come late adolescence, that is muted; they're more mature, will let go of some of those labels, and look inside themselves – and to the family around them. At the centre of that are questions – and this generation will question everything, which is something we should encourage. 'They're curious about themselves:

"prove it to me" is what young adults are thinking. Show me because I'm not going to just believe you,' Mitchell says. Sometimes that leads to very 'black and white fixed views of the world', as any parent will know. 'And I have found the worst thing I can do as a mother is fight against that black and white thinking. I feel like it is undermining the confidence they're bringing to the table,' she says. It's their voice, and it might be a little rough around the edges, Mitchell says. Undeveloped. In need of nurturing. 'But I can hear it coming around the corner. And I really feel like we need to try to champion and honour even some of those really big bold statements they make because it's their attempt to be adults and they're puffing out their chest and they're saying, "Look at me, I'm arriving." And we want to go, "Gosh, welcome in, you know, like, let me open the door to adulthood and let me hear your voice."'

The role of parents is raised repeatedly in the discussion about confidence, and the theme that underlines each of those discussions is how confidence can be stunted by parents catching their children before they fall. The names are numerous. Cotton-wool parents. Helicopter parents. Lawnmower parents. But it's a point to which every expert returns: the role parents can play in developing – and how they can hinder – their teen's evolving confidence. Dr Archard says schools put enormous effort into helping girls understand themselves, and use all sorts of data to ensure purposeful programs. What about parents? 'I think what needs to happen on the parenting side is to allow girls, in particular, to not have a perfect life. They're not learning the skills they need to learn regarding conflict management or disappointment,' she says. 'There's still way too much saving of children, and particularly for girls. If we're not allowing them to develop their voice and their conflict-management and problem-solving skills, we're not allowing them to develop their resilience, we're not allowing them to develop their confidence. If we don't develop confidence and resilience, then anxiety is the flip-side of that. That work needs to happen from the beginning with parenting.'

The examples given of how parents make their daughters' decisions for them run to pages. What they eat. When they eat. What sport they do. What subjects they choose. What order they put on their university course choices. And those pop up in each state, in metropolitan and rural areas, and in public and private schools. This is not differentiated by area; it is more by generation. 'I think we're saving our children more and more. We want a smooth path for our children,' Dr Archard says. Parents are thinking of how to make their daughter's life perfect, 'in that moment' and not thinking of 'how that plays out when she's 25 or 30 and hasn't learnt the skills she should have [learnt] as a teenager.' Parental engagement is different from parental involvement, but educators explain how each year some parents line up to complain about the choice of school captain or rowing captain or cultural captain. They write letters to argue over half-marks in assignments worth 25 per cent. And many do it even without their daughter's knowledge. 'Let's just take captains' positions,' another school leader says. 'I've had so many complaints and often they just filter up to you too; you don't get that direct phone call. Parents need to be able to validate and acknowledge that it's okay that their child wanted that position, and that it was disappointing that she didn't get that. But then what's the opportunity their daughter could take hold of? What's the opportunity to actually show leadership without the leadership badge? That would be a better use of time, than phoning the school.' Dr Terry Fitzsimmons from the AGEC says gender-neutral parenting, and allowing children as many experiences as possible, can also help to encourage confidence. The level of 'cotton-wooling' is astonishing. 'We're not designed for that. We learn by doing and we learn by failing. We learn by making mistakes and, yes, there's a bit of danger attached to that. But the downside is horrendous if we end up with a generation that doesn't understand who they are and what they can do.'

So is there a correlation between confidence and leadership at both the school level and the CEO level? Or is confidence second to other important 'soft skills', such as empathy and teamwork and critical thinking? 'Confidence is just as important as it ever was and confidence and leadership go hand in hand,' Dr Fitzsimmons, who did his PhD on female CEOs, says. 'You can't be a CEO and not be confident – that's a given.' While leadership has changed over the past 20 years, confidence remains a key part of the toolkit, that includes trust and collaborative thinking and a whole lot of other things. But boards need their CEOs to be able to make decisions. Resilience is also critical, he says – a point made by his PhD, which showed that of the 30 female CEOs he studied, all but two had suffered major trauma in their lives. 'That has always stuck with me,' he says. 'Two people could suffer exactly the same thing. One will give up; the other can keep going. Or one will go off the rails and never recover and the other person will become tougher and harder and continue.' In addition to individualised personality traits, he believes a support network is crucial to process failure. 'One of the things that's really important about the study we did is that once you have a level of self-confidence, it's harder for it to erode. But the reverse is true too. So in adults, it's so much harder to get confidence. If you've already got high self-efficacy in your teens, you're far more likely to maintain that when you get into the workplace.' School principal Kim Kiepe remembers a lesson in failing, and exactly how her father supported her. She went for a driving test and was required to do a reverse parallel park outside Government House in Brisbane. It's a wide road, but steep. 'He failed me straightaway because I couldn't do a reverse park down a hill,' she says. 'I was a mess.' The driving instructor drove her home. 'Dad stood at the top of the steps. I just walked up sobbing, and we stood in the kitchen together and he put his arms around me. And he said, "Don't worry, darling. You're not used to failing."' Can she do a reverse parallel park on a hill now? Yes, she says. Her first boyfriend taught her. Her father's point was simple. Failing is part of learning – and it's important to understand that.

The traits of a successful CEO are numerous and confidence is crucial. So is leadership, in a transformational, collaborative and collegial way, along with other attributes such as strategy, street smarts, integrity, stewardship and social capital. The last of these, while on a tangent, is interesting. 'It's not who you know, it's who knows that you know,' Dr Fitzsimmons says. 'And there's a distinction between those. You've got to have a circle of people who can vouch for your credentials.' He's not the only person to raise the spectre of 'imposter syndrome' here, which he says affects males and females. 'It's not limited to gender. It's any minority – whether it's racial or language other than English, or religion or any of those things, it's where you don't look like the main group, yet you get a role in the main group,' he says. Girls pepper their chats with this phrase. They feel like imposters. Some described not 'deserving' a position. 'To an extent, nearly everyone feels that way from time to time,' Dr Fitzsimmons says, including those given the job of CEO. 'If you look outside, the connection to competence is your ability to understand why you're there. So do you actually have the experience this role requires? Do you have the qualifications this role requires? What do others look like in this role? The more you understand that, the less likely you are to feel like an imposter.'

While confidence ebbs and flows from primary school through to high school, new adventures, a touch of failure and an ability to bounce back are unanimously supported as stepping stones to self-assurance. So can you see it – in the way someone walks, or talks or holds themselves? The common view is not really. It's more about doing than talking. About self-belief and the ability to 'have a go'. Reverend Dr Anita Monro runs Grace College, a residential facility at the University of Queensland. It's made up of a large number of first-year students who come straight from city and country schools across Queensland. Does she know, as they walk out of school and into college, who will succeed and who will not? 'We do pick the ones that we might have to keep an eye on,' she says. How? 'Through the level of confidence they show.'

The good news here is that confidence levels can grow. 'Often the ones we've picked out as vulnerable have perhaps had circumstances determining that,' Dr Monro says. She says she tells them they've already succeeded at school. So they have the skills to succeed elsewhere. And the growth in confidence is huge between February and December of that first year after school. That's irrespective of whether they work or study, and whether they live at home or else-where. 'At university, by the end of first semester, they've done some assignments, they've got results and they think, "I can do this."' Of course, everyone has 'glitches' along the way. 'But generally the glitches don't come in first semester, because everyone's fairly focused,' she says. 'It's in the second or third or fourth semesters.'

10

Going places: The bid for independence

The first solo driving trip is always the hardest, at least for many girls' parents. With their red Ps slapped onto the back of your car, they'll reverse out of the driveway and disappear around the nearest corner. They've done their required number of hours. They've passed the driving exam. They've been told, repeatedly, about the statistics that show when a learner driver first gets their P plates, their risk of a serious crash jumps six times higher than other drivers.[1] You remember them nodding. Scary, you thought, and hoped they thought the same. You've told them, over and over, how important it is not to speed, or how they cannot have a single drink and drive. They know not to answer their mobile while in the car, and to take extra care in the few spots of rain threatening a bigger deluge. After dark, they've promised to call you as they leave the party on the other side of town so you can lie in bed and estimate how long it will be before you hear the garage door open and they return to the safe embrace of their own bedroom. Driving, a rite of passage for teens on the verge of adulthood, is a tangible developmental milestone bigger than almost all those that precede it.

As toddlers, they'll take that first step before reaching out for an adult's hand. The same will happen on their first day at school. And as they travel through those childhood markers – from their first friendship bust-up to puberty to having access to social media and then choosing the subjects they will focus on in senior school – most will have an adult, almost always Mum or Dad, by their side. Even for the long stretch of driving heading up to their P plates, they will have an adult strapped into the passenger side. Look here. Watch that car in front of you. Take the first left at the roundabout. Slow down. Slow down. Slow down. Some will prefer to do that driving training with Mum, but in this project most said they opted for Dad. Why? He was more chilled. He didn't yell/scream/cry/berate/tell them what they were doing wrong constantly. He even made it fun, some say. 'One of my learners said, "My mum holds onto the Jesus bar,"' NRMA driver trainer and assessor Noor Sheerazi says. The 'Jesus bar' is the bar above the passenger side window. Sheerazi says learner drivers take on the messages of those teaching them. 'But they've got to learn from both parents. They shouldn't be learning from one. The reason is every person teaches you something extra than the other person,' she says.

For fathers, teaching daughters to drive can be gold: 100 or more hours in a car, with their daughter just as she's ready to take off on her own. It's an opportunity to savour, but also to bond, to problem-solve and for her to know he'll always be there, in the passenger seat, ready to guide her for life. But as she reverses out of that driveway by herself for the first time, everyone knows this milestone is different from the others. This is the end of rearranging timetables to drop her off and pick her up from the part-time job she used to save money so that one day she could have her own car. This is the end of those late-night drives to pick her up from her friend's 16th birthday party. Those early morning wake-up calls to ferry her to sport training are gone. She has her P plates and, in a show of fierce independence, she's disappeared around the first corner.

That path to P plates and beyond is different for every teen. Some girls grab their learners the moment they can, and count down the hours until they can take the car for a spin solo. They will sit the driver's test days after the minimum requirements are met.

'I'm a P plater like a cool kid.'

'I have 80 hours, woohoo.'

'I have my licence. I love it!'

'I have got my learners. I have also got my motorbike licence. So I'm learning to drive.'

'I drive myself everywhere.'

These teens exude confidence and believe their parents provide them with the independence they deserve, as teens on the verge of adulthood. In rural areas, girls sat and passed their driver's exam early. In some cases, they had been driving around the family farm for years. In others, they knew their licence was the ticket to university an hour or two away. Others saw it as a reason not to use public transport, a view influenced by COVID-19. 'I live in the inner city in Melbourne and I could get the train but I don't want to with COVID. Driving offers another option,' one 16-year-old says.

Asking questions of our girls for this project threw up so many themes, and in driving, three distinct groups surfaced. The first group comprised those keen to get their licence and use it, and often they did so at the first opportunity. The second group made their driving decision around study. 'I have my Ls, however I'm pausing learning to drive until after studies at school are completed,' was an answer given repeatedly. 'My parents didn't let me take my first Ls test until I turned 17, and then my time was taken up by studying, and then we couldn't really go anywhere last year,' another said. These students might have started learning, and then the Year 12 study load swamped their free time. Or their parents were the arbiters of how quickly they were eligible for a licence. 'I'm not allowed to drive on busy roads yet, so I drive out to Tullamarine but my parents are often busy so I haven't done much practice at all,' another 17-year-old offered. Others drew up a list of priorities for their final year, and a driver's licence was stamped firmly on it – but below study and sport and free time. It could wait. But it was a third group of girls, aged 17 and 18, that presented as a surprise: girls who did not want to drive. It made them anxious. Some had waded through the requirements, pocketed their licence and put it in the bottom drawer. Others did not want to do that either.

'I'm super scared of it, so I only have two hours.'

'I currently have a fear of driving ... I've only driven twice.'

'I stopped due to driving anxiety. I plan to take it up some more in my gap year.'

'I am 18 and still on my learners, but I am too anxious to start driving.'

'I got into an accident on my Ls so I stopped driving for a year, but now I'm close to finishing all my hours.'

Mothers also raised this reluctance by some daughters. 'I encourage her to go for a small drive by herself each Sunday, but she just says she has the licence, she doesn't need to drive,' one mother explains. Psychologist Carly Dober says cultural communication about women and driving, and common tropes about how hopeless women are, and young people being 'dangerous' drivers due to their inexperience behind the wheel, could account for some of this. 'How many times have you heard people make fun of a woman driver in a car crash, or driving badly?' Parents are also nervous about their children driving for the first time, and that could instil a disproportionate fear about the experience and encourage avoidant behaviour. 'I would encourage parents to instil confidence in their soon-to-be drivers, and encourage them to arrange private lessons and remind them that driving is a skill, much like anything else, where practice makes a good habit,' she says.

NRMA driver trainer and assessor Noor Sheerazi says that while she doesn't see a difference between males and females, other factors play a role. Rural children often had more driving experience. And those who played sport, for example, learnt quickly. That makes sense. Spatial awareness and hand–eye coordination are important in driving. She also sees the anxiety factor more in sensitive personalities. 'When we're born we don't know how to walk, and we can't remember each time we fall down. So we keep trying,' she says. But a sensitive new driver might think of the experiences others have had and 'not want to have those negative experiences'. She tells the story of one student who accidentally reversed into a tree, with a parent in the car. 'That girl could not forget the noise,' she says. 'The noise sat there in her ears.' For four years, she would not go near the speed limit; such was the impact of that experience. Her advice? Encourage them. Allow them to be a learner driver again if they wish. 'But you have to create situations like "Can you move the car?" "Can you grab the keys and go get some milk for me?"' The P plater has to feel needed, that they need to run that errand.

The journey to drive is a telling analogy of the journey to independence. At 18, our daughters are adults and should have learnt the independence that allows them to make decisions by themselves. We might remain a sounding board, but we want them to be able to fathom for themselves the best way forward. Whether that's the amount they drink at university or work parties, to walking home after dark, to saving money and travelling afar, we want them to make thoughtful decisions. We want them to enjoy life, laugh often and take risks that are calculated and deliver a benefit. We want them to travel and learn and love. But we also want them to understand coercive control, the value of superannuation and the importance of mentors and friends. That requires allowing them a gradual independence, just as learning to drive does. They are in control of the vehicle, but with an instructor close by. And then, after being tested both off and on the road, they are granted greater freedom: the right and power to drive by themselves. But it's with a big red P plastered across the car, as a warning to those around them. This person is still learning to drive. It's new. And it's wise to be kind to them, to understand they might make mistakes and to be able to respond to that quickly. In this project, girls often used the word 'adult' as a verb. 'I'm not ready to adult.' Or 'Isn't it their [parents'] job to adult?' Or 'I need to practise adulting.' They see adulthood as unlimited independence. It's not based around age. It's based around freedoms. And many want more of it.

'My parents are controlling and won't let me get my licence so that I have that next level of freedom.'

'I know it is a privilege but also, I think as I get older, I need to become more independent in order to grow more and become more mature.'

'I'm not the same little girl anymore and I want to be creating my own life stories. I would like them to allow me to have more freedom.'

'[I] would like my parents to trust me more and allow me to go places with friends such as parties. I would like my parents to allow me to do things without their constant *input – such as let me go about my day and study without constantly saying, "Shouldn't you be studying?"'*

'Trust me. Let me spend time with friends. Have co-ed friendships. Let me go on walks by myself. Not track my Instagram. Let me spend time in my room. Teach me life skills – how to cook, change a tyre, communicate my opinion. I'm jealous of my friends being able to do stuff.'

'I'm 16, almost 17, and I'm not allowed a job and my parents constantly are checking up on me.'

'My parents have not prepared me for the real world.'

'My parents don't let me do anything independently, which is frustrating because I don't have the skills I need to survive in the adult world.'

'My mother is a helicopter parent for sure. She treats me like a child even though I'm going to uni next year.'

'I live in the same street as my school so I don't have my Ps and my mother doesn't let me catch public transport to places I haven't been before. I feel quite suffocated sometimes.'

Certainly COVID-19 has had an influence here too. 'I feel like I haven't really had a chance to be an adult. Living at home 24/7 makes me feel like I have regressed into a two-and-a-half-year-old waiting to go to school,' one

17-year-old commented. But an irony showed through in their answers too. Despite their pleas for more independence, and better practice in 'adulting', many also eschewed the knowledge or know-how to put that into practice. 'Although having independence at 17 is great, I also love to feel like I'm still a kid – like getting my mum to book my doctor's appointments and return my online orders. I feel like it's good to still be babied sometimes.' That reference to doctors is repeated by many girls, who at 16 and 17, and even at 18, still prefer their mother to attend an appointment with them. 'I've scraped the front of my car [against a parked vehicle] in a car park,' another 17-year-old said. 'I was really responsible and put a note on, to call me. I tried to organise it by myself. But I couldn't. I couldn't adult that much.' Similar examples were given in relation to booking a driving test, applying for a tax file number, lodging university course applications and writing a résumé. Byron Dempsey, founder of the Driven Young podcast, says the topics of consent and money also showed a strong thirst for knowledge. 'They don't understand money psychology and the importance of saving. I think a lot of people think the property market is so difficult to get into now, they don't even bother trying. And as a result, they just spend their money.' The difference between good credit and bad credit; good debt and bad debt; stocks; environmental, social and governance (ESG) factors; and compound interest were also topics that many school graduates did not understand.

Author Michelle Mitchell says every parent has 'a different risk tolerance', and that helps to determine how strict they are with their children. 'Some parents are just more fearful of things in the world and others are more confident in their kids' ability to manage them,' she says. 'But whatever parents do, they've got to let the rope out slowly.' What concerns her most, around the granting of independence, is the line 'when you turn 18'. 'Nothing magical happens then,' she says. The brain doesn't change overnight. Nor does their assessment of risk or their ability to critically analyse a social media post. 'They might get their licence one day, but their ability to handle things doesn't just change overnight,' Mitchell says. 'Whatever parents do, they've got to be prepared to just gradually work with the process and not just let go all of a sudden. I feel like that can be a real risk factor.' Girls agree. 'If they slowly give me independence, I will not rebel,' one explained. Mitchell says parents tend to justify 'hanging on' to their daughters. 'They justify making decisions for their girls for longer. They justify them staying at home for longer,' she says. Why? 'I think because we don't see them as strong and as resilient and as independent as they really are capable of being. I think one of the hurdles our girls have to jump as they become older is the hurdle that says,

"If I'm weak and fragile, I'm going to get along better at work or people are going to like me more. If I play second fiddle instead of standing up and being myself it's going to be a ticket into things." They have to be able to stand on their own strengths,' she says.

Educator Dannielle Miller says parents also have to pick their battles and not become 'hysterical over small things'. 'If you sweat the small stuff, they'll never tell you the big stuff.' We need to understand the autonomy they have over their own decisions, even those with which we disagree. 'For example, when my daughter was 16 she wanted to have her ears pierced twice. I didn't really want her to. But I explained to her that it was her body, her ears and her choice. Similarly, she's got two tattoos. She knows I don't like tattoos. But she's 22. Now, if she wants to draw on her body, that's her choice.' Miami State High School principal Susan Dalton says, 'I always adopt the philosophy of really connecting with parents on a parent level – as opposed to as an educator.' She wants parents to know schools are walking with them, not judging them. Both want strong, smart, curious and kind graduates. 'Each child is totally different and unique and I actually see parents struggle more in Years 11 and 12 than in those junior years – without a doubt. They are genuinely worried about the kids.'

Whether it's parental worry or teenagers wanting to feel safer, apps tracking family or friendship bubbles have exploded in popularity – and controversy.

'My parents track my location so I constantly feel like I have to make decisions based on what they want.'

'I'm often not allowed to hang out with my friends. They track me on Life360 even though I'm only at school or home or my two jobs.'

'Stop tracking me. It's an invasion of my privacy. Let me create my own boundaries.'

'My parents allow me a lot of freedom; however, they have my location on Life360. I feel like part of being a teenager is doing things your parents wouldn't necessarily like you doing – for example, going to parties.'

'I'm supposed to experiment. How do I do that while I'm being tracked?'

'When you try to talk about it, it's about keeping you safe. I don't want to be safe all the time. I got into a friend's car and I had to lie and say I was studying. It creates enormous anxiety.'

'Mum knows what I'm doing. She panics. And then that breeds lies.'

'My parents were the chill parents until halfway through 16. I told [Mum] everything. Boys. Friends. Now I tell her nothing. Life360 means she just asks questions.'

'I'm scared to ask if I can go on a date. She'll be going past the restaurant or wanting to know where he lives.'

'Mum has become addicted to where I am. She's now living my life. I'm scared of asking her whether I can go out – so I just lie about why I am somewhere. If I catch up with a friend, and we go somewhere on the spur of the moment to a park for a picnic, she sees where I am and I'm grounded.'

'Every two hours I turn it off and she can't track me. She is so distrustful. I'm just saving data.'

Let's come back to the issue of trust in just a moment. But is tracking your child recommended? Or a sign that a parent can't let go? Does it breed distrust? Or does it ensure that a busy family can operate by knowing where everyone is at any point in time? There are two answers to almost every one of those questions, depending on who you ask.

If it's negotiated, why would there be a problem? It might help students working late at the library feel safe, one expert in teenager behaviour says. Another, equally qualified and highly regarded, said she despises tracking apps.

'It's awfully intrusive,' she says. 'Basically, if your partner did that, that would be considered stalking and coercive control. It sets them up to believe that if someone loves them, they get to monitor them. I think that's an atrocious message.' The next stop is two senior educators, between them responsible for thousands of girls. One says she uses Life360 – an app that allows a voluntary group to know where each member is at all times – with her family. The other says she couldn't countenance it. So next I head for a parenting expert and a social media researcher. And here there is a symmetry in views. To both of them, it depends on the reason for the app's use. Are parents using it to track their children? Or to check on them while they are driving from Point A to Point B, rather than calling or texting them? 'I still track my 21- and 18-year-old, and they are absolutely fine with it because it was a conversation we had early,' one expert said. She doesn't believe either of her children are up to mischief, but it's a way for the small family unit to check on each other's whereabouts. 'It's not about knowing where they're going. They can go where they like. But they can also see how far away I am from picking them up from footy training.' The key here is that it is mutual and voluntary and used for practical purposes. It's not used to spy or track – and that needs to be understood and agreed upon with teens. From my research, if there is a hint of distrust then it can never work.

Trust. Trust. Trust. It is a word that pops up repeatedly. Mum doesn't trust me. My parents have no trust in me. Why don't my parents trust me? Experts say that's a call by our teens to be given enough latitude to make decisions. They will make mistakes, just as we have. But they won't learn unless we trust them enough to try. Remember the first cake you baked? Few would nominate it as their best. That came with practice, massaging the ingredients, changing the temperature or the time it was in the oven. Adulting takes practice too, and mistakes are inevitable along the way. The girls expect that.

'I wanna be able to learn from my mistakes and to be able to say that I've lived a life with no regrets.'

'The bubble wrap is unforgiving and doesn't prepare me for the outside world. I want the choice to attend university in New South Wales instead of the closest one to home. I want the chance to make my own mistakes.'

'Let me enjoy my teenage years rather than holding me back and making me watch everyone else have the time of their lives.'

'I think that's a part of growing up – making mistakes and learning from them. I feel like my parents don't really let me make mistakes.'

So what do they want to do? What's the 'independence' they yearn for? At 16, the word 'trust' peaks. They want to be trusted to make decisions – from riding public transport to planning their own study to choosing their own clothes. Many also want to be treated the same way their brother is treated at 16. At 17, 'driving' was the most common answer, but so was having a boyfriend, keeping their phone in their room, deciding what parties they could attend and until what time, and even walking the dog at night by themselves. At 17 and 18, money also surfaced as the glue that bound girls to their parents. 'I want financial independence but I won't until I finish uni,' one said in a comment that mirrored many others. Indeed, some girls opted not to study after Year 12 so they could seek financial independence. Even at 16, that money tie was strong. 'I have to rely on my parents because of money,' a Year 11 student said. And there were social and political deviations at this age too, as you would expect. 'I wish they would trust me and my opinions over their own when it comes to decisions about my body,' one 17-year-old says. 'For example, they don't want me to get vaccinated, but I do.' Dr Danielle McMullen, a GP in Sydney's inner west, says young women need to develop a relationship with a GP. 'You remember to bring them in for their check-ups when they're little kids because they've got immunisations and that kind of stuff. But it is helpful to have a check-up in those later years just to touch base and so that they understand that they can go to the doctor confidentially as well,' she says. Children can access their own Medicare card from the age of 15, she says, and that is something Dr McMullen knows some parents find confronting. More often than not, the daughter will want their mother, in particular, at the appointment at that age. 'Sometimes they just want an external person to give them a bit of support. And they might want the freedom to just say words, use their own language, talk to someone without Mum or Dad watching – even when Mum and Dad already know what it is that they're talking about.' That doesn't mean they're keeping secrets; they are just creating networks and partnerships that will hold them in good stead down the track.

Kids Helpline counsellor Josie Tucker says she sees the 'struggle for power' between parents and teens in some of their calls. 'We see the parents in some cases pushing back or really locking down and we certainly hear a lot of conversations about power or about fairness.' She uses that word 'fairness' often. 'It is something that is very important, certainly in my work with teenagers. At certain times, they're expected to be very responsible, very independent and other areas are taken away from them.' Young people are good at understanding when things make sense, and when they don't. 'And when decisions are arbitrary or they are treated as much younger, that's a real challenge [for them].' Tucker labels 'fairness, consistency, and communication' as the 'equalisers' in the power dynamic between parents and teens, who want to participate in processes if they understand how they work. She says she, as an adult, can see how parents might have arrived at a decision. But sometimes we forget that teens are still navigating and learning about the adult world, and faced with a decision made on their behalf, they want to know that it is 'fair'. Creating shared decisions works wonders.

Given that many children are opting to stay at home well into their twenties, should we begin encouraging them to leave earlier, to seek independence? 'I think we can push them away while they're still at home,' Brisbane school counsellor Jody Forbes says. 'It's important to try to get them to adult even if they are staying at home and so making decisions and getting their own bank accounts and getting Medicare cards and making sure they go to the doctor because I think parents are increasingly [disempowering] girls by being helicopter parents,' she says. Encouraging them to 'adult' encourages their development, she says. 'So we have to consciously say, "Well, you're nearly 18 so you can make your own hairdressing appointment." Applying for a tax file number, registering to vote, doing a first aid course are also other steps towards independence.'

Of course, the road to independence might be as filled with potholes as some of our suburban streets after heavy rain. Let's take the irony thrown up by lockdown in Melbourne, for instance. Principal Linda Douglas says her research data showed the girls gained 'a real sense of independence' during distance learning. That flowed into an increased student voice and student agency because the school was asking students what worked well and what could be improved. 'The girls really grasped that and started to have a greater voice in what the learning could be like, what worked well for them,' she said. That independence meant girls were setting up their own study systems, working on what their needs were and alerting teachers to that. Take this comment from one Year 12 student as an example: 'My marks are better because I am an independent learner. I have focused on my needs not the needs of everyone in my class.' But that stellar display of independence in learning was not matched in other ways. Girls reported that their parents – particularly their mothers – mollycoddled them, treated them as pre-teens, checked up on them constantly and packed lunches while they were learning from home.

11

The gender agenda

In a big public school in Queensland, the 17-year-old captain wears an oversized 'they' badge. They made heaps of smaller ones too, by themselves one weekend, so anyone who wants to discard the 'him' and 'her' at school feels welcome. In another school, a private all-girls' college, the female captain wears pants when almost everyone else chooses the regulation skirt. Why? She wants younger students to know that they should feel comfortable wearing them too if they choose. In Melbourne, a teacher is petrified that one of her charges will be subject to physical violence if their parents discover they are using a traditional boy's name at school. Only a few kilometres away, another teacher at another school has set up a LGBTQIA+ 'safe room'. And she makes sure she visits it, to hang out at lunchtime. Back in rural Queensland, hundreds of kilometres from specialist medical services, a 16-year-old googles 'how to become a boy'.

Gender identity is broadly defined as how someone sees their gender, how they show that to others and how they want others to treat them. And to accommodate the diverse ways a person can express themselves, it has added more acronyms and words to our vocabulary in recent years than almost anything else. AFAB (which means 'assigned female at birth'). Body dysphoria. Cisgender. Intergender. Third gender. Agender. Pangender. Non-binary. Bigender. Gender nonconforming. Genderfluid. And a dozen more. For teens seeking to find themselves, it can be complex and tortuous and lonely and certainly liberating. For parents, it can be confusing and shocking and filled with grief. Many find it unacceptable even. For schools marketed to a single sex, it is posing enormous challenges as toilets and uniforms and sports competitions are navigated. 'The level of distress I see among gender-questioning and trans young people is like nothing I've ever seen before,' Victorian teen psychologist Laura Lee says. 'It's a conversation we need to have as a community, but even for those girls who are heterosexual or who are cisgender [a person whose gender identity is the same as their sex assigned at birth], they are absolutely still wanting to be able to express their identity – and that's where I know uniforms are being increasingly talked about and increasingly contested.'

We will look at uniforms in a moment, but how best can gender identity be explained? We know that all children develop their own identity. It starts young, when they might look outside their families to see how other families work, and as a teen a girl might step back from the mother they don't want to emulate. They pick up bits and bobs along the way as they decide who they are, and where they fit into the world. Gender identity is simply part of that. And gender identity is different from sex. Gender identity is whether your identity is male or female. Sex relates to anatomy. Let me pass the discussion over to child and adolescent psychiatrist Dr Stephen Stathis, who is also the medical director of child and youth mental health services at Children's Health Queensland. Dr Steve – as his patients call him – knows he's a male and the thought of identifying as female makes no sense to him. A decade ago he might have called himself a bloke. Now, to be more precise, he is a cisgendered, heterosexual Anglo Australian male. 'That's just my identity,' he says. But different people in different cultures have different ways of identifying. It's not just dictated by clothes, for example. There's 1001 other ways that you might identify as male or female. 'In Australian culture, it is not uncommon for females to cross their legs when sitting down. Males rarely do,' Dr Stathis says. And when your gender identity matches your gender orientation, everything fits. 'But if my gender identity is incongruent or differs from gender orientation, that's where conflict can occur.'

'Single-sex schools are based on an assumption that they are all girls. That's not true, even if our parents think it is.'

'Lockdown was good for thinking. It helped people come out. There's also been more exposure in the media. Representation of the gay population has also opened the door – and maybe the minds of others – so non-binary [people] and others can find their space too.'

'I'm gender-fluid. Most of the time I'm a girl, but sometimes I'm non-binary and sometimes I'm a dude.' [Almost in the same sentence, this student says one of their sisters is dyslexic. Neither is a label; it's just who they are.]

'I know lots of girls who are having trouble with sexuality. They are bi-curious. Half are really accepting of that. We are friends because of who they are, not that. The other half of the year group are really weird about it.'

'There are a lot of teachers who don't know how to cope with [gender issues] because they haven't been taught. My PE teacher told me there was a transgender girl in Year 7. They didn't know what change room to use. I told them to let them use the girls' room. She'd be safer there. These are teachers. They asked the Year 12 students what to do. They thought we would be more accepting of it.'

'People just want to find their place in the world and be comfortable in the world. We don't want to be who people expect us to be. We want to be ourselves but often we are afraid to do that. We need to foster a better atmosphere.'

Six comments from dozens on this topic, collected from 16-, 17- and 18-year-olds. The level of introspection shown by teens in this project was marvellous. They think deeply and their candour is as delightful as it is unexpected. 'I can't prove this, but my sense is actually that they're leaving space for everyone to explore,' West Australian psychologist Majella Dennis says. 'It's really about bringing the awareness that everyone's exploring out into the light.' Dennis has worked with young people in both Queensland and Western Australia, and consults to all-girls schools. 'In the past three or four years I've just really found it to be much more normalised, much more accepted in fact among adolescents.' A Victorian educator puts it this way: 'We all went through an experimental stage of asking, "Who am I?" I think this is an emotional experiment of students asking, "Who am I?" They are not just willing to go with a societal norm – but [want] to question themselves as part of that journey.' Another educator, Deborrah Francis, says it is also part of students finding their voice on their own terms, not those of their parents. 'I'll give you a perfect example. We had a student recently who said, "We would love a person of colour as a school psychologist."

Now in my mind, as a young child, no student would ever have made that comment.' About a year ago, Dennis ran a program directed at Year 9 at an all-girls school. 'They specifically requested not to be addressed as girls,' she says. 'At the beginning of the session we asked "What are your expectations and what are some shared values that we want to uphold?" And the students requested that they be referred to as students or people, but not girls.' While the request came from one student, the consensus was immediate, with nodding and clapping. That was the first time Dennis had seen that reaction. Head of the Alliance of Girls' Schools Australasia Toni Riordan, who is also principal of a Brisbane all-girls school, says she sees Year 11 and 12 students' strong passion for social justice, where they want to protect others. Most were passionate about advocating for or being allies to those transitioning or questioning their gender identity. 'I think that's probably different to their older sisters and mothers,' she says.

Dr Steve Stathis remembers, about a decade ago, seeing a young child who was adamant they were 'in the wrong body'. They also had diabetes and depression. 'I had never seen this before,' he says. They had 'gender dysphoria', which was termed gender identity disorder until 2013. The case was complicated because of the child's speech and language problems. That meant Dr Stathis had to research language so he could adequately explain to the child what they were experiencing. 'You have to really understand what you're talking about to do that,' he says. A few months later, he used the case in addressing a group of GPs and paediatricians on the topic of mental health in young people with speech and language problems. At the end, the questions were rapid fire. 'One hand went up about gender dysphoria, and then another, and then another. No one had questions about speech and language but everyone had questions about gender.' He agreed to use the small practice he had at the time to see some of the concerned GPs' patients. Soon waiting times had exploded to almost 18 months. To see an endocrinologist for possible treatment options took another nine months. The Queensland Government, in this case, then funded a gender clinic, and similar clinics now operate in other states, including Victoria and Western Australia.

So has gender dysphoria always occurred at this rate? Dr Stathis's answer is as honest as the expression he wears on his face: 'That's the big question because there has been a significant escalation in the numbers of young people presenting with gender diversity and identifying as transgender, and there has been also a change ... I am also seeing children who, as young as three or four, clearly identify as the other gender.' He knows this is a complicated issue for teens – and their parents – to grasp. 'In Anglo-Australian society, what you can do as a little girl is much broader than what you can do as a little boy,' he says. A young girl can wear shorts and play rugby, enjoy rough and tumble, ride a bike and muck up. 'And everyone grins and says, "Oh, isn't she a tomboy."' He doesn't like that word, but knows it's in common use. 'But a little boy puts on a pink tutu and he's off to see [me].' Historically, the number of boys being referred to gender services is bigger than the number of girls. 'But now we're seeing a big increase in the number of girls, specifically in adolescence,' he says. Why? 'We don't know.'

Not every gender-diverse child has gender dysphoria. 'When I was a young person, you might dress up in black and identify as Goth and you might have even had a piercing,' he says. 'It is normal for young people to test boundaries. Adolescence is about individuation and identity. Who am I in this big, crazy world? And pulling away from your parents? We all did it. We all tested boundaries. So it's not uncommon, in my view, within the general population in schools for young people to be testing, questioning their gender, just as they question many, many things, whether it's their sexuality, climate change, the environment, politics, whatever.' In this research, it was common – particularly in private all-girls' schools. Maybe that is a coincidence, maybe not, but the issue surfaced less in co-ed and public schools. With the passage of time or professional help, many teens don't continue on the journey to changing the gender they were assigned at birth. To do that, in Dr Stathis's words, teens have to be 'insistent, persistent and consistent'. 'By the time [they] come to see us, most of these young people have been identifying as their preferred gender for a period of time.' Age is irrelevant here in terms of presentation. 'I've seen children and adolescents of all ages,' he says. But it can be very relevant to treatment. 'Because in early puberty, to do nothing is to do something – which is to allow them to continue to develop in their natal gender. And if you allow them to develop and, for example, their voice breaks – that's permanent. If you're a natal female, and you allow them to develop and they develop breasts, that's permanent; it will likely need surgical intervention.'

It is important for any treatment to be supported by a 'developmentally appropriate, family centred and affirming approach', he says. 'By affirming, I mean the importance for a healthcare professional to initially simply listen to the young person and the family.' From a mental health viewpoint, the majority of adolescents who are gender dysphoric – up to 90 per cent – have comorbid mental health problems. 'I've seen the most horrible things. Just listening to them, allowing them to be heard, implies a deep respect for what they have experienced.' For those adolescents who proceed, there are three specific stages. The first stage is where puberty is blocked. This is totally reversible, and is given by injection by a paediatric endocrinologist or specialist doctor. 'Treatment centrally blocks puberty in the brain. There's few side-effects,' he says. It allows the young person to develop emotionally and cognitively while they consider whether to continue with treatment. 'I've had young people who started this stage and then have said to me, "Dr Steve I'm not transgender. This isn't for me."' The second stage is where a patient might begin their chosen hormones. A teenager identifying as a male would begin testosterone, for example. And the third stage requires surgical intervention. These three stages have become more challenging in Australia since a 2020 court case overturned earlier laws, as the consent of both parents is now required for each of those stages.

Putting our heads in the sand won't work here. Without confronting this issue, some teenagers are driven to risky behaviour – males asking female friends to source oestrogen from their GPs. T parties, or testosterone parties, where testosterone is purchased online from China and then injected. Dr Stathis has seen transgender young people self-harm, or binding their breasts with duct tape in an attempt to hide them. Their skin came off when the duct tape was removed. Others could not bring themselves to use a tampon or a pad – and used pull-up nappies that leaked – meaning that one week in four, they skipped school.

That no doubt points to how difficult this issue is for parents, as well as their teens. 'Even the ones who are absolutely supportive will say to me, "I've lost my son. I'm fine with my daughter, but I've lost my son [or vice versa]." As a parent, I can understand that. There is grieving there,' Dr Stathis says. He's a parent of two teens and he says he tries to imagine how he would respond if his daughter or son came home and decided they wanted to change gender or identify as non-binary. 'But if you push back, they may also push back harder. This has always been the case. Rather, despite how fearful or unconvinced you as a parent might be, you have to approach it in a curious, kind and understanding manner,' he says. Recent Australian studies would put the transgender population at about 1.3 per cent, meaning that many young people, like their parents before them, are 'testing the boundaries' and don't present as consistent, persistent and insistent. That statistic again: 1.3 per cent. Another point here is the broad agreement, when researching this, that gender might be on a spectrum, but throughout history has not been recognised as such or has been stigmatised. Dr Stathis? 'There's always been right across the world – "the third gender" – or it has been explained in different ways, by different groups. So it's nothing new. But it is something that's being tested.'

That's certainly the case in schools and in lounge rooms across the nation. Let's go back to school uniforms for a moment. The irony of a situation where girls are told to be themselves and run their own race, but dress identically and conform in other ways, is not lost on students. 'I think there's a huge mixed message to say the very least, a huge message for girls who are told to embrace their individuality, but only in this way,' psychologist Laura Lee says. 'I have a lot of girls talk about wanting to do things that would make them feel so much more comfortable in their own skin, as simple as wearing their hair a certain way, or a certain colour that they're prevented from [wearing], and I think that rule feels as though it doesn't have a relevant purpose in this day and age.' Psychologist Majella Dennis says she sees two students struggling with school refusal. 'One hasn't been to school in a year and it started around a uniform, and them being really uncomfortable. It was a tight white skirt in primary school. And this particular student developed early and that combined with going through puberty – it became a massive issue for them.' She continued onto high school where the only option was a skirt, or 'an ugly pair of pants that were clearly designed to put a big asterisk above their head to say "I'm different".' Dennis isn't the only person to raise this. Several school counsellors, backed by students, say schools adopting unisex uniforms had chosen something particularly unfashionable – in colour or style – to deter students from wearing it. The problem, they say, is that those brave enough to do that feel as though they are publicly marked as 'different' because the takeup rate is so low. 'Our school captain deliberately wears pants,' one student says. 'She's not questioning her gender and lots of people who choose them aren't – but she wants to make the point that if you are, you can wear them and not stick out because the school captain wears them too.'

Many also raised the ironies that are worn alongside their uniforms. 'We're taught to be modest, and then they put us in these tiny little athletic uniforms with pleated little skirts,' one student says. I think I can hear Dennis nod down the phone line. 'It's massively contradictory and they put them in competition with each other in just about everything, and then tell everyone they need to be kind and compassionate with each other.' However, she's not against uniforms and sees the role they play. 'I think the gender divide that the uniforms highlight and perpetuate is a bit outrageous in this day and age.' She's right. Even if you look at the economics of uniforms worn in girls' and boys' schools. Girls' uniforms have more pieces, vary often between summer and winter, and are more expensive. One Melbourne teacher raises the same issue but says uniforms also bring 'a sense of common purpose of values and an identity in a different way'. Still, there needed to be choice within it, she says. 'I think it's worth listening to the students . . . I could learn from my students here.'

Uniforms are only one issue being discussed by school leadership teams and school boards. Unisex toilets. Swimming carnivals. Change rooms and sports competitions are all being discussed as they struggle with a phenomenon that is enveloping young people. Parents have a stake here too, with many already lobbying schools against any change. 'Their argument is that they've chosen a single-sex school and it has to remain that way,' one educator says. And this from a school leader: 'I'm appointed to run an all-girls' school, and that's what I am doing.' A third said this: 'You go to a gender-specific school because you "identify" as a girl or a boy. If you don't identify as that gender, then you stand out. And that's not what the spirit of the school is about.' A fourth says the issue kept her awake at night, and she wasn't sure how the school, parents and students would end up on the same page. And a fifth says, 'From a principal's point of view, it's not just the gender identity of students. There are staff who are struggling with that as well. And that has an effect on the teaching and learning environment. I think as a society, we've moved a great deal, but we have to move more obviously. Some schools can manage that very well. Others struggle with it. And that's usually around how their communities view those types of matters.'

'We have to strike a balance,' Dr Stathis says. 'We have to be absolutely supportive of young people who are questioning their gender, or who are gender-fluid or transgender. That needs to be a bedrock. We have to accept, support and champion diversity.' But we also need to recognise how challenging the issue is for schools and parents, and the community at large. 'So my view is, yes, we need unisex toilets; yes, we need to have open dialogue; and yes, we need to listen to the challenges of young people who are in schools.' He dismisses concerns – usually from parents – that an adolescent who identifies as male might have an advantage in sporting competitions. Dr Stathis says it is the opposite for adolescents who have not entered or who are only in the early stages of puberty; many are disadvantaged because the early stages of treatment involve blocking hormones. Arguments over change rooms are also scare-mongering. 'The majority of gender-diverse or transgender people are very private. They are not going to undress in front of everyone. That's the last thing they want to do.'

So what does Dr Stathis tell young people who are transgender, gender-questioning or non-binary and attend single-sex schools? 'I say to think about your gender, but not too much.' Each student is more than their gender. 'Gender is an important part of who you are, but it doesn't define you,' he tells them. And many of them say they want to stay at that school because of other factors, such as the friendships they value. 'The majority of transgender young people or gender-diverse people don't want to stand out and so they would rather not push things too much,' he says. 'I have to say this, though: if you are a transgender female, you should be allowed to go to an all-girls school because you're identifying as a female. If you're a transgender male, you should be allowed to go to an all-boys school because you identify with them.' But he accepts this carries risks for both the young person and the school. Transgender young people rank among the bravest he knows. 'I get emotional when I talk about this, because I've seen how hard it is. Their peers might be accepting, but it is still difficult. This is not just something you pick up overnight and say, "I'm just going to try this on." This sense of identity is something that lies deep within them.'

'We need to listen better, and in doing so communicate that we have a trust in the adolescent to do this exploration, which is a developmental task and that's not going to be linear. No matter what happens, we're the adults and should be the wise elders,' Majella Dennis says. That's her advice to parents. And to schools? 'It's really important to progress and to be well researched and to connect to the community.' The student voice is so important too. Victorian psychologist Carly Dober says parents also need to be given the 'space and the opportunity to voice what they're really going through because for some it can be grief, it can be shock, it can be loss, it can be confusion, you know, a lot of self-blame and self-doubt'. This journey is one where adolescents are trying to 'practise what it is like to be an adult' in their families and communities, like their school. 'If you invalidate that, and you send them a message that their ideas are unimportant, their feelings are unimportant, that can lead to a whole host of mental health challenges and physical health challenges.' At one end of that is suicidal ideation or suicide, but it can widely create anxiety, stress and a distrust with their parents. Indeed, the figures around gender dysmorphia are heartbreaking. Almost one in two transgender or gender-diverse people have attempted suicide. Four in five transgender people have reported self-harm. About 70 per cent report that they have no support at home, and 80 per cent of transgender young people report discrimination.[1]

Psychologists, everywhere, have stories of parent–child relationships being ruptured on this issue. It can be a particularly vexed issue for those from cultures where very traditional roles are assigned to males and females. One school psychologist told me of a student who has been grappling with their gender for three years; they are now in Year 11. 'They're petrified to tell their parents because they overhear how their parents talk about this. They've come out at the school and their peers have been very supportive, but [they] have to pretend to be a different person when they come home.' This is not a lone story. At parent–teacher interviews, several teachers told of their fear that they would forget to use the birth name of their student. 'You know, it's one slip and it could be very nasty,' one educator said. Another said, 'It's incredibly taboo, particularly in Asian cultures. It's quite shameful. I work with a big Southeast Asian community and they don't seek help even when their child is actively suicidal because it might bring personal shame to the family. They feel that if their child is experiencing mental illness, then [they] obviously didn't try hard enough.' Universally, the advice to students is to find someone they can trust in the first instance, seek professional help and connect with queer peers. Parents should also seek professional advice. 'They can then have their own independent place to talk about it and be their true unfettered selves. And they can have the resources to then support their child through this period, to get them to lean on their social supports, and also to read relevant research, to seek out evidence-based research,' Dober says.

Dr Stathis says the two factors that significantly impact a transgender or gender-diverse young person's mental health are the support of the parents and the support of their peers and school community. 'If you don't have those, mental health issues arise,' he says. And the issue is not going away. In five years, I ask, how will this debate play out? 'My view is that what is going to become increasingly topical will be the whole concept of non-binary, which is rapidly escalating.' Gender-fluidity is also more likely to be an issue. 'They may change or say, "I don't feel comfortable as either gender" or "I feel comfortable as both",' he says.

12

Consent and what we all need to learn

In this school science lab, the stuff you'd expect sits on high-top tables for the Year 11 class about to get underway. But this is a sex education class, and the focus is on a foam structure that looks a bit like a penis. It's sitting atop one of the tables, with a couple of condoms by the side and the lesson is focused on how to use a condom. 'We were standing around watching, thinking this is nothing like real life – but no one would say that,' a 17-year-old says. That story shows the startling divide between the delivery of sex education in some schools – where it is routinely delivered too late, and focuses on the role of women not men, and even abstinence – and the real world, where young women are forced to navigate assault, toxic masculinity, slut-shaming and coercion. 'What is missing is consistent sex education across all schools,' one 17-year-old says. 'There are different standards everywhere. One school gets something, someone else gets fear-based abstinence. We need discussions about bodily autonomy where we can report things when we are young. We need sex education that is factual and relevant and inclusive, and that extends to diverse communities that we don't always talk about, like the queer community. And we need to talk about stealthing.' That's just one of the terms many parents might not know, but is the act of secretly removing a condom during sex, when the consent was based on the use of a condom and the person giving the consent believes it is still in place. Victim blaming needs to be addressed too, another 17-year-old offers – and you know she's sitting on a story that keeps her awake at night. 'The biggest issue that needs to be covered is the importance of feminism in our world,' a peer in another state says. Adopting feminism would prepare girls to take on the sexual assault, harassment and bullying that are part and parcel of their lives. 'It also allows us to face the issues of workplace equality and the lack of body autonomy. At a young age, girls are already susceptible to outrageous remarks and inequalities, and are already being objectified and degraded,' she says. As a young woman, she says she sees women begging to have the choice over what happens to their own bodies. 'I see women constantly objectified and ridiculed in the media over their appearances and I see us already having to fight for equal pay with male colleagues.' She's 17 too, and wants the world to be equal and modern and inclusive – and strongly believes it is not.

'They're really progressive when they teach kids how to put condoms on,' educator Dannielle Miller says wryly. 'It doesn't really explain how to have a conversation about wanting him to put a condom on or what happens when he takes it off. I feel like we're setting a pretty low bar.' Miller says students are tired of 'dumbed down' versions of sex education that were too stuck on the 'consent issue'. 'Most young people intrinsically understand what consent means and what lack of consent means,' she says. 'They're not stupid. We need to look beyond "consent" and actually position that in a broader framework around all respectful relationships.' Miller, who received an OAM for her services to education, women and youth in 2021, says teens need to understand when their boyfriend is controlling, or if the relationship has isolated them from friends. 'The stuff they don't know is stuff around coercive control, and information on trauma responses. It's not just fight, flight or freeze. It's also appease, which is a particularly female response to trauma or dangerous situations, where we try and calm that person down or we can be very pleasant to them. Because we feel if we do that, then we can get away and keep ourselves safe.' That exact way of thinking is mirrored in some of the accounts of girls who have been sexually assaulted. 'He kept pressuring, almost begging me, and didn't stop even after I said multiple times I don't want to or "no, stop". I felt I had no other options so eventually I said, "Yes but could you please make it quick."' That's one girl out of almost 7000 who penned their experiences at the request of Chanel Contos, a former Sydney schoolgirl who this year won the fight to ensure earlier and better consent education is delivered in Australian schools.[1] 'It's a valid response,' Miller says. She says some teens feel guilty because they 'didn't fight him off or didn't run away. But that was actually a strategy to keep [them] safe. That's valid. You don't need to feel guilty about that.' Another educator, who asked not to be named because of the pushback surrounding alcohol and sex, says girls often 'accepted' what happened to them because they were drunk. 'I'm sorry, but if we have young men who are lining up to have sex with a girl who's unconscious on a bed, that has nothing to do with alcohol being provided. It's got to do with abhorrent behaviour by a group of the young men.'

Over decades, the need for sex education – beyond abstinence and how a condom works – has been talked about and delivered in haphazard ways by reluctant teachers. But the guts of the research for this book shows teens want the whole story, not just parts of it, and they want it delivered by experts who they can question. They want to be informed and empowered. Remember the cup of tea analogy? Some schools have been considered progressive for explaining sex was like being offered a cup of tea: you could decline or accept, change your mind, stop drinking at any time, and prefer different varieties. Talking to girls, they see that's a bit outdated too – it is viewed as too simplistic, too genteel, and failing to address issues directly. Besides, how many teens drink tea? In 2022, it's 'FRIES', and no metaphor sits around it. It's just an acronym that addresses many of the nuances around consent. Coined by Planned Parenthood, it stands for Freely given, Reversible, Informed, Enthusiastic and Specific, and allows direct discussions around stealthing, cajoling, guilt-tripping and many of those more nuanced issues that need to be understood.

That need is driven by what is happening to students in private and public schools, co-ed and single-sex schools, in regional areas and cities. It was early in 2021 that Chanel Contos posted her Instagram story asking followers if they or anyone close to them had been sexually assaulted by someone from an all-boys private school when they were at school. A day later, she had more than 200 affirmative responses, prompting a petition demanding more holistic consent education in Australia. It led her to set up the Teach.Us.Consent.™ platform, where people could share their anonymous testimonies about sexual assault. By Christmas 2021, Contos had 45 500 signatures – and almost 7000 stories. By February this year, after addressing state and federal ministers, Contos had won an agreement to overhaul sex education in class. 'I have lived in three different countries and I have never spoken to anyone who has experienced rape culture the way me and my friends had growing up in Sydney amongst private schools,' she told followers on her site. According to the Australian Institute of Health and Welfare (AIHW), almost two million Australians have experienced at least one sexual assault in their lives, from as young as 15 years of age.[2] Reading the testimonials of those who have contacted Contos is heartbreaking.

> 'After he raped me, him and his friends threw the condom around the room and made jokes about me.'

> 'After he had sex with me, he got up and left me in the room and then left the party with his mates.'

Two stories out of 7000 but you simply need to ask a teen in order to find others very easily, perhaps even closer to home. Rapes in sheds, at parties with people metres away, in bedrooms, in cars. Sober and scared. Frozen. Numb. Drunk. The next day shame. Guilt. Nightmares. Slut-shaming. And not knowing where to turn. In this research project, incidences were raised voluntarily and repeatedly.

> 'I had a male student touch me inappropriately and I asked to not be around him but they kept him in my classes and said to let them know if more happens. Isn't once enough?'

'A lot of stuff has happened to me where I've looked back and realised that it was really not okay. I'm only 17 and I already value a guy's satisfaction over my own comfort, like when I'm in a relationship it feels horrible not to please a guy if he asks for that, and immediately my mind goes to, "if I don't then he has to find that somewhere else surely".'

'So many of my friends have been raped. They've hidden it, every single one of them. It's like "teens can't control themselves", "you were looking for it", "boys will be boys". One of my best friends is burdened so hard here; I've seen how it affected her. She's living her life without dealing with it because it's not taken seriously.'

'I love co-ed schools because I get along with boys as well. But it's hard when I've never been in a relationship and I've never done all this stuff and there's this pressure. I'm behind them. I'm not as good.'

'I would not go to my school if it was my choice. It's a co-ed school. Girls are objectified, and boys harass them.'

'It's like what you are meant to do, not what you are comfortable with.'

'I don't know a single boy that doesn't regularly watch porn, and I've had guys get out laptops and start watching

it while we were doing stuff, or like trying to show me what they want me to do.'

'I lose sight of my self-worth when it comes to guys, because you just crave their approval. That might just be a me thing. I'm not sure.'

'Recently my ex and I broke up, in June, and honestly sometimes I still get really upset about it. And like I know it's a teenage relationship so it's obviously dramatic and we are still kids and blah blah blah, but the emotions I feel are so vivid and explosive that it feels like the most important thing in the world, when clearly it's not.'

'Boys get away with asking girls for photos and harassing us and constantly sexualising us. I feel uncomfortable around lots of boys because they are very disrespectful and look at our bodies especially from behind. Some don't even talk to some girls at my school because they say they are really ugly.'

So how do they rate schools and their parents in addressing their needs in this area?

'There is no sex education at school. None. We have no knowledge.'

'Gender, sexuality and women's rights are not talked about enough.'

'We have had presentations on consent at school but they are filled with misinformation and quite frankly don't do shit. These school presentations have not prevented count-less rape and sexual assault experiences ... it seriously is a joke.'

'We are taught through science, but it's not in a way that you can apply it in a situation.'

'My school poorly handles concepts around sexuality and sex education. They have never taught us anything regarding sexual education or finding our own identities and often react poorly to same-sex relationships and those who do not identify as cis gender individuals.'

'I made a survey and sent it out to my school; a few women replied saying they had been sexually assaulted (including myself) and the school did nothing about it.'

'My parents never discussed any sex education topics. I learnt everything from my friends.'

Students say any sex education eschews inclusivity, and actively excludes consideration of some groups, including transgender, gender-diverse and sexually diverse young people. Overwhelmingly, they voice support for LGBTQIA+ inclusivity. This is supported by a study in South Australian schools that found about one-third of LGBTQIA+ students never had 'any aspect of LGBTQIA+ people mentioned in a supportive or inclusive way during their relationship and sex health education'.[3] Girls also believe they are unfairly targeted in many conversations, when the focus should be more on the behaviour of their male peers.

> '*I don't think that parents or the school are educating them on the issue enough. Instead they are educating girls on how to prevent it and how to report and act on it.*'

> '*Can we talk about the way teen boys treat young women?*'

Those two comments deserve a focus. Teen girls are angry that the focus is on their role, rather than that of the boy who is often the perpetrator. (In this project, there was no claim of a girl assaulting a female partner.) They wonder why boys' schools are not putting the same emphasis on consent and the issues around it. And they see it as another telling example of societal inequality. The story of how to put a condom on a piece of foam is a stellar example. Is that a girl's job or responsibility? Dannielle Miller says girls are feeling rage and frustration that much of the education provided in the past has been superficial, shaming, judgemental or gender stereotyped. 'And they really want to have much more sophisticated and nuanced conversations that are very authentic and direct on this topic,' she says. Psychologist Nicole Young says teaching around sex education does not reflect contemporary times, and that is across government, Catholic, co-ed, single-sex and independent schools. 'You have to go beyond just the formal teaching to how are we changing the culture and the conversations that staff are having, that the community is having, that young boys and girls are growing up hearing and witnessing at home, in football clubs and at school,' she says. 'And those conversations around intimacy and concern and bodies and differences and equality and all of those things should be happening from day dot.' Cyber safety expert Susan McLean agrees that there can be enormous pressure applied by boys. 'There is a reluctance to say no, because if you say no you're frigid. So to them being frigid and not liked is actually worse than being called a slut.' Byron Dempsey hosts a podcast titled Consent and Sex with former police officer Brent Sanders; it was sparked after Dempsey recorded five million views on his Driven Young podcast, talking about consent. It is the same issues as those raised by students and health officials that are capturing his audience – age, alcohol, definitions, online dating and the consequences. He says he's learnt that some boys have a preconceived idea that 'someone who commits a sexual assault crime is like an old white man in a trench coat in an alleyway'. 'They think, "Well, that's not me, therefore I'm not a rapist." That's not the case.' He says some ignore the pressure they put on girls until they say 'yes', and then believe that equals consent. 'However, if you manipulate them, if you coerce them, if you put pressure on them over time and they say "yes", that's not consent because you've manipulated them. Because they got the "yes", they don't consider themselves a rapist.'

Asked about what they wanted included in the talks provided at school, girls also asked for details around sexual health. Urinary tract infections, thrush, menstruation, along with the difference between ethical and hardcore porn (almost three-quarters of boys aged 16 to 17 years and one in three girls aged 16 to 17 years reported having viewed pornography in the past 12 months[4]), technology, contraception, pleasure and how sex makes them feel. 'We haven't been told about the emotional side of sex,' one said. 'How it gets inside your brain,' says another. This is supported by an online survey on sex education conducted by the Commissioner for Children and Young People in South Australia that tapped into the views of 1200 young people aged from 12 to 22 years, who pleaded for content 'to move beyond puberty, anatomy and the prevention of pregnancy and diseases'.[5] That survey included female, male, non-binary, transgender or gender-diverse, sexually diverse and culturally diverse young people, including those with a disability. And the verdict was similar. They want sex education that teaches them about healthy and unhealthy relationships, how to protect themselves from violence, the complexity of consent, how to access support, image-based abuse including pornography and the interplay between sex, drugs and alcohol.

Young women such as Chanel Contos, 2021 Australian of the Year Grace Tame and Brittany Higgins, who blew the lid off political sex abuse in Parliament House, have turned the dial here. Each of them, driven by her own personal experiences, has used her voice to allow her younger sisters to be heard at home, at school, at university and at parties where they've been ignored for too long. As discussed elsewhere, being heard can draw criticism from those who don't like the message. Grace Tame is a perfect example. On receiving the Australian of the Year accolade for 2021, her determination and courage in forging legal change around sexual assaults was applauded. Groomed at 15, she was repeatedly sexually abused by a teacher. Despite the trauma and heartache that brought, she used the national accolade to acknowledge victims, encourage other young women to speak up, and to force account-ability among those who write our laws. The impact of the courage she's shown should not be underestimated.

Neither should the work of Angie Wan and Dr Joyce Yu, a pair of school friends who set up a not-for-profit organisation called Consent Labs in 2016. It was a response to the experience of teens living at residential colleges and universities in Australia, and last year they spoke to more than 10 000 Australian school students in Years 7 to 12, parents and university students. Angie Wan says the thousands of cases described to Chanel Contos were not surprising. 'It was still obviously incredibly harrowing to read through those testimonials, but they were experiences that myself and my peers had already lived and that was the entire reason why we started Consent Labs,' she says. 'It's surprising how many students will have basic questions, even around what constitutes a healthy relationship. They're not able to identify the characteristics for themselves, which is quite alarming, particularly in that 16 to 18 age group.' Susan McLean, who is also a former police officer, provides talks on the role of technology in consent. 'I can remember being at a girls' school, and I had a 15-year-old ask me what "rape" was. She didn't actually know,' she says. She also routinely sees girls believing that 'yes' once means 'yes forever'. 'They don't realise that consent is finite; it's not ongoing and they do not understand that it can be removed at any time.' She says it can be heartbreaking. 'I think how have you got to 17 or whatever, and no one has sat down with [you and had] any sort of conversation about any of this? How can any young person protect themselves if they're not educated?' That's at one end of the spectrum. Wan says that at the other are students wanting to support peers disclosing sexual assault or asking whether they can seek support. She says that, whatever the level of knowledge, a 'crisis point' has been reached, which warrants detailed conversations around respectful relationships and consent education.

At the centre of any consent education has to be the issue of coercive control, which has popped out of headlines in Australia since Hannah Clarke and her three young children were brutally murdered in a suburban street in Brisbane, in 2020. Hannah's ex-husband had been tracking her, stalking her, and on this morning he jumped into her car, as she prepared to ferry her children to school, held a knife to her throat and ordered her to drive off. He then poured petrol over his wife and children and set all of them alight, killing Hannah and her three children before stabbing himself to death. In the months that followed, I spent time with Hannah's parents Lloyd and Suzanne. They are down-to-earth, caring and clever, but they hadn't understood that term – coercive control – until they'd lost their daughter. They'd known their ex-son-in-law had been telling her what to wear and who she could see, manipulating and intimidating her to the point where she was scared and sometimes isolated. That fits the definition, but 'coercive control' simply hadn't been part of their vocabulary. Thanks to their efforts, jurisdictions are now acting to ensure coercive control is punishable. Other moves are also afoot, with two Australian states moving to better define consent. For example, in New South Wales, and thanks to the advocacy of Saxon Mullins (who in 2018 gave up her anonymity to reveal a 2013 sexual assualt and the later criminal trials and appeals), the Crimes Act will be changed to ensure consent is not assumed – it must be clearly given by words and actions. Legislative actions to ensure the requirement for affirmative consent and to make stealthing explicitly illegal are also planned in Victoria.

One in three young people, aged 12 to 20, reports being a victim of dating violence, according to Dannielle Miller. 'While teen boys are just as likely as girls to have experienced some measure of abuse, girls are four times more likely to report being frightened and hurt by the aggression they experienced,' she says. Psychologist Majella Dennis says coercive control and family violence are on a continuum. 'We need to be able to recognise red flags,' she says. 'We need to be talking about healthy and unhealthy relationships, whether it be friendship relationships or dating relationships, the whole spectrum in between.' Boundaries are a big part of this. In the cold light of day, away from other influences, what behaviour will a teen girl accept? And how will she explain that? It's no different from drawing boundaries around friendship in Year 5. Do they accept a friend bullying others? Who allows them to sit with them on some days and not others? In previous research, for my last book, *Ten-ager*, on ten-year-old girls, that was a crucial part of developing healthy friendships. And it's no different for 16-, 17- and 18-year-olds – although probably just a tad harder.

School counsellor Jody Forbes also encourages students to tune into their feelings, which can be red flags or cues that boundaries are being crossed or violated. They might feel afraid, uncomfortable or resentful. 'Pay attention to how you feel and to your gut instincts,' she says. She shares a story that shows, unlike other creatures, humans will sense danger yet still walk right into it. 'You're in a hallway waiting for an elevator late at night. The elevator door opens, and there's a guy inside, and he makes you afraid. You don't know why, you don't know what it is. Many females will stand there and look at that guy and say, "Oh, I don't want to think like that. I don't want to be the kind of person who lets the door close in his face. I've got to be nice. I don't want him to think I'm not nice." And so human beings will get into a soundproof steel chamber with someone they're afraid of, and there's not another animal in nature that would even consider it.' Others describe this as a type of 'good girl' behaviour. They don't want to rock the boat or draw attention to themselves. The widely held view – in girls' school especially – is that more needs to be done outside girls' schools, and particularly in boys' schools. Brisbane principal Toni Riordan also worries that girls might change when they move from an all-girls environment to other environments. 'My sense is – and this is just what I'm picking up from students – is that when they move into that social circle with boys, they defer.' Others agree. This is the 'good girl' syndrome in action. Parenting educator and author Dr Justin Coulson says boys are neurologically between 18 and 24 months behind girls at school graduation, and there is still an expectation that 'boys will be boys'. 'I don't know how else to say it – but there's just an acceptance that boys are going to goof off, do dumb things, get themselves into trouble and that's part of being a boy and part of growing up. Girls aren't expected to do that. And they generally live up to their expectations.' He says girls have told him that while the boy 'did the wrong thing, [she] was the one feeling dirty'. 'I remember one girl just saying, "I don't want to be a girl anymore, because I don't want boys to look at me; like they just want my body."'

A parent's role here is changing, and they are embracing the need to educate their daughters. That's important. By the age of 16 or 17 years, two-thirds of young people in Australia have been involved in a romantic relationship. While about 30 per cent approached for this project said they had a 'partner', other analysis suggests higher figures. For example, the latest National Survey of Secondary Students and Sexual Health states 34.3 percent of Year 10 students and more than half of Year 12 students (55.8 per cent) reported that they'd had sexual intercourse.[6] It's not always an easy topic for parents, though, and it carries added layers in some families, particularly those of certain cultures. But it's necessary. In this project, some partnerships were a week old, while some were three years old. Interestingly, in Melbourne several responses pointed to relationships becoming serious very quickly. This was explained by hard lockdowns that only allowed visits from a small number of people, or within a limited radius. That meant some girls were talking to their partners, online, for hours every day – and in several cases, parents agreed with that relationship becoming more physical earlier than they might outside lockdown. They wanted their daughter to maintain connections, but also understood that the partnership had matured more quickly than it might otherwise have done.

So how do you talk to a teenage girl when you can see an unhealthy romantic partnership developing? Dr Coulson says to pick a neutral place, and ask permission to have a chat about it. Then, as non-judgementally as possible, raise concerns by using facts, not thoughts. What you see. What you hear. Not what might be. And then listen. It's a difficult place, as one father told me. His eldest daughter was dating someone who would turn up late, then not turn up on occasion, and had begun to speak down to her, and even comment on what she was wearing. He told me he confronted him – and his daughter packed her bags and moved out.

Interestingly, the national debate about sexual assault, consent and coercion prompted some girls to look at the relationship their parents shared too. 'For some it was a big paradigm shift,' one psychologist says. They saw their mother's unequal role and came to the conclusion that their relationships, down the track, would be healthier and more balanced. 'Some then saw their dad through a very different prism. How jarring is it when you notice that perhaps your mum is being financially abused? Sexually abused? But you have options that perhaps your mother didn't.' No doubt exists, though, that an increasing number of parents want consent to be dealt with by experts. 'Parents have also gone on a bit of an education journey in the last 12 months, and realised that these issues around consent are things [about which] young people might have to struggle when they're in their twenties,' educator Dannielle Miller says. It's an area crying out for genuine cooperation between parents, students and schools.

Party scenes

In a world where we champion equality, our liver stands out as a big handicap for girls. And it's an important thing to know, given how crucial it is to our health. Without a functioning liver, we cannot survive. So what does that mean next Friday night, when a 17-year-old is downing a cruiser at a party at your own home, or an 18-year-old, as a rite of passage, is off clubbing? In short, it means young women are often far more affected by alcohol because of the difference in the development of their livers. Livers in males develop earlier, around 18 to 19 years of age. But the female liver takes longer, and is not fully developed until the early twenties. And that has a couple of consequences. First, young women between the ages of 18 and 21 might be drinking to excess, relishing those years of freedom where they are legally able to walk up to a bar and ask for anything from a watermelon cruiser to a martini. According to Paul Dillon, expert on teen alcohol and drug use, that puts strain on an organ that is underdeveloped. Other factors complicate this too – from women not producing an enzyme that breaks down alcohol to having average lower body weights. The damage is compounded when girls have been drinking regularly, earlier. The second factor is that the underdeveloped liver means alcohol remains in a young woman's system for longer – and that can have crushing consequences while she is on her P plates. Dillon has a list of stories where girls have lost their licence while believing no alcohol would be found in their system. 'These girls are really great kids who would never ever consider breaking a law,' he says. 'In one example, a young woman finished drinking and went to bed at 11 pm on a Friday night. 'And she got busted for mid-range drink driving at 5pm the next day! They really do have to be super careful.' He says often, at a talk, a girl will say that she 'can drink any guy under the table'. And that might be true. She might walk and talk and act more sober. He asks her this: 'But will you be able to process alcohol as quickly as a guy on average? No, you won't – and it's important you understand that.'

Dillon is the director and founder of DARTA, Drug and Alcohol Research and Training Australia, and author of *Teenagers, Alcohol and Drugs*. Each year, he works with hundreds of school communities to address drug and alcohol use by teens, and says he can see the role competition plays with teen girls. 'They're hanging out – a lot of them – with slightly older guys and trying to compete or keep up with them in a whole pile of different things.' He says he can see the resentment build sometimes when he starts to talk about the physical differences between sexes and what that means to them. It's the push for equality, not peer group pressure, that is driving some drinkers. 'It is widely accepted by most people. It is a common myth from parents about peer pressure; from my experience, no one is ever peer pressured to drink or vape,' says one 17-year-old. Others hint that males have entitled views around female peers drinking. 'Some of the girls in my group, including me, like to drink while the boys are very judgemental of us drinking.' But none of that changes the facts. 'Alcohol affects them more. And in terms of harm, they're going to be more harmed by alcohol,' Dillon says. You can hear, in his voice, how much this worries him. 'In Years 7 and 8 and 9, young men are more likely to have consumed alcohol than young women. And then it changes, it flips, and all of a sudden at 15, girls are more likely to drink alcohol than their male counterparts.' His comments are based on the 2017 Australian Secondary Students' Alcohol and Drug survey. The good news is that fewer high school students are drinking alcohol overall. Some are declared non-drinkers and that group – at least anecdotally – is growing. 'I really hate drinking and everything associated with it,' one 17-year-old says. 'I don't enjoy getting drunk,' another says. 'I hate seeing my friends change. They become different people,' says a third. And those comments are more common than they might have been a few years ago.

But this 2017 survey of about 20 000 secondary students aged between 12 and 17 years showed that at 16, more girls than boys had consumed alcohol in the previous month (46 per cent compared with 43 per cent). It flipped a year later, when 55 per cent of boys had drunk alcohol in the previous month, compared with 52 per cent of female students. Thrown together, 16- and 17-year-old girls consumed more alcohol than boys in the previous month, with an average of 5.5 drinks.[1] And their preference tended to be 'alcohol energy drinks'. Dillon says that a few years ago he took a walk around a hospital liver ward with a mother and medical specialistwho had been at one of his presentations. She told him how her work had changed dramatically. She used to work with older men, and now regularly patients were younger women with alcohol-related liver disease. Some were in their twenties.

It can be hard for 18-year-olds to understand this, when the societal message runs so strongly counter to it. Visit a bottle shop, and you can see the lure of colourful pre-mixed spirits. They're marketed like cosmetics at a big retail store. Purple, pink and green hues cover the wall, with guava-flavoured, pineapple, watermelon, raspberry, zesty lemon and pink grapefruit flavoured cruisers all on offer. Many sound – and taste – like soft drink too. A hint of mint? Or ginger? It's all on offer for our teens to pre-load, or drink at parties, clubs, pubs or at home; anecdotally, in the first year out of school, consumption jumps.

'I'm 18, so I can do what I like.'

'No study. No curfew. It's just money holding me back.'

'I get smashed, but I've studied hard for a long time.'

'I've never vomited or had a hangover. I'm known as the mum of the group.'

At 18, all that is legal. But where are 16- and 17-year-olds consuming alcohol, and who is providing it?

'Only at parties.'

'At parties.'

'I did get smashed [at a party] on the weekend but I don't usually.'

'I drink to cope with anxiety, anywhere.'

'At home with my parents. They're chilled.'

'I buy my own alcohol – no big deal.'

'Once I got into Year 12, my parents allowed me to drink. They buy it.'

'My parents buy it but I have friends whose parents don't allow them to drink so they get others to get it for them [including girls as young as 14].'

'My partner is 18 so alcohol is no problem.'

'In Australia, drinking starts at 16. Overall our class is pretty chilled. You see some kids at other schools and they are legless. It's [different from] going to a party and having a drink compared to getting smashed. We have small parties and a few drinks.'

'We are the generation where everyone wants to try something.'

'I think a good 70 per cent [of] Year 11s in my region specifically drink and 50 per cent have vaped. I feel like our generation is very carefree in terms of wanting to give everything a go – good or bad.'

Those last two responses bring me back to the visual smorgasbord on offer. Just like their parents, they want to push boundaries and make a few mistakes while trying something new. Statistics suggest almost 12 per cent of girls aged between 14 and 19 have recently used cannabis[2] and only 3 per cent have recently used ecstasy, although 10 per cent of 17-year-olds had used it at some point.[3] From this research, that figure might now be higher, as girls at public and private schools in almost all cities raised it as their party choice – in many cases ahead of alcohol.

MDMA. Methylenedioxymethamphetamine. Ecstasy. E. Some girls describe it as gifting them the best night of their lives. It wasn't like holding a vape, which looked a bit sad, or downing cruisers that added to calorie counts. E made them feel on top of the world. And because it was a tablet, downed early in the night, they'd get away with it. That's the story of a limited group – those who volunteered information during this project. But it backs up what others, including Dillon, are finding. 'It was the one drug that they thought they could take [where] they felt they were more in control, if that makes sense. You didn't necessarily look tragic at the end of it,' Dillon says. He sees another big – and dangerous – attraction with ecstasy, too. 'If we want to be really, really honest about MDMA/ecstasy, the vast majority of people who use that drug have, the first time they take it, the most incredible night of their entire life. The experience is so profound, [even] life-changing.' That presents policy-makers and health educators with a specific problem around messaging. Teens are told ecstasy is dangerous and can kill you. And then they look around at a music festival where people are having the time of their lives. 'The message they've been getting and the message they're actually seeing – they don't match,' Dillon says.

Ecstasy is a gateway drug for good girls, in some cases. They don't want to be a 'drinker' and despise those who vape. Ecstasy allows them to join in, seamlessly. They see that it doesn't change their world the next morning. They don't have a hangover. No one is commenting on their behaviour. And, according to some counsellors and health educators, they then wonder 'What else have they lied to me about?' And that can lead to other risky behaviours. One expert who visits schools says sometimes schools are 'staggered' because it might be the school captain or a school leader, among the most unlikely, that are caught with ecstasy. In this project, I was routinely told that teen girls almost never pay for ecstasy. It's given to them by someone older, usually a boyfriend.

'Vaping is a massive issue in our school.'

'Vaping is pretty normalised.'

'Several of my friends are addicted to vaping.'

'Most of my school friends are underage and drink, but not a lot of them vape.'

'Vaping is gross.'

'Vaping is big in our bathrooms at school, but not with my friends.'

Vaping is growing, and those doing it are becoming younger and younger. The Resilient Youth Australia 2021 Student Resilience Survey Cross-Sectional Report showed that 18 per cent of girls in Year 11 and 18 per cent of girls in Year 12 said they sometimes, often, always or almost always used e-cigarettes. A year earlier, in 2020, only 10 per cent of Year 11 female students said that, and 14 per cent of Year 12 students.[4] While many girls eschew vaping as 'dangerous', 'stupid' and 'ridiculous', the figures for 2022, given the jump in the previous year, were expected to be higher. That means while a big chunk of 16- and 17- and 18-year-old girls abhor vaping, another group of girls have become committed vapers. That struck me, wandering along the Esplanade at Surfers Paradise during Schoolies Week in 2021. While some might dismiss it, other young women were inhaling without a care in the world.

The research for this book threw up dozens of surprises, and vaping was one. We know it's a problem. We know it is largely unregulated. We know we don't know the composition of vapes. But do we really understand how pervasive vaping has become in just a few years? 'I've got families and schools I'm working with, students in Year 5, who are vaping,' one expert says. And that is not uncommon. Ask at your school. Students in Years 7 and 8 and 9 are routinely being pulled up, disciplined and suspended over vaping in the toilet between lessons, after school in the bus line and even, defiantly, in the open playground. This should frighten us all, and be the impetus for a mass change in thinking about how we handle vapes. 'It's a massive issue,' one 16-year-old says. 'But it's a specific cohort. There's a real problem in Year 8. We get the blame. I think it's a lack of education. Not just at this school.' Educators largely agree; certainly those found vaping are more likely to be in Years 8 or 9, not in Years 11 and 12. '[Those who are] getting caught in schools and getting into trouble are the younger ones, basically because they're stupid,' one educator says in reference to them deliberately flouting rules, doing it in toilets next to staff rooms, or out in the open at lunchtime. 'The older ones – they're not taking them to school.' But they are doing it elsewhere, he says, as evidenced by the number of parents contacting him because they are worried their children are addicted to nicotine.

The designs, flavours and colours of vapes hide their danger. They are marketed to young children and teens. Big vaping companies, like Big Tobacco in their parents' day, are prepared to spend money and attack public voices who speak out against vaping, and their means of making a profit. If their attention is to silence their critics, perhaps it is working. If this sort of threat existed in some other way, we would have politicians and policy-makers, parents and health officials all calling for immediate change, increased regulation and a greater focus on what teens are inhaling each time a vape is confiscated. Largely unregulated, a huge percentage – maybe more than 90 per cent – of disposable vapes come from China, where the industry is not well regulated and companies can make half a million vapes in a day. Late in 2021, it became illegal to buy nicotine vaping products from overseas websites (as well as locally) without a doctor's prescription. Health officials hope that will change the trend in usage, but many remain sceptical.

The lack of transparency around ingredients, as much as how they reel in teens, is also worrisome. Health officials say they can contain the same toxic cancer-causing chemicals found in regular cigarettes. 'This includes the highly addictive chemical nicotine, heavy metals, ultrafine particles, volatile organic compounds and some flavouring chemicals that can be harmful to health,' a Queensland Department of Health guide explains.[5] 'It's difficult for consumers to know exactly what's in their e-cigarettes – for example, nicotine has been found in e-cigarette liquids claiming to be nicotine-free.' One teaspoon of commercially available liquid nicotine can cause irreversible damage or death to a child. Other ingredients that may be acceptable for use in foods could be harmful when inhaled as a vapour.

Sydney GP Dr Danielle McMullen says that while traditional tobacco smoking has declined, she has found the takeup of vaping by young adults concerning. 'We just don't know what's in half of these little vape sticks. It's not just water and nicotine, because nicotine doesn't taste like blueberries,' she says. The nicotine levels in some were higher than in traditional cigarettes. One NSW Health study found that 70 per cent of vapes actually contained high levels of nicotine, even though the label did not state nicotine as an ingredient.[6] The long-term impact of vape ingredients is unknown too. 'The young adults I've spoken to – they know it's not good, but it's socially acceptable and it's cheap and [they think] it kind of looks cool,' Dr McMullen says. 'So even though they know that they're doing something they don't want to be doing and that's dangerous to their health, they don't know quite how to stop either.' There is no doubt that teens understand how dangerous tobacco smoking is: it has been drilled into them since birth; some have seen parents or aunts or uncles or grandparents try each New Year to give up; and others have seen loved ones die as a direct result of smoking. And, as discussed earlier, vaping and drinking can be a divisive factor in friendship groups in those final years of school. So how do we mute the power of marketing here, and the takeup of vapes? Laws can always be beefed up, but we need teens to understand how a flavour in food when heated to 350°C, as happens in the 'vaping' process, can present problems. We need them to understand what they might be putting into their bodies. And how that might turn their life upside down.

Parental role-modelling keeps popping up as the anti-dote to behaviour around drugs and alcohol. And that's difficult at the age of 17, when teens are on the verge of adulthood. Take for example how alcohol is dealt with in the lead-up to an 18th birthday. As Paul Dillon says, 'If you have views about alcohol that you don't want your child to drink until they are of legal age, do you wait until the moment you know midnight strikes on their birthday?' Or how do you deal with a 16th birthday party when some of the invitees might be 18? 'It's a really tough one,' he says, 'and I think every parent has to make their own decisions in these areas.' Educator Penny Golding highlights the impact and unpredictability of COVID-19 here, especially around lockdowns. That presented difficulties for parents too, as evidenced by the increased sales of alcohol. She says that, like other parents, it made her think about how she was dealing with the stress around pandemic changes. Whether that response is reaching for a packet of chips or a glass of wine, it is worth considering the value of role-modelling. Showing joy, not being serious all the time, making time to laugh and connecting with loved ones all played a role. Teens saw it, and some of it rubbed off.

Being honest, up-front and communicating views clearly are all part of the answer provided by every expert consulted about how parents deal with drug and alcohol issues when their children are on the verge of adulthood. It's recognition that one size doesn't fit all, that families have different priorities and different views. But there are also laws, as Dillon points out. For example, if your daughter is having an 18th birthday party, it is illegal in every state and territory to provide alcohol to minors – those aged under 18. 'I get asked by parents all the time, "What should I do?" and I say, "Well, look, I can't give you the answer to that. I can tell you, number one – the longer you delay your child's first drink, the better,"' he says. 'Number two: you are legally able to give your child alcohol. That's absolutely no problems in your own home, if they are with you.' But that doesn't include stocking a crate with vodka and driving your child to Schoolies' Week on the Gold Coast where they are sharing a room with someone who isn't 18. Or celebrating the end of school with a big party and vodka slushies.

'My parents allow me to drink as long as it's not a school night.'

'They provide me with two drinks for parties and then we buy more.'

'My parents can't pick me up. My parents want a drink on the weekend.'

'My mother thinks I'm the most innocent child to walk the earth. Others are genuinely impressed by how much I have her fooled.'

Whether girls are 16 or 18, they are still learning limits. They will push boundaries, just as their parents did before them. But times have changed. Children, as social demographer Mark McCrindle explains, often act – and are treated – younger for longer. Perhaps the world's not as safe a place. But, on average, girls are prepared to talk to their parents more – and that's a nugget of gold worth millions, which parents perhaps should draw on. Take this one example. Girls are asking visiting experts to schools how much they can drink with the medication they are taking for anxiety or depression, or even the contraceptive pill. Why would that question ever come up at school, Dillon asks? Before their first drink, they need to understand the interaction between medicine, and/or the pill, and alcohol – and parents need to address that. 'Some have been on medication since they were 12 and 13 and 14, particularly anti-depressants or anti-anxiety medication. Now they are young women, and they – or their parents – have not had a discussion with the doctor when refilling that prescription five years on,' Dillon says. 'No one seems to be having that discussion with kids.'

Other conversations around parties are also recommended. Knowing where your teen is, and who they are with, how they are travelling to a party and coming home, and what curfew they have are among the top tips. Dillon goes further, suggesting parents talk to the party hosts, ask questions about alcohol and adult supervision, and have the name and contact details of at least one of their friends. He suggests parents also monitor how much money their teen earns (or is given) and how they are spending it. Dr McMullen says it's important for teens to 'have a safe place; a place that they are home', and to know that they can call their parents at any time of the day or night. 'If they're feeling unsafe, or they think they've gotten into a situation that they're worried about, they need to know they can call their parents,' she says. 'I think that really plays a big part in how kids behave and in keeping them safe – because kids will experiment. And they need to know that they're still allowed to call out for help.'

14

Finding balance

A teen girl needs to be a deft juggler. Like her mother, often she needs to be skilled in time management, able to meet the demands of school, sport and cultural pursuits. And then, just as she hits her mid-teens, a few more balls are thrown at her to make balancing everything just a tad more difficult. Social media. ATAR. Decisions about what to do next. Friendship foibles. First dates. Parties. Driving practice. Rising anxiety levels. And for the next couple of years, she needs to find the balance that ensures none of those balls goes crashing to the ground. 'There's an issue of hypocrisy,' one 17-year-old says. 'We're told you need sleep. You need to relax. You need balance in your life. You need to look after yourself. And then you have five hours of homework!' That quest to find balance is talked about constantly. The quest to be a 'whole' person.

To reduce anxiety. Encourage a healthier life perspective. Ensure an equilibrium in work–life balance that is vital for our young as they climb into careers and partnerships, and perhaps having children. No one doubts the importance of balance. But is it possible when time is gobbled up by hours' more study than they've needed to do previously? When competitive sport requires increased training? When cultural pursuits wipe out weekends for workshops and practice? When part-time jobs are seen as their ticket to buying those new jeans and gaining confidence at the same time? When friendships and relationships need to be nurtured, and hours disappear with the lure of scrolling through Insta and Snapchat? Something has to give, and even the best jugglers will need to reduce the number of balls they have in the air. Or see them come crashing down.

'It's complex,' says Adelaide principal Dr Nicole Archard. 'But it comes down to doing some of each of those things. That's really important because being physically active is just as important as doing your homework and socialising with friends.' She pinpoints skill-building, time management and lowering expectations as areas that might help girls find a balance. Flicking through social media reels turn minutes into hours, she says, and they also need to learn to say 'no'. It is fine to decline an invitation from a friend to go out; it is okay to say 'no, I actually need me time now'. Once again, this issue of perfectionism comes up. It is perhaps the theme song of this cohort's lives. Dr Archard raises it this time, talking directly to the girls. 'You don't have to be great at everything. You don't have to be perfect at everything. You don't have to be everyone's go-to best friend all of the time. You don't have to be the straight A student all of the time. You don't have to make sure that you're in the top sporting team all of the time.' It is a valuable skill to be able to put boundaries in place, and say, 'I don't have to be the best at everything that I do.'

Scarily, and too often, sleep is the first 'activity' to be sacrificed in these teens' busy lives. Half of 16- and 17-year-olds are not getting enough sleep on school nights, and a symmetry occurs between shorter sleep periods and higher rates of anxiety and depression. Bad sleep hygiene, poor routines, the lure of the smartphone's blue screen, homework and caffeine intake are all blamed in research. And catching up on weekends just doesn't work; that 'yo-yo' pattern is blamed for disrupted sleep, and creates further problems. The Sleep Health Foundation and the Australasian Sleep Association say the pandemic made it harder for all of us to be sound sleepers. It used research to explain that as many as 46 per cent of people reported poor sleeping during the pandemic, compared with one in four pre-pandemic. Its 2020/21 report says poor sleep impacted 'mental health, consistent with the higher rates of anxiety and depression observed during the crisis'.[1] 'In addition, circadian timing phase delay ("evening" type) has become increasingly prevalent, especially among our young, exacerbated by disrupted routines and emerging patterns of increased late-night digital device use during the pandemic.'[2] Moreover, the direct links between 'sleep disturbance, mental health, and increased suicide risk are further exposed in the context of this current crisis'.[3]

That's the research, but our teens' lack of sleep stood out like a bad juggler on centre stage during this project. Australian Department of Health guidelines suggest teens aged 14 to 17 years require between eight and 10 hours of sleep each night. So how much do they get?

'Seven hours.'

'Six hours but I know I should have nine.'

'I get seven to nine hours but I feel as though I need more.'

'I wish I could be less tired. I'm tired no matter how long I sleep.'

'I like to study late and then I have to get up early to get to school, so maybe six hours.'

'I don't get as much sleep as I should. I stay up at night on my phone or watching shows because I don't get much of my own time during school life and workdays. I sleep for six hours.'

'I go through stages and I know my friends do the same where one week you won't sleep at all. Another you go to bed before eight.'

'I can't fall asleep before 1 am even if I try.'

'During the week I get six hours and ten hours on the weekend.'

'I can't get my brain to switch off. I wish I got more hours of sleep though and [for them to] be meaningful hours of sleep.'

'No matter how hard I try I can never get to sleep until around 2 am. I wish I could go to sleep around nine or ten.'

'Five hours.'

'Typically I get around six hours of sleep. I usually finish my homework and go to sleep by midnight. On the holidays, I usually get around ten hours.'

The teens are honest in their assessment. They know they are compromising on sleep. They know they want more sleep. And they've even considered what the hurdle to more hours and better sleep might be. My question to 1000 teens was, 'What is affecting your sleep?'

'Study, phone. My brain won't switch off. Procrastination.'

'My brain just thinking. Anxiety. Gaming.'

'Thoughts running around my head at Olympic pace – all the things I've never said. Crying. Studying. YouTube.'

'Sometimes I just cannot sleep because my thoughts just won't shut off.'

'Anxiety. Snapchat. Instagram.'

'Worrying about things like friends and tests and grades.'

'Overthinking.'

'I FaceTime a boy until 3 am because I study all day.'

'Relationships are stressful. My phone.'

In a cruel irony, many teens would get the amount of sleep they needed if they didn't have to rise so early. The science is unequivocal, but in layman's terms, teens can become night owls; their bodies are almost primed to stay up late and sleep more deeply into the morning. Their sleep drive builds more slowly, which means many teens don't feel tired enough to go to bed until late. Their bodies also wait longer to produce melatonin, the hormone that helps promote sleep, according to the American Sleep Foundation. 'If allowed to sleep on their own schedule, many teens would get eight hours or more per night, sleeping from 11 pm or midnight until 8 or 9 am.'[4] But here's the problem: school starting times. And catching up on the weekend – and the inconsistency in sleep routine that delivers – might exacerbate sleep schedules. 'If I had a magic wand, the thing I would ask schools to consider is shifting the times that schools run,' says Sydney-based educator Dannielle Miller. 'We have this weird 9 am to 3 pm kind of thing that we've stuck to and there's not really any research that supports that,' she says. It simply clogs roads and leads to queues of tired teens dawdling through the school gates. The idea of changing school times is raised and dropped regularly. Indeed, in February this year, and on the back of COVID-19's remote learning lessons, the New South Wales Government flagged an intention to trial an overhaul of regular school hours. Many schools have played with trials. Some schools, particularly overseas, have moved to more permanent changes. But in Australia, largely it's been tricky. While school drop-off times choke up roads, they also 'fit' in with local communities: bus and train timetables, parental drop-offs on the way to work. They mean families don't have different children starting school at different times. In short, this concept has repeatedly been put into the too-hard basket, and widespread acceptance has failed despite regular calls by health experts and researchers.

'I see tired students a lot more than I used to,' says Andrew Pierpoint, the president of the Australian Secondary Principals' Association. Some schools have taken to introducing 'sleep hygiene' lessons; others are sending notes home to whole cohorts with tips for teens to sleep longer and better; and individual families are being targeted in some instances because teachers can see the tiredness in how their teens cope with classes during the day. Tasmanian psychologist Nicole Young says school surveys highlight a concerning lack of sleep. 'I think young people don't have good sleep hygiene and I think that that probably comes back to parents losing some element of control around technology and screens and those types of things,' she says. That's backed up by girls' responses. At 16 and 17 and 18, it's not really possible to have phones removed from bedrooms. Some teens are living away at university or in other accommodation. But even at home, by that age it is harder to have control over what time children turn off their phones and shut their eyes. Young says the hard work needs to be done when young people are being introduced to technology. 'How do we use it? When are we using it? What are we missing out on? What does sleep hygiene look like? What are the boundaries?' Girls need to have those answers before they are 16 and 17. But what if they don't? The teens need to understand the impact of lack of sleep. What is it stealing from them? Certainly, she says, the tie between anxiety, stress and a lack of sleep has been delivered by research, over and over. 'Sleep is so important in so many areas of development – in terms of our energy, our attention, our ability to regulate our emotions, our stress, even our ability to digest food.'

Often during this research, I was struck by the insight our teens offer. Much is said about their inability to analyse critically what they see on social media, and to understand the nuances of mature thinking. But most of them do, I'm sure. It's just that they struggle to apply that to their own lives, or they choose to ignore it because of the pull of the now, the instant gratification that colours all our lives. Sleep is for later, when now they could be talking to friends or texting a new romantic interest or even studying that last chapter the teacher hinted might be on the exam. 'I wake up extremely tired,' one girl said. She recognised she had to address it, and would – eventually. 'There is too much on my plate.' That 16-year-old knew she had to drop a ball soon; the difficulty was deciding whether it would be netball or the cello. She wasn't too passionate about netball, but loved her team. She'd happily have foregone the cello, *but* her parents had hired one for the whole year. How was she going to tell them? Time poverty umbrellas these teens, and decisions on how to fix it require giving up something that they often love.

'I gave up swimming. I'm not quite smart and had to drop something to fit in tutoring. I was a good swimmer.'

'I stopped cross-country. It just phased out because I was really tired. Now I do no exercise.'

'I stopped gymnastics. The stress. Competitions. Time-consuming.'

'I've dropped netball. It takes too much time. I need to work on weekends.'

If sleep is one of the balls being dropped by these teen jugglers, another is exercise. Sometimes it's abandoned because the student has not made the top team. They've seen sport as competitive, not social, and they'd rather direct their efforts elsewhere. Sometimes it's because of that 'perfectionism' factor. They can see they're not going to win, so it's best not to compete. Other times, they follow their friends; it was social, and the fun was sucked out of it when friends quit. And often it is because that's the ball they've chosen to drop. No juggler, however experienced, can keep an infinite number of balls in the air at the same time. But what is missing here is a consideration of how sleep and exercise can make the balancing act easier; how it can reduce stress and anxiety and bring a level of calmness to a juggler's performance. 'Anxiety is really driven by unpredictability,' says anxiety expert Dr Jodi Richardson. 'Uncertainty. Lack of sleep. Oh my goodness, so much. So much. Difficulty getting to sleep, staying asleep, quality of sleep, which is in turn affected by social media activity.' And exercise? 'It is almost a panacea when it comes to anxiety because it's the natural end to the fight or flight response.' How does that work? When we become stressed or anxious, cortisol and adrenaline are released into the bloodstream as our bodies prepare to fight for our safety or to flee. Dr Richardson says that anxiety could simply be a teen waking up and realising, 'I haven't got a present for a friend for their birthday on Saturday.' But the body and the brain react in the same way whether threat is imagined or perceived or real – and the fight or flight response is initiated with the expectation that we will do something physical. 'We will actually fight for our safety or we will run – so short-term, high-intensity exercise can help utilise all those fuels that the body's prepared and primed to move,' she says. There are other reasons why exercise is so powerful in managing anxiety. 'Another one is that it promotes the release of a neuro chemical that puts the brakes on the stress response,' Dr Richardson says. GABA, also known as gamma-aminobutyric acid, is a natural chemical that acts as an anti-anxiety neurotransmitter. And all the reasons aren't scientific, either. Those with anxiety can also benefit from the social side of sport. 'It creates opportunities to have a talk and have a laugh and lean on relationships – if it's a team sport.' The role of sport has already been discussed; in creating independence and friendships and a whole set of skills. Its role here is just as important. But that often ends with Year 12 graduation because sport connection tends to be through school, not the community. 'And so when school ends, sport ends because they haven't built those networks in community sports,' Dr Richardson says.

Of course, many girls continue to play sport after Year 10. 'I play water polo, netball, basketball. I sing and am on the environment committee,' one 16-year-old says. 'I play badminton, soccer and do choir,' says another. And it was due to COVID-19, not by choice, that others dropped the sport ball. 'I do nothing now due to COVID, but I was doing boxing for the school before,' one says. 'COVID has stopped all my co-curricular activities,' says another. And 'before it was cancelled due to COVID, I played netball'. But these are teens motivated to play sport, join a team, win competitions. Many others in this cohort have simply stopped. 'You remember Wednesday afternoon sport, don't you?' The question is posed by school principal Andrew Pierpoint. He gives the example of one big town which has four state high schools and 19 private schools. 'We all used to play sport on Wednesday afternoon and the primary kids used to play sport on Friday afternoon. The primary stuff is still going but the secondary stuff has fallen in a heap.' He's right. I can remember growing up in Dalby, west of Brisbane, and 'wagging' the compulsory sport afternoon. It was overlooked, and most of the time I was 'wagging' it in the library or at my house nearby with my debating team. On occasion, you'd bid farewell to teachers as you walked out the gates. Pierpoint says 'students voted with their feet' by doing similar things; they dismissed involvement in it – and it ended. 'I think there's a great deal of research that says students who are active and who are not necessarily fit but are active and get out and have a run around the paddock are academically more able,' he says. 'There's a truckload of research around that.'

Melbourne principal Dr Toni Meath says keeping teen girls moving was a key motivation during lockdown in Melbourne, especially when 5-kilometre rings locked down homes. 'We actually sent them out in neighbourhoods for learning,' she says. As an example, film competitions focused on neighbourhoods were held across the school. That had the added value of some students becoming a bigger part of their local communities, which they often only saw out the window of a bus or tram on the way to school. The school also held 'eight before eight' each morning – which meant eight minutes of exercise before the clock struck 8 am. And activities were focused again at midday. 'I really wanted to keep them moving and fit and getting fresh air, even in winter,' Dr Meath says. Like other schools, Dr Meath held non-screen days where even staff were encouraged to not access computers. Across at Carey Baptist Grammar School, Kellie Lyneham says her school is involved in a compulsory Saturday sport competition, meaning all students participate in physical activity at least twice a week. 'As a mother and as an educator, I can see the many, many benefits to that because that protective behaviour is an expected behaviour.' Some students – male and female – struggle with it, and the key is to offer a broad range of activities. Increasingly, schools are trying to make sport or exercise a part of every teen's schedule. At Brisbane's Moreton Bay College, for example, exercise is encouraged as part of a specific strategy to strive for balance. 'We're trying to offer that consistent message to the girls,' principal Janet Stewart says. The title of the school's wellbeing framework is 'Keep Learning'. 'It's not to keep learning at the expense of other things,' she says. 'You're only going to keep learning if you feel really good, and you can only feel good if you're active. All of that learning is dependent on them being able to balance their lives in a healthy and holistic way.'

Disordered eating was discussed in Chapter 8, but it is worth revisiting because time poverty often also impacts eating habits. Uber Eats deliveries to after-school study centres skyrocket around exam time. Dr Danielle McMullen says girls' thinking can confuse parents. 'It's often a bit confusing for parents because on the one hand their daughter won't eat dinner with family or doesn't want pasta because she's decided she doesn't want to have carbs, but will stop at the servo with her friends and have a big slushie and bag of chips and a Mars bar,' she says. Then they'll talk about wanting to look slimmer. 'To adults, sometimes that doesn't make sense. There's a lot of social pressure that these kids are under to look a certain way, feel a certain way but they aren't necessarily supported with easy healthy food options around it,' Dr McMullen says. She's so right. Look at the offerings at tuckshops and sports events, and in vending machines. 'So the best thing families can do is make sure that healthy, easy food is on offer, that fruit is around the house and that snacks and healthy options are available after school,' she says. And that adults are modelling that behaviour – in terms of both cooking and eating together. Educator Dannielle Miller says she worries that we are 'setting up our young people sometimes to a different standard than the one that we live'. 'If you asked most busy working professionals, they'd probably say their diet isn't great. They don't get enough sleep either. Role-modelling is part of it because there's nothing teens hate more than hypocrisy. They have a finely tuned radar for double standards. So their parents constantly being on the phone and drinking coffee and not getting much sleep – and then saying they should be going to bed earlier and eating better – that's going to ring fairly false.' Dr McMullen's wish is that teens are educated about healthy choices. She sees many wanting to be vegan, for example. 'You can have a healthy balanced vegan or vegetarian diet, but it takes a lot of effort,' she says. 'You need to understand food nutrition. It's often helpful to get some advice from a dietician to help with meal planning.' And that's because while Oreos might be vegan, 'you can't live on chocolate biscuits'.

Psychologist Laura Lee uses the HAES principle when talking to many girls and their parents. HAES stands for Health At Every Size, and it's made up of a group of health professionals promoting a definition of health that is not centred around weight. She explains the principles: weight inclusivity, health enhancement, respectful care, eating for wellbeing and life-enhancing movement. That means moving for joy, for example, rather than specifically for exercise. Girls get it, but it's new for many of their parents. 'It's really different from how we might have been raised,' she says. 'Engaging in discussion that promotes health and moves away from eating restriction or exercise for weight loss is really critical to girls' wellbeing. The damage that can be done, and the trauma that it inflicts when parents make comments about their daughter's body weight or shape or size cannot be overstated.' It's more about being in tune with their body than knowing the healthy food pyramid off by heart. Lee says girls are not educated about gynaecological health and period pain. 'It's an area that girls are very poorly informed about,' she says. Period pain is often underestimated. One principal makes the point that a male student is able to get special exam consideration for a urinary tract infection, but girls could battle similar hurdles each month. Miller remembers being up all night in agony every month. 'It was extreme. But the truth is that when you're younger, your periods can be really irregular, and a period pain you experience can be really extreme,' she says. An Australian study conducted by the Victorian Women's Trust found almost 60 per cent of respondents said a day off to rest would make their period a better experience every month.[5] And the SA Commissioner for Youth and Young People said that while the effectiveness of menstrual leave policies had been debated across the world, employers in some countries, including the United States and India, had adopted policies allowing women to take a paid day off during their period. 'In Japan and Korea, such leave is embedded in legislation,' the report said.[6] In 2020, Scotland became the first country to make period products free, and in the same year Victoria became the first state to provide free pads and tampons to all government school students. A report by the commission found that stigma, emotional stress and discrimination can envelop young women, and called for more understanding, better education around menstruation and the development of specific menstrual wellbeing policies.[7]

Iron deficiency can also be a struggle for many young girls. 'We see a fair bit of iron deficiency . . . once a period starts and women are losing iron every month,' one GP says. They say that can be exacerbated by diets low in meat. 'That, along with their growing bodies and menstrual losses, means you do often see iron deficiency.' That can make it difficult to focus, and provide less tolerance for exercise. Signs that a teen might need an iron boost could be difficulty in focusing or concentrating, less exercise tolerance and a sense of fatigue. This GP says that is often 'an entry point to talk about eating behaviours and nutrition' with teens.

Martine Oglethorpe is a youth and family counsellor at The Modern Parent, and has a strong interest in living with technology. She says that search for balance is particularly important as we move on with COVID-19 hopefully in the rear-vision mirror. That's because of the reliance on technology for information, entertainment, socialisation, education and work during lockdown. 'It's played such a huge role in our lives that we need to make sure that we're getting back some balance – which, particularly for young girls, is an active lifestyle,' she says. Oglethorpe worries that activity is 'hugely lacking' for many young women, and that it will be harder now because of the significant break. 'They've had that break from it, and to now get the motivation to go back is really difficult,' she says. During lockdowns, the smartphone replaced connections that might have been derived from a weekly basketball match or going to the gym. 'All those sorts of things were taken away and so they were largely replaced or continued to be exacerbated by the use of the devices as other ways to connect and remain connected, which works on one level. But I think it means you're missing out on those other ways of connecting.'

Oglethorpe says she's been talking to parents whose daughters were talented sportswomen but now can't find the motivation to go back. 'It's just gone – like it's too hard because it's no longer part of that routine and I think every time we take something out of routine, it's hard to get it back. And that's why I'm always about building habits and routines into our life so that they become just something that we do. When they're not, it's really hard to build them back when they get older and they're now in charge of how they spend their extracurricular time.'

15

Success: A new outlook

Marni's mum was dux of her school. 'She's so intelligent. She did pharmacy,' her daughter says. But it's not a boast. 'She's not once said to me that she loves her job. Seeing that, I want to do something that makes me happy. I want to feel excited about going to work every day. I don't want to feel trapped.' Marni encapsulates how many girls at 16 and 17 and 18 see 'success' as something very different to how their parents continue to define it. To Marni, her mother's stellar career might be admirable, but it does not equate to the 'success' that she and her peers chase. She sees her mother's identity as based around netting a career, not a job, having a secure and growing income, and securing a roof over her family's heads, usually with expansive views. But that sixteenth-century definition of 'success' is more akin to its Latin origin, meaning result or outcome or advance. For this cohort, the dictionary definition has changed to something more like 'feeling content'. Of course, there are exceptions, but only a handful of girls in this project immediately described big houses, grand jobs and their own Wikipedia page as ingredients of 'success'.

> '*I will probably judge myself based on the kind of position I am in (e.g. what kind of job, how much money I am making, if I have bought a property).*'

> '*If I am happy and wealthy and have many assets.*'

Most did not use the terms 'money' or 'wealth' or 'assets'. Staying true to the values they hold dear, impacting others' lives, giving back, a healthy work–life balance, being fulfilled, being creative, pushing personal boundaries, maintaining 'solid' contact with family and friends, having 'passion' for what they do and loving life all trumped material success. Perhaps that's naive – and a few years outside home trying to pay an electricity bill will change that – but the teens repeatedly raised the difference in the meaning of success between generations.

> '*Teachers think it's grades. Parents think it is about opportunities and good careers. I think it's about doing something I love.*'

'When I think of success, I find it hard to define. It's not getting a lot of money or cars or houses. It's more about completing your own goals and doing what you want to make yourself happy.'

'Financial stability is crucial – but so is having meaning in life.'

'Money is important to me, but I'd rather be in a job that makes me happy and feel like I have fulfilled a purpose.'

Marni and her peers are not focused on the extra income afforded by careers that lead to a bigger office and a larger home. They see how their parents are running businesses, working late at night and catching up on reading on the weekend. They are also seeing their mothers, in particular, packing school lunches and juggling household chores with work responsibilities. 'That's not success. That's work. And you can't judge one by the other,' says a 16-year-old.

So how will they judge success later in life?

'If my heart is happy and I'm healthy inside and out. A life that energises me.'

'You can have a poor job and still be successful because you're happy.'

'If I can look in the mirror and like who I see – physically, mentally and emotionally.'

Parental 'pride' was also nominated by several girls – almost all from Asian backgrounds – in determining whether they would later judge themselves as 'successful'.

'If my parents are proud of the work I have done.'

'To see my parents with pride in who I have become.'

Perhaps it's another irony that 'financial security' is missing from their answers when it – along with an unclear future – is one of the issues they worry most about. Byron Dempsey, founder of the Driven Young podcast, joins this cohort in bristling at the word 'success'. It might have Latin roots, but its traditional relevance, he says, amounts to nil. Zero. Nought. 'It's so subjective – if you love your life and you think you're successful, then you're successful,' the 23-year-old says. 'If you're a bus driver who has an amazing family, you don't make much money, but make enough and you travel with your family – that could be success.' Parents know that, but some parental experts wonder if our daughters hear us say it enough. And certainly girls want us to flip that age-old view that sees success as a synonym for a high-status and highly paid role held by attractive people who travel the world in their spare time. They want to hear us – specifically – tell them that success doesn't require you to wear either 'expensive clothes or a Rolex watch', as Dempsey puts it.

In research where ironies are popping candy, here's another one. Despite all of this, girls in Years 11 and 12 especially are studying harder than many of their parents are working. With exams looming, they will set the alarm for 5 am and still be staring at a computer at 10 pm. They will have a private tutor for biology, stress out over a chemistry paper and worry that their mark for modern history doesn't match those of their peers. They will hand in draft after draft after draft. Their ATAR is seen as a life decision-maker, a make-or-break number. One number, delivered in the lead-up to Christmas, which doesn't distinguish between naughty and nice. In their minds, it distinguishes between the winners and the losers, those able to nab the path they want and those who hit a roadblock. So why do they put so much focus on exam triumph when their future is described almost wholly in terms of being happy and valued and balanced? How do they reconcile that?

'It's just ingrained in our heads,' Sally says. 'Everything we do at school is to prepare us for Year 12. The teachers even say that. So as much as you want to "enjoy" your final year, it carries an overriding pressure.' Meghan agrees: 'It is hard to reconcile. But it's just the traditional timeline of life. You finish school, then go to uni and then you do this and that. We're on the first part of the long journey, which hopefully will bring happiness.' But are you happy working so hard? 'It's putting happiness on pause [in

Year 12], because ultimately the happiness is there – you have to wait for it.'

Leadership expert Dr Terry Fitzsimmons says he's found that girls are also taught about 'success' differently from what their male peers are taught – and that carries messages about how happiness and their careers are later seen. 'The boys are told – especially the elite boys – that they are the future leaders of this country. They're going to be prime minister and they're going to be the top in their field. The girls are told that they're going to be very successful in their careers. They're going to be great lawyers and great doctors. Can you see the difference? One's leadership oriented and the other is career oriented.' This is a crucial distinction that we shouldn't underplay. Dr Fitzsimmons' research is used widely, and he's been working in this area for decades. He says the evidence also shows that boys have an 'earlier and better understanding' of career and education. For example, in Year 7, about 15 per cent of girls don't know what their parents do for a living, or what degrees they hold. In Year 11, the number of girls who still aren't certain of that information sits at 9 per cent. 'Yet for the boys, it was only 5 per cent in Year 7,' he says.

Certainly it's at a very young age that students are encouraged to focus on deciding what career they might pursue. Who hasn't had a child come home and disregard the career choice of their parents? But as young as Years 5 and 6, attention is focused on what they might want to 'become' after school. 'I want to become me,' one 16-year-old retorts, when telling the story about surveys she has filled in since Year 6. That focus on the future is powerful – and is used by some schools to pinpoint students' strengths and weaknesses, encouraging them towards particular subjects. In many, many cases, that opens their minds to new possibilities and opportunities. But is it too much, too early? Psychologist Majella Dennis says it's important to see this whole discussion through the eyes of students. 'At 15 you choose your subjects so you can choose your career so you can choose your life,' she says. 'And – obviously this is just anecdotal – but I had a few students come through with extreme anxiety around subject selection at the end of Year 10 being really concerned that they would end up homeless because they couldn't make the choices they saw everyone else making about their future careers.' Dr Fitzsimmons says one surprising finding in his research was 'how locked in career interests were by Year 7'. That meant 'whatever interventions we're going to put in place in the future [have to happen] much, much earlier'. He'd also like to include a debate about many other gender issues, including why women continue to be paid differently for roles that require the same or more effort than men. 'That's the whole boilermaker-childcare argument: same credentials, same effort and way more responsibility for childcare providers – yet they get paid woefully. We've got a lot of work to do in that space.'

That focus on career continues unabated through high school. Appointments with the school guidance officer, famous alumni invited back to talk about their 'successful' career trajectory. Science and maths subjects pushed, particularly with high-scoring young students – and increasingly, in the view of the girls, at the expense of the humanities. As outlined earlier, this has created a division in some schools where those studying history and art and music and economics are seen as 'not quite as academic' as their maths and science peers. 'Oh, I thought you were quite clever but you're not doing maths and science,' one girl says she was assessed by peers. None of this is an argument against early conversations about careers, but these clever teens, about to move to university or other study, or to start looking for jobs, see fulfilment through a different lens where work is only one factor. And they are asking for that discussion to run parallel to the discussions around high ATARs and job security and career trajectories.

Despite all this – and it's another irony in the search for work–life balance – they agree that comparison and expectation are key drivers of their daily senior school schedule. It's hard not to compete, many say, even though they emphasise that they want their friends to do well too. They just can't help 'placing' where they sit in a group. And that can bring brutal self-judgement and anxiety, and even lower a ceiling that girls will put on their own potential. Geelong psychologist Laura Lee explains that it is 'the innate human drive to compare'. 'It's that social comparison that we all engage in and that we've all been engaging in for a long, long time. We call that our caveman brain – when we were cavemen and cavewomen, and we needed to belong to a group because it was safe to be part of a group where one person hunted, one person built the fire and so on. We started comparing then, because our role in a group back then was literally life or death, so we would look around that group and go, "How am I performing compared to the rest of this group? Do I still have a role to play?"'

Take, for example, a class of clever Year 11 students, who all study Maths Methods. All of them hit 90 per cent in an exam, except one, who records 78 per cent. The teachers are almost unanimous in how they describe that student's response. She believes that she's performed poorly, despite the 78 per cent, and the fact that Maths is not her strong suit. She takes on the messages delivered by those around her, even if they are unintentional, and might make the decision to do General Maths instead. During this project, girls explain this 'type' of thinking repeatedly. Beautifully non-judgemental of their friends, their self-judgement is harsh and relentless. They'll believe others before they believe themselves. Self-doubt is a constant foe, lurking in the shadows each day, ready to bring shade at any opportunity. And they know it. 'I'm my own worst enemy,' one 16-year-old says.

Victorian educator Penny Golding says parental role-modelling is worth remembering here, and sometimes parents embark on their own competition in a bid to provide opportunities for their children. Like others, she says the focus should be more on the strengths of individual children, 'working out what's the best fit for them and maybe not what the Joneses next door are doing'. At the moment, the focus is on school results and ATAR and subject selection, when it might be better to ask, 'What's the best version of success for my child?'

Expectation, irrespective of whether it comes from parents, the school or, for many, the girls themselves, also plays into how they see success and their future. Certainly, parents want their children to finish Year 12, and many encourage their children to nab a strong ATAR, aware of the focus employers and universities, schools and the community at large put on it. That in itself ignores the values of trades and non-university courses offered through TAFE and other organisations. 'My father says I need to make something of myself. What does that even mean?' one girl asks. Lee says parents' expectations and how they might explain them play a strong role in how girls see success, later. 'You've got some parents whose girls feel a lot of pressure to perform academically or financially and then you've got parents who talk about significant success in terms of meaning and satisfaction and happiness and fulfilment,' she says.

'There's too much pressure on Year 12s and school tells us the only way to be successful out of school is to go to uni and get a really high ATAR if you want to get a good job and live a good life.'

'I'm 18 and I need to have my future sorted out.'

So what does the future look like for this cohort? Matthew Peter is Queensland Investment Corporation's (QIC) chief economist and a regular commentator on where the economy is headed – and he is optimistic about where this generation of students will land. 'My view is that the labour market outlook for young females at the moment is the best that women have ever faced in Australia in the post-colonial era,' he says. While that doesn't mean it is where it should be, female participation rates have jumped from 44 per cent in the 1980s to 60 per cent in the early 2020s. Over that same period, male participation has fallen from 78 per cent down to 69 per cent. 'So while there is still a gap, women have narrowed it.' Peter says women still dominate the traditional areas of health, education, administrative and accommodation services, and have not been able to wholly crack the male-dominated and typically higher-paid areas, such as financial services, IT, transport and construction. Indeed, female representation in those areas has dropped over the past two decades. 'That employment share really is the thing that needs to change,' he says. But he feels strong optimism based on how the labour market has shifted to a 'more pro-women backdrop', driven in large part by the move towards environmental, social and governance (ESG) standards, a term used to measure corporate behaviour and performance. This is a salient point. Businesses and governments are now promoting women because they're either required to, or because they see the benefit in doing so. And it's spreading its tentacles across sectors. Home offices, flexible working hours and increased childcare support are also helping to dismantle age-old forms of discrimination.

The uncertainty delivered by COVID-19, and repeated and lumpy lockdowns, have helped create an uncertain future. Teachers see it in the questions asked by their senior students. Psychologists see it in their long waiting lists. Parents, too, talk about the 'uneasiness' and 'uncertainty' and 'fragile' future their teen girls are facing. Lee says the impact of COVID-19 has been huge on young women, and they are trying to remain positive. 'I think there's a sense of "This is where I'm at right now, it's difficult and I need to grit my teeth and get through that,"' she says. And that's particularly been so in metropolitan Victoria.

Golding sees that students' sense of security and their hopes for a future have been diminished. Some just don't feel secure; COVID-19 robbed that surety from them in the last two years of school. 'Some are saying, "Well, why would I try to go to a university course that's going to be online? I don't want to have university online, I want to have life with people.' She wonders whether this generation will mirror their forebears in the 1970s and decide to do things 'their own way' by being innovative, and true to themselves. 'I think they'll be looking for that opportunity once they can, and I think it will be amazing to see what that involves. I don't think we're going to be as locked down in our pathways anymore and it's going to be [interesting] how well systems cope with that.' Social demographer Mark McCrindle shares that enthusiasm. 'Much of the narrative we hear about the future for young people is negative, from climate change and the future forecasts to the economy and the volatility to the downside of technology, particularly the technologies that this generation uses, the anti-social nature of them, and the fake news and all of that. So almost all the key areas of their life and their future are couched in negative terms.' But that hides a strong optimism. 'They see some of these challenges, but . . . we're bringing a comparative lens that they don't have. These are the only times they've ever known and this is the only place they've ever known and this is the only age they've ever been through this particular time.' This is their life, without the comparison their parents can make. 'They also bring this youthful idealism – it's almost a trait of human life – to look forward into the future. I see them not only as optimistic but with great opportunities.' 'The world's always been an uncertain place,' economist Peter says. 'We always have threats to our future. We can't allow ourselves to be overwhelmed. Threats come and go. The economy retreats and recovers. I think what young people can do is position themselves as best they can to [deal with] the conditions presented to them.'

Peter understands why they might worry. COVID-19 continues to sit as a big influence on their future plans. The climate outlook is depressing. They look at their parents' home and know affordability might be a lifelong struggle. And certainly housing affordability is a problem in the Sydney and Melbourne markets especially. 'The growth in those cities over the past decade has really been astounding. Melbourne's population is now 40 per cent higher than just a decade ago and one thing that that rapid growth is causing is higher levels of population density compared with most other capital cities.' For example, in Melbourne about 450 people live in a square kilometre. In Brisbane, the nation's third-biggest city, only 145 people share the same space. 'The problem is that living close to the CBD in Melbourne and Sydney is prohibitively expensive – and that's a feature of most capital cities around the world. Young people can't live where their parents lived anymore.' But he allays concerns, at least in part, about them having to deal with out-of-control debt levels. Yes, government debt has skyrocketed. And household debt is about 200 per cent of disposable income when, 30 years ago, it was only 75 per cent of disposable income. But the issue is not so much the debt as the ability to service it, he says. 'So if we go back to 1991, you paid 13 per cent mortgage on the home loan compared with under 3 per cent today, and that means you today could be carrying a debt of almost five times what you carried back in 1991.' The unemployment rate back then was also double what it is now. It was 10 per cent versus 5 per cent [now]. What that means is you can carry more debt now, assuming interest rates don't rise.'

Economically, the picture painted is cheery, and the position of our daughters is strong. Almost half don't go on to university study, and many of those females typically end up in lower paid administration, accommodation and service jobs. But that appears to be changing too. Traditionally, males were favoured in jobs like construction and mining because of physical strength. 'That's no longer the case,' Peter says. 'Technology has changed and you don't have to be a six foot two hulking male to be in any of those industries.' In a world of digital currency, where we will not need cash or credit cards and where transactions will be stored in blockchains, 16- and 17- and 18-year-old girls are at the front of the jobs queue.

From Peter's analysis, the opportunities for young women in the future fall into three big areas. Climate change headlines his list. It will provide a catalyst for well-paid jobs that, importantly, will also deliver satisfaction. He nominates digital technology as the second area. 'That's really exploded over the last decade, and we're still to harness even a fraction of its capability. And that technology is evolving faster than our ability to keep up,' he says. Households will crave the ability to analyse data, and this cohort is positioned in the right place at the right time. Leadership is his third area, and where he believes women will have an unparalleled opportunity in business and politics. 'That role, up until very recently, has been overwhelmingly the domain of men. It's traditionally been acquired by men on the job by recruiting through the ranks, and via networks – but that's what's changing.' Businesses are now providing formal leadership training for staff, and women are taking that up with enthusiasm. 'The world is finally ready for women in all leadership roles as a norm rather than the exception. Young women can take advantage of that now,' says Peter. This project has shown me that our daughters are queued up at the starting line, and ready to own those opportunities.

16

What's next?

Exams. Tick. Graduation. Tick. In some states over the past couple of years, families have filled halls and shed a tear as their daughters walked across a stage to pick up that single sheet of paper, signalling the end to schooling that began 13 years earlier. In other places, where COVID-19 stole ceremonies and cancelled graduations, the final bell acted as the full stop on school. Goodbye. And good luck.

For as long as they can remember, the girls have been told to believe in themselves. To reach for the stars. That they can do anything. And now it's that time. But what comes after school? And how do they determine the path they wish to take? 'I know so many who are anxious about it – because they don't want to leave. All they've known is school,' a Year 12 teacher says. 'Since I was five, I've got up and put my uniform on and gone to school. Now it's over,' says a recent graduate. For some, that brings a stunning sense of freedom that might begin with a week of celebrations, known as Schoolies, which attracts more than 15 000 17- and 18-year-olds to Queensland's Gold Coast, as well as other areas around the nation. For others, it signals the beginning of their working life. Lucky enough to secure employment, they put their holiday off and head straight into the workforce. A big cohort will wait a few more weeks for that ATAR score to lob before knowing whether they've nabbed the course of their dreams, or whether they'll have to find another way to make their dreams come true.

That road from school to university, for better or worse, is now a well-worn track. Many in this generation of girls will be expected to follow their parents and head to university. In earlier research I did, it was explained to me as 'expectation inflation', where we – as parents – want something better for our own offspring. We 'expect' more. And the road to university is a stellar example here. Many parents – particularly women – might have been the first in their family to attend university. They might have crashed through that historical barrier where boys were more likely to further their education, post-school. Some might have been helped over the barriers by their own parents, wanting more for their children. But fewer expectations existed for women, and these girls' mothers might even have had to argue their case to get there. In my case, that entailed enlisting teachers to convince my parents that I could succeed at university. That was a big leap for my parents. How would I survive in a big city? How would they pay for my lodgings? What type of career would I pursue? Would this mean I'd never return to live in the home they'd made in country Queensland? My story is not special; many women of a similar age, with daughters graduating Year 12, might also have had to plead or cajole, or at least ask, to go on to university study. Now, having experienced that and often the wonderful career paths it delivers, we want our daughters to take a similar journey. The difference here is that many parents 'expect' their daughters to attend university. In some cases, it's non-negotiable – a simple extension of school. In many cases, according to school career counsellors, parents will have a strong say in the path chosen by their daughters.

To many girls, parental support – emotional and financial – is welcome. Some parents will have put money away, just like school fees, to ensure their daughter can attend a university in a city hundreds of kilometres away, or live in a university college, or so that she doesn't feel pressured to work and study at the same time. In other families, the student takes on those responsibilities, juggling work and university assignments, and sometimes a whole lot more, including the care of a sick parent. And while the paths to university (and indeed post-school life generally) differ between students, making the decision about

'what's next' can be filled with anxiety and even fear, for all.
Consider these comments, which reflect hundreds of others.

> *'When I finish, I don't know what I'll be doing. That's
> scary.'*

> *'It seems like the be-all and end-all. We've done all this
> work to open opportunities and now we have to pick one.'*

> *'My parents will tell me. I want to do music and science.
> But Mum says just focus on music and then you can go
> back to science. It's at an impasse. She made me do a
> tertiary workshop at the Con [Conservatorium of Music].
> I didn't want to do it. I ticked that box for her.'*

> *'My dad's telling me always that we will have four careers
> so why are we being made to pick one. I'm not too
> stressed. I'll pop out something.'*

> *'How will I make that decision? I'm sick of thinking of it.'*

> *'TAFE or uni. I would like to do construction at TAFE;
> however, my parents push me for uni as my brother never
> had the opportunity to go – so they make it almost a guilt
> thing where if I can go I should.'*

> *'I recently picked up a traineeship in a job that I really
> enjoy and my parents were very against it. [They believe]
> students who can't do well in school do traineeships,
> not students like me.'*

'I don't think the pathways beyond Year 12 are clear and I don't think the schools make it transparent. My school just pushes the ATAR. Other ways to get into university are not discussed.'

These comments could run for pages. A belief that schools – public and private, co-ed and single-sex, rural and metropolitan – encourage tertiary education over all else. A belief that they need to make a decision too early and that it will determine their trajectory for the rest of their lives. A belief that the focus is on getting the best possible school results to open opportunities, but stunted discussions on what those opportunities might be.

'I feel the moment you hit Year 11, the only thing people ask is what are you doing after Year 12. I'm trying to deal with Year 11. That's enough.'

'It's just hard when I have no idea of what I want to do. I put all this pressure on myself to work it out. My parents are fine and just want me to enjoy and do what I want. But I have no idea of what I want.'

'I definitely think schools could work to make us feel like individuals. I am from a multicultural background. It's weird how we have to know what we want to do, fit in a box, ship off to university and it's not their problem anymore.'

'I wish I knew what I wanted to do. It would be so nice to have a goal I was working for. I choose my subjects based on what I would enjoy. I'm glad for that, but I don't know why I'm doing them now.'

'Everyone says just play it out and see what happens. But just say it doesn't happen?'

'I'd be more confident organising a meeting with a career counsellor if it was face to face. I haven't had anything like that; there's been no encouragement to do that.'

'Telling students there are other pathways and that there are other ways of getting where you want to be is really important,' Miah says. 'Telling them there is one pathway is not very helpful to anyone. It's not just me who thinks that.' She says all her friends are determined to get high ATARs because 'we've been told you need it to get a good job and be a success'. In reality, she knows that's not true. 'But when you hear that all the time . . .' Miah wishes there was a place to go to find out everything. A one-stop shop that could provide all the answers. She found, for example, a changed prerequisite, in small print, that added a requirement of Maths from 2023 to a course she'd been coveting for years. The problem was that she'd dropped Maths, which had not been required previously. Perhaps an education broker is a missed opportunity? Someone who listens to the student, opens their mind, provides the prerequisites, stays in touch, helps fill out forms – from subject choices to scholarship applications, who knows when early entry opportunities pop up, and who is available in that tricky three months after school. An individualised service, as opposed to a school guidance counsellor, whose diary is likely to be brimming with appointments from students of all high-school years.

Most principals spoken to during this research agreed that the focus on university entry is all-encompassing. In some cases the perception is that schools are responsible here, because they have an eye on rankings, fees and future enrolments. Certainly parents play a role too; they want their child to achieve, and that ranking is proof of success in their eyes. A ticket through to the next door. But girls are also chasing it, even though they know there are other pathways. 'I've put in so much work. I'm not going to take early entry. I want to feel as though I deserve it,' one says. Like his peers, Brisbane principal Dr Andrew Cousins sees that. And he knows most of the students at his school will receive an ATAR. 'My question – whether it is a drive by students or by parents – is whether it's the right decision for them for their own self-efficacy and wellbeing.'

Byron Dempsey advises listeners to his Driven Young podcast that if a particular course, requiring a degree, is their passion – unashamedly go for it. But he reminds teens that not all traditionally successful people followed the path to university. Richard Branson. Steve Jobs. Oprah Winfrey. Ralph Lauren. Dempsey says he asked himself several questions in Year 12. Is this pathway right for me, despite what others say? Can I make a living while travelling the world and meeting people? Do I have to buy a home and settle down by 30? Do I have to earn lots of money to be successful or happy? Can I become rich without working nine to five until I'm 70? Everyone will answer those questions differently – and the path less travelled can be rocky. All Dempsey's friends went to university and made new friends. But in the end it was the right decision, for him. His advice? Question everything. Research. And make a decision that suits you.

'I really want a gap year, but it's less likely now. Even going around Australia is much harder. It is a bit uncertain. You can't really make plans because they'll change. Even choosing unis, if it's in a different state, you can't get back to your family.'

'I wanted to take a gap year before uni, now I'm not sure I'll end up going to uni. I need a break.'

'I wish I could do a year on an overseas exchange to Italy but my family said a big fat no.'

'I want to go to university to be a primary school teacher but I'm not sure I want to go straight away.'

'I'm taking a gap year even if it's in my room watching TV.'

'Uni. But first I want to take a gap year to fricken' relax and figure out who I am.'

The gap year. That twelve-month break is not financially possible for all, but for many students this is seen as a circuit-breaker. A time to gather new experiences and work out what you really want. It can be a magnificent teacher. A holiday companion. A life determiner. A year-long course in languages. A reward. A challenge. An opportunity. But COVID-19 has killed many of the possibilities a gap year traditionally brings. School principal Anna Owen, like many others, says that while not all gap years are 'created equal', the gap year delivers those who take it a maturity that later helps them thrive. Melbourne educator Penny Golding says the gap year has been instrumental in helping students 'discover themselves and find their own journey'. She says she worries that COVID-19's impact on that, along with a loss of casual employment for teens during lockdown, means some students are now 'languishing'. Asked to describe that, she says some students might be 'failing to thrive' in terms of different opportunities and discovering themselves, and learning from those activities that life might naturally put in their pathway. How do they know who they are if they haven't had life experiences? 'We learn through interaction with others,' she says. This point was mirrored by many others.

Julie Shaw is deputy principal of Pymble Ladies' College (PLC), an independent girls' school on Sydney's Upper North Shore. During lockdown, she hosted a webinar on gap year options for students and how these had been impacted by the pandemic. Her views provide a refreshing look at how schools are trying to disrupt old ways and forge a new path forward, despite a global pandemic. Pre-pandemic, students would pack a jumbo jet and more than 300 of them, from different schools, would head to the United Kingdom to all sorts of experiences, organised through a local travel agent. COVID-19, the increased cost of visas, decreased opportunities to save due to declining part-time work in Year 12, and decreased opportunities available in the United Kingdom made her look elsewhere. 'So we became involved with Australian schools that would generally take [gap year students] internationally. And we tried to provide opportunities for girls and boys among independent schools to find employment in Australia and New Zealand.' For example, a student at her school might take on a paid role at Queensland's Whitsunday Anglican School. The school decided to replace the dying gap year with its own innovative program, working with a travel agent to send students elsewhere in Australia. It provided them with opportunities – often paid employment – and granted them experiences like those they would have had pre-pandemic. Other schools have followed suit, with some offering accommodation for gap year students in their boarding schools. In other cases schools have 'gap apartments', and in yet others students find their own lodgings. PLC's English teacher and head of senior Nikki Wyse says the school also ensures it stays engaged with its Year 13 students, who routinely return throughout the first few years after graduation to help current students with the transition. 'It's about giving the girls roots and wings,' she says. 'They have to have their strong roots so they feel they belong. We know students learn best when they feel they belong. But they also need to be confident to spread their wings and fly.'

Dr Amanda Bell, AM, who has run both schools and a university residential college, says she would love to see more work around post-secondary planning in schools. In some schools, students are simply slotted into interest areas, which their personality might not suit. 'I think the goalposts have shifted a lot. And I think that post-secondary planning needs to start at least at the Year 9 level. It needs to be encouraging them to think widely, look carefully and [understand] what it means to make a considered choice.' Parents needed also to be educated around options because often they might encourage their child to do a particular course because it represented a solid degree for the last generation. 'These kids are very impressionable about that,' she says. She spent time interviewing girls at the beginning of their first year at university. 'And in Year 12 they would have got fabulous marks in English, history, a language and something else. And they've chosen commerce!' She'd ask whether they had considered a first degree in humanities, for example. But the answer aways came back the same: 'An arts degree doesn't get you anything.' Dr Bell says a 'leadership of self' is almost as critical to understanding a 'leadership of others', and girls need to understand their own agency to take responsibility and make things happen. Choice and leadership and exercising restraint need to be taught along with soft skills so that by the time the girls reach Year 12 they understand that the decisions they make are well informed and suit them as a person.

Melissa Loveday is the careers program leader at Mount Alvernia College in Brisbane. She lost her parents in her senior year and didn't complete Year 12. She finished it at TAFE before completing a Bachelor of Arts and then teaching. She has since attained a master's degree in education leadership and career development. It's a story she tells students. 'My advice is that it's not the end of the world if you don't get the results you want because there are plenty of ways to get to the end and it isn't necessarily always linear,' she says. She urges students – and their parents – to educate themselves about all the options available after school. It was no longer a choice only between university and work, with TAFE offering many different pathways. And she says students should not be choosing a career based solely on their ATAR ranking. 'For example, if a student gets a top ATAR but really wants to do teaching, parents might say, "Well you got an ATAR above 90 – maybe you should be considering law, or maybe you should be considering something in the health field" when it actually doesn't align with the student's interests,' she says. This echoes the views of the girls surveyed. Repeatedly, many parents want the career to match the ATAR, not their daughter's interests. 'It's having trust in young people that they know where their heart lies and what makes them happy,' she says. Educator Dannielle Miller encourages parents to listen to what their daughter might be saying. 'If you're doing it because it's a chore or pays well, or you think it's prestigious ... that's going to be very draining. That will wear off fast,' she says.

'Getting closer to university, my parents are upping the pressure and everything is far too much to handle no matter what I do.'

'I want to be successful so I have to go to uni.'

'No choice. My parents say university.'

Social demographer Mark McCrindle says both schools and parents need to ensure students understand there is no 'one pathway'. Education policy is directed at getting 90 per cent of students completing Year 12, and 'then the majority off to university'. 'But at the same time, if we look broadly on a macro scale, we've got skill shortages.

We've got a challenge around some of these key sectors like trades and construction, for example. And, of course, technology is going to find it hard to replace those jobs ... so structurally we've got issues – but beyond that at an individual level you've got people now who are following this broad direction or indeed incentive. Yet it's not for them, and that's why we have such a dropout rate at university when those structures are over,' he says. That expectation can be more direct when it is cultural. Several educators raised this as a concern. 'Parents do want results. When there is that financial burden for a lot of families [in paying school fees], the expectations are high,' one says. 'We are living through it at the moment,' another says. In many families – particularly those from India, Sri Lanka and China – there can be a 'real disjunct between parental expectation and what the child is actually capable of', another says. 'And so we are tending to nurture at school, provide the equipment but also trying to bridge the gap between parental expectations and a child who feels so much pressure and can't perform her best because of it.'

I love Dr Justin Coulson's take on this. 'Once they know what lights them up, going to university will be an absolute thrill if what lights them up requires university,' he says. 'If what lights them up doesn't require university, look at how much time, energy and money they're saving.' He says the focus on university has travelled too far. 'Who's at fault? We need to point the finger at pretty much everybody who's involved in education. That's the school education system. The parents who have the very best intentions for their children and know that education is going to help their children to do well. And it's also the kids who put pressure on themselves because they feel like they've got to live up to this expectation. It's the legislators. It's the bureaucrats. It's the last couple of 100 years of educators who have created what we now have. It's the universities. It's the employers. It's the whole society.' He says fewer than one-third of Australian adults have a tertiary qualification. And he routinely asks parents, 'How many of you are doing what you thought you'd be doing when you finished school?' Between 70 and 80 per cent of adults were doing something different, and say they are happier now. Then he asks, 'How many of you are actually doing what you left school to do?' And usually 70 to 80 per cent of adults put up their hand and say, 'Actually, I'm doing something different. And I'm much happier now'. 'So just knowing that there's room to change and that not everyone has a degree is really important,' he says.

Author and podcaster Byron Dempsey says he believes that push towards university by many parents and schools is simply how many parents view 'success'. 'This is how previous generations have been conditioned to believe what success is and they think university is the best thing to set someone up for life – and maybe it was 20 or 30 years ago, and it still is a great option nowadays.' Melissa Loveday says that while students actively consider career choices when choosing subjects in Year 10, they change many times before Year 12, when most settle on a course. She says it's important to meet the prerequisites for courses they might consider and have an understanding of what different courses entail. And that sometimes throws up a challenge. For example, students might think that studying psychology means talking and helping people – when the first year is directed more at science and statistics. She agrees that swapping subjects after Year 10 is difficult. 'It's quite difficult to change . . . you need to have consistency across all units, so typically we'll change students quite early in Year 11,' she says. Loveday says those who haven't made a decision about what to do later are not usually disadvantaged. 'The advice is . . . to choose a broad range of subjects so that they get a finger in every pie and see where their strengths are,' she says. And to choose subjects where they have a 'demonstrated capability'. If a student is not excelling at Maths and Science, for example, they have a good indication by looking at their Year 10 results.

All this focuses pressure on students. What will I do? Who will I be? And that will change many times over their lifetime. But during this project, the number of Year 12 students who felt anxiety about 'what's next?' was overwhelming. They see success differently from their parents, as discussed elsewhere. They understand, in theory, that their first choice post-school is not their last choice. But sometimes the messages they hear around that don't match the reality.

'I chose the wrong subjects in Year 10 and now it's too late.'

'I am so worried about the end of this year. I don't know what to do.'

'I'm so scared I wake up and can't breathe. What's next?'

'Who you are in high school is not who you have to be for the rest of your life.' That's author Rebecca Sparrow. 'Once you walk out of those school gates for the last time, you get to reinvent yourself. I think that's really important. Whatever label or identity you had during your school years can be shaken off.' The decision now is not a decision forever – it's just a decision for now. It was simpler a generation or two ago: a trade or university. A lucky few managed to travel on exchanges overseas. Others went interstate to university or to live with relatives. Nursing and teaching topped the list for female students. That landscape has changed – partly because of COVID-19 but also because of a host of other issues. The pressure for some students to meet their parents' expectations. The pressure for some to meet their schools' expectations. And their own. My impression, after speaking to experts, is that we are narrowing how our daughters see the opportunities instead of handing them a clean, crisp white sheet of paper – and encouraging them to own their future. The opportunities and the challenges. The path forward, which will be littered with passion and pitfalls.

The importance of those three months post-school kept me awake at night. Many girls felt lost. Others decided to party for 12 weeks until university began. They put off seeking work as a reward for working so hard at school. Slept in too late. And stopped all those habits school and parents had instilled over many years. With university or TAFE or work looming, perhaps this is the time to ensure she is a good driver, has a tax file number and a registration to work with children, her own Medicare and, if able, a private health care card, is registered to vote, has learnt to cook ten basic meals, knows how to change a tyre and a fuse and has done a first-aid course. Certainly understanding consent and time management, how to care for her mental health and the importance of a positive mindset, along with financial literacy, will also ensure she is ready, with the confidence and ownership needed to take the next step. Some of that will even involve 'unlearning' what she has been taught at school. That's because what lies beyond the school gates doesn't always have a correct answer, and that work is more a team effort than a solo one. And, as Byron Dempsey says, they will never again have to raise their hand to go to the toilet.

Navigating campus life

Josie struggled for 30 minutes to find her tutor's office. He'd told her where it was, vaguely, and now she was heading there, armed with her assignment draft. Eventually, the winding corridors led to his office, and with a fair amount of pride she hand-delivered her work. 'It's a draft?' he asked. Yes, she told him. 'I might wait for the final copy, if that's okay,' he replied. She tells the story with a mix of humiliation and incredulity. Amaya goes to another university, in another state. 'Do you know the lecturers don't go through your drafts? It is SO different to school,' she says.

University life. Post-Year 12. Year 13. Whatever it's called, COVID-19 has turned tertiary study on its head. As lockdowns spread, students moved from campus into their bedrooms, hunched over computers on beds or at a desk a couple of metres away. Group assignments were done online. Open-book exams meant many students didn't venture onto campus at all. The upheaval wasn't limited to lessons. The pandemic and the universities' response meant the social life their parents had enjoyed no longer existed; university, as a playground where teenagers practise being adults, closed its doors. Dating switched to social media apps, often away from big groups. 'Would you write a book on 18-year-olds in their bedrooms?' one mother asked me last year. 'She doesn't come out. When I ask, she says she's studying. But that can't be healthy?' For many young women, even in their third year now, they've only known this version of university life. 'Mum always talked about it as this wonderful time of life. Work hard. Play hard. Meet new friends and networks that will set you up for life. I don't know any of that,' Rebecca says. 'It's very different from what I expected,' another girl offers. 'I thought it would be more like the movies, which was naive to believe, but that was my only experience as none of my family have attended university.' Educator Deborrah Francis says, 'That's exactly the scenario I'm living through. I join all the other mums in saying it makes me very sad because my university years were fabulous. They were the years where you really find yourself, you find your tribe and I must admit that I'm very worried about the social degradation of these adolescent children.' Many of us will agree with that sentiment. We want our own children to have the university time we enjoyed. Kids Helpline counsellor Josie Tucker says, 'They're grappling with that "Who am I?" and "How do I fit in?" and once that really big structure gets stripped away, it's "How do I exist independently in the larger world?" It's really challenging and often not taken very seriously because many adults will put on various coloured glasses and talk about the best years of their life.' She says we need to be watchful of that because it ignores the contemporary climate where uncertainty has narrated a new normal in our daughters' academic and social lives.

Two themes stood out in the stories of first-year university students. The first was the 'isolation' many felt: off campus, away from friends, stuck in their bedroom, being treated just as they had been at school. No in-person lectures. No meeting new peers. 'It's just so isolating,' Maria says.

> 'Uni is entirely online. As a result I am very lonely and haven't met anyone.'

> 'When you go to uni, you come home and it's a different environment. One is for learning and one is where you belong. That's now changed. You constantly think you should be doing work.'

The second theme was the challenge posed when the structures at school have collapsed. Most of the difficulty around university life didn't come from coursework.

Indeed, many students found focusing on subjects they liked enjoyable, and with reduced contact hours, the work was 'easier' than in Year 12. But fewer structures – and safety nets – exist. No longer are numerous drafts of assignments provided with feedback. No longer are there constant reminders of when an assessment is due. No longer are notes sent home reminding students to have two pens and a calculator and a transparent ruler ready for an exam. No longer is the day divided into 40-minute learning chunks, with 'spares' in between where study is encouraged and supervised. No longer does a bell signal it is time for morning tea or lunch. In theory, it sounds unthinkable that young adults don't know when to eat or what study is required, but when they are hand-fed, as many of them are at school, cutting that umbilical cord has significant consequences. 'The lecturer has 500 students and doesn't care if your dog died on the weekend. You're not going to get an extension,' author Rebecca Sparrow says. Dr Amanda Bell, who has headed girls' schools and a university college, says: 'The schools have become these kids' worst enemies when it comes to independent learning in a way because – and particularly with girls – they want to do it right.'

Assessing and providing feedback on drafts is commonplace in Years 11 and 12. Teachers even say they respond to emails and drafts at weekends, with some putting aside a number of hours each weekend when students can communicate online and receive instant advice. If students are that keen to improve their work, they explain, their role is to assist. In some cases, that leads to multiple drafts of an assignment being given feedback. That might not be helping the students in the long term, says Dr Bell. 'When you go into the workforce, nobody's going to keep looking at myriad drafts of a report,' she says. Careers program leader Melissa Loveday says the focus on pastoral care is often behind students being 'hand-held throughout school'. 'We have drafting processes and exemptions. At uni, they have to stand on their own two feet and that's a real struggle,' she says.

That strict school structure hides a hard landing. And it's not only schools where structures are propping up students. At home, students work around rules and times and family processes. Nightly reminders that phones should be out of bedrooms. Being woken for early morning extra-curricular activities. Encouragement – sometimes even financially – to study. A ride to a part-time job. Lunches packed. Early morning lifts to the rowing sheds. Parent–teacher interviews where weaknesses are identified so they become strengths. Then all that is ripped away in the three months between school graduation in November and the start of university life in February or March.

I put this question to about 200 first-year students: is university different from what you expected?

'Yes. More *freedom, choice, time.*'

'*It's way better than school.*'

'*It's actually harder than school, but I love it. You don't feel [like] a non-equal person.*'

'*I was expecting my classes to have people [who] were all the same age as me – that was a bit of a shock on the first day. In my first semester, it was also a relaxed environment, which I wasn't expecting.*'

'*There are no in-person classes – so how do you make friends?*'

'*Uni life? Disappointing. It was going to be all the things high schools are not. I was going to be able to park on campus, wear what I wanted including more than one earring in each ear (scandalous, I know), without being told off and being treated like an adult, not a child. That doesn't really matter when everything is on your laptop.*'

'*All my classes and interactions with my friends are now online. I feel very, very disconnected.*'

'*I didn't expect it to be so self-driven. You don't even have to turn up if you don't want to. You choose your own timetable, which can be bad if you go out and then sleep all day.*'

Nikki Wyse, head of senior school at Sydney's Pymble Ladies' College, says students can be startled by the reduction in care once they leave school. 'One of the girls was just saying to me that if you ask for help at university, it's there. But no one says, "I noticed you're struggling. I noticed you are not turning up." And I said, "Oh, do you think we smothered you too much?" She said, "No, no, no, no, I'd never have got through Year 12 without that".' PLC operates a buddy program where a custombuilt website allows Year 12 students to talk to recent graduates and to seek advice about pathways to university. The school also has a group of GPs visit the school's senior students. 'And they go in small friendship groups and can ask them anything,' Wyse says. There's no teacher in the room and it allows students to seek medical advice on any issue they might like – whether it's how to apply for their own Medicare card or go on a mental health plan. It's part of a wider effort to instil confidence for post-school challenges. 'I think a lot of girls are very lonely. They are observers rather than participants in life. They watch other people's parties unfolding and wonder why they're not invited.' Providing confidence through soft skills could also help in little ways – like enabling them to introduce themselves to others at university. This is not just the domain of private schools. Corinda State High School in Brisbane, for example, has guidance officers call every student about their ATAR, ensuring their preferences are correct and helping to change them where necessary. And then, in the first term after graduating, those who weren't offered a university place or recorded a low ATAR are helped into training or to find another pathway. The school's principal Helen Jamieson says it has provided stellar engagement. 'For the first term, we spend time ringing kids back, setting up interviews, looking at programs like TAFE, getting them into Certificate 3s. It's intensive and it's all funded by the school,' she says.

While COVID-19 has been a villain here, structured school lives have been growing over recent years, driven by two strong factors. The first is a determination to respond to the mental health challenges facing many students. Indeed, that's another area where girls say they suffer post-school. Psychologists see a spike here too, in those first couple of years outside the school grounds where teachers and counsellors aren't canvassing classes for those who need a quiet moment or a friendly chat. Kids Helpline also receives a spike in calls from Year 13 girls, a recognition that this year can be a tough one, and it's often done alone.

The second factor behind increased school structures is the race by schools to head the league table of results that the media like to trumpet. More help, better feedback and multiple drafts can do that. Certainly, anecdotally, the hand-holding is done more often in big private schools that record a greater number of high ATARs than other schools. Many students also have up to four tutors, for different subjects, in that final year, adding further layers of support. Psychologist Majella Dennis says the current education system can provide students with a 'real sense of burnout'. 'They've worked their butts off to get to the pinnacle of all pinnacles – their ATAR – and then they get to uni and they've got nothing left. Nothing.'

Reverend Dr Anita Monro's residential college at the University of Queensland was female-only until 2022, when it opened to all students. She sees the folding school structures as a challenge for many freshers. Time management needs to be learnt. Workloads need structure. No one is encouraging them to rise early or watch a particular lecture. She encourages parents, as well as schools, to discuss how that might unfold. 'Sometimes Mum and Dad are so anxious about everything being done, and done on time, that there's not necessarily the space for them to discover how to do it.' She says parents sometimes find it hard to let go – and will even call the office if they hadn't heard from their daughter for two days.

Female students who are the first in their family to attend university are also more likely to struggle with mental health issues compared with their male counterparts, according to research by the University of Queensland and University of South Australia. That research, released late in 2021, found 40.9 per cent of females experienced mental health impacts compared with only 3.8 per cent of men.[1] Associate Professor Garth Stahl, from the University of Queensland's School of Education, says that being the first in a family to go to university often leads to 'an increased level of grit and determination'. The study looked at experiences between genders. 'The stark contrast between men and women reporting mental health issues is concerning, and could mean a variety of things. First and foremost, it shows that mental health continues to be a gendered issue,' Associate Professor Stahl says.

Anna Owen, who has headed schools in Canberra and Queensland, says the solution does not lie in disbanding school structures. 'They don't really sit down to a big bowl of consequences until they hit first year uni,' she says. 'But we are always going to support students to do their best. We will do that extra 10 per cent to make sure they don't self-destruct in these really important years while they're at our school. We shield them from their own adolescent weaknesses sometimes. I think the worst outcome would be if we started removing some of the structures that we have in schools, entirely.' The focus, she says, should be on rethinking how to apply them.

University colleges can provide a stepping stone to adulthood, where girls live with peers, under supervision, and are encouraged to make new friends and become part of a college community. But only a privileged few can afford a college room – and almost all freshers, wherever they live, will be challenged by the freedoms on offer outside their home. Alcohol. Parties. Drugs. Sex. 'And they have to make choices,' says Flo Kearney, who heads Women's College at the University of Queensland. A former principal of Somerville House in Brisbane, Kearney has 130 new first-year girls come into college each year. 'There's so many decisions to make – to organise themselves, there's access to alcohol and other drugs, nightclubs ... they're exposed to experiences that they've never been exposed to before. At school, there was always some guidance. There were rules – and even though they didn't like the rules and might complain about them, they provided a framework.' Reverend Dr Monro says that first post-school year can also be confronting. 'It's completely new to most and it's unexpected and so they come from school where they've been the leaders,' she says. 'And then they're in a new environment and they're out of their comfort zone. They need to find their space again.'

Certainly, for many first-year university students, their bedroom provides the physical space where they listen to online lectures: at a desk, but commonly propped up on their bed. And that, over recent years, has fed isolation and a lack of connection. A slight irony pops up here. This is the online generation living their lives onscreen and on social media – but faced with a tertiary experience delivered almost wholly online, they are struggling with it. Perhaps that simply illustrates the value of real-life connection. Josie Tucker, from Kids Helpline, says the organisation has received an increased number of calls around 'connection and purpose'. Dr Danielle McMullen urges parents to consider Year 13 as a key developmental stage at the start of adulthood. 'Often moving out of home, getting a job, starting university – all of those are quite high-pressure situations and people need support because everyone stuffs it up a little bit. And they've got to have a safe space to land.' She says COVID-19 has magnified problems, but isolation and disengagement have been growing over recent years as increased numbers of students self-fund their university courses, or move out of home to be closer to full-time work or study. That has made engaging in the social life promised by university increasingly difficult – and this was the case even before COVID-19. Vice-Chancellor of Sydney University Professor Mark Scott, AO, agrees, saying COVID-19 has revealed 'an underlying condition' about who is engaging in university education and how. HECS fees mean many young people are working several jobs to pay their way, wanting to graduate in shorter periods 'because they're clocking up significant debt'. The risk is that the university experience is becoming a bit like a 'Service New South Wales experience' where the focus is on 'getting in and getting out with the relevant piece of paper'.

COVID-19 has certainly increased the sense of isolation felt by first-year students. 'They've been looking forward to leaving school, going to university, having that freedom, that independence, that decadence to be able to study subjects they really want to . . . as well as the social life that goes with it,' Dr Amanda Bell, who has headed schools and a university residential college, says. 'And that has sort of fallen a bit in a heap.' It's also come on top of the traditional school rituals – from assemblies to formals to year cohort trips – being cancelled. Touch points or markers are important for this group, says Dr Bell, because they are the tangible steps 'from one point in time to another which signifies moving from school girl to young woman, moving intellectually from the scaffolded and walked beside by teachers to being mentored and tutored at a university level'. But COVID-19 has meant that those rites of passage at university – from first relationships to toga parties to meeting hundreds of others, sleeping in and choosing tutorial times – have also been cancelled, on top of all the milestone events at school. 'However, they've still had to submit all the same kind of work requirements, and they've had to pay all the same university fees,' psychologist Carly Dober says. 'So it's just been all input, no fun.' Dr Bell says it begins to 'separate the students who are innately resilient and capable of flexibility and adaptation and [who] respond to change in a positive way'.

National union of students women's officer Georgette Mouawad says, 'We've noticed a massive effect in terms of participation.' Fewer students are participating. Many are not forming the same bonds that they would have in previous years. Second-year students are acting like first years – because they missed that experience in their first year. She has noticed the isolation personally. 'It's the most important time of your life and it's the opportunity to network for whichever field you decide to go into after you graduate,' she says. She saw a difference between her in-person and online classes: fewer friends and less collaborative learning.

Friendship has been discussed elsewhere, but an important factor here – one raised repeatedly – was the chance to reinvent yourself at university. School psychologist Nicole Young says many girls hope to find their tribe at university after failing to build a close network of friends at school. Year 13 is sold as a new beginning where they can move away and recreate identities and find new opportunities. And that has been stolen from many. Others who managed a move were then locked down – and missed friends' birthdays and grandparents' funerals. They were by themselves, cooking their own meals, without the support of friends or families. 'The mental health impacts of that are going to be huge for the next few years,' Young says.

Those teens who continue to live at home, whether they are working or studying, can face other challenges – particularly if their parents treat them as if they are still at school. Dr Bell says that isn't a criticism: parents are simply trying to care for their children. 'And they are trying to be independent. They're not sure how to do that in a context that doesn't physically take them away from the home.' Girls explain that too: trying to forge a pathway into adulthood, but living by the rules their parents established years earlier. Mouawad says two other factors were apparent with the girls continuing to live and study at home. First, they were doing the same chores and making the same contribution to the household – despite the fact that they were also full-time university students. More worrying was the change in how sexual assaults were occurring. Sexual assaults have been a well-publicised scandal on many campuses, and universities, faculties and colleges now focus considerable time and effort on ensuring students are given advice. The National Student Safety Survey, released in March 2022, found one in 12 university students were sexually harassed and one in 90 were sexually assaulted in the past 12 months. The figures for female, transgender and non-binary students were much higher than those for male students and 50 per cent knew the perpetrator.[2] How those disclosures are dealt with, and assaults prevented more broadly, are issues that continue to be discussed. But Mouawad says online classes have created other problems. 'Now that education is finding itself in the home, we've still got students experiencing new forms of sexual violence ... mostly online forms of harassment,' she says.

Of course, an absence of structures, isolation, disconnection and barriers to meeting new friends are not the only challenges faced by first-year students. Delayed diagnosis of mental health conditions, diseases and neurological disorders such as ADHD, autism, depression and endometriosis is another issue facing first-year students in particular. A lot of these students are studying without any adjustments or accessibility plans, and navigating undiagnosed conditions and the health system, Mouawad says.

So what experience is likely to encourage teens to embrace university in any form? And what skills underpin the ability to grow and adapt to the changes post-school? Reverend Dr Anita Monro says that when a student knocks on her door asking for assistance, it's usually as a result of her 'naivety'. 'They don't know what they don't know and what they think is safe isn't necessarily safe,' she says. Anxiety also remains a significant challenge in Year 13. 'You don't have that deadline of working towards an ATAR, but it's every semester. And it comes out particularly in those last few weeks of semester,' Dr Monro says. 'If they've got a good grounding in things as simple as referencing, then they're not going to be as anxious about putting that assignment in,' she says. Three university college heads, in three different states, also nominate confidence as a factor in successful first-year students. 'They're comfortable in their own skin,' one says. Flo Kearney says 'character and values' also play a part. 'They have a sense of who they are. They've worked through some of these things them-selves.' She says most students will hit speed bumps along the way and need to make decisions. And that will help gift them a stronger sense of self. A common theme develops around those from city and country areas too, with rural students often taking a bit more time 'to get their heads around the requirements of the university sector', as one expert describes it. But they are also less competitive, and more 'likely to have a go at fixing things when they go wrong'. Dr Monro has headed a residential college for almost a decade, and has seen a major common theme during that time: 18-year-olds now have 'less life experience' than their older sisters.

That hits the mark with social demographer Mark McCrindle. He says that with the whole focus being school retention rates, university access and opportunities, graduation rates are all about 'skill markers not around the social development or around life development'. 'We can have increasingly educated young people who can study online and tick the qualifications, but without the same development in life and social skills,' he says. Character development is essential. So is resilience. And so is being able to respond to a fast-changing society. That is needed so we don't end up with a 'hollowed-out generation that have the ticket, have the qualifications, but haven't been able to fully thrive' in that developmental life stage. Dr Bell agrees: 'We haven't seen a black swan event impact younger people like this since the war, where the enemy is known,' she says. 'Here it's unseen and unpredictable.

And it operates by stealth and there's a degree of fear of not knowing what the impact is going to be.'

Professor Mark Scott, who headed the NSW Department of Education and served as ABC managing director before taking on the post of Sydney University Vice-Chancellor, knows the challenges faced by universities to recreate modern-day engagement. 'I met my wife at lunch on the lawn at the University of Sydney,' he says. 'The great friends I've made who have stayed with me were the friends I made in university. I knew none of them when I walked in the door on day one, but they were all there waiting for me. We just had to find each other.' Universities need to provide students with that sense of belonging and connection again. 'And we're worried that some of the students starting in third year have had two disruptive years and those who are starting first year have had two years of schooling dramatically disrupted,' he says. The University of Sydney this year boosted grants to student organisations, clubs and societies to lure students back on campus, which was vital. 'Campus is where all the other magic happens – friendships, exposure to different people with different ideas, and courses outside your own; a place for you to explore other interests – so you need to get that physical presence,' he says. That should be music to the ears of parents and students.

The way university is delivered also needs to be disrupted. 'When I was a student, you had to be at the lecture because if you weren't at the lecture, you'd have to rely on some other friends' terrible notes and you really missed out on what was going on. Now with more and more lectures being recorded [and you can] catch up later, is there a compelling reason why you need to get out of bed and get on a train? Or can you just do it all later on?' Professor Scott, who is also on the board of the Sydney Theatre Company, says if no one turns up to performances, the audience is delivering a message. 'In a post-COVID environment, if you're going to take an hour of a young person's time and you want them to get out of bed and be there by nine o'clock in the morning, you're going to have to really think how you make that an engaging and interactive experience,' he says. 'The line I keep using is that you want the university experience to be truly a transformational experience for these young people because you're not just taking their money. You're taking the most precious years of their life. They will never have this time again, we know that. You've got to make it exciting and compelling and engaging. And then at the end of it, they should be bereft that they're leaving.' It's a sentiment that both the students and their parents would embrace.

18

Words of advice

Sometimes you find what you are looking for in the most unexpected places. Keys, for example. And advice it seems too. Adolescence is a tunnel. Sometimes dark and impenetrable. It's the light at the end that acts as the guide. And that's how 16- and 17- and 18-year-olds – but especially the last two cohorts – describe their parents, particularly their mothers, when it comes to looking for advice. Asked who they rely on most, almost half nominated their mothers – a far cry from the answers given when this cohort was 14. Back then, and even years earlier, friends were girls' counsellors-of-choice. Mum and Dad's advice was seen as old-fashioned and too conservative and judgemental, and not based on any understanding of anything. Perhaps it's because those teenage years start earlier that girls are walking out of the tunnel of adolescence a bit earlier too. Girls in Year 7 are now having to make the choice about whether they agree to vape with a friend. Body image issues are skyrocketing at that age. So are mental health issues, particularly around eating disorders and self-harm. Those years from ages 12 to 15 are tougher now than they were for a girl's big sister only a few years ago. That puts 16- and 17- and 18-year-olds in a tricky place. Some are fighting entrenched problems. Some feel the weight of the world on them. Some are struggling to breathe between study and the pressure they often apply to themselves. That's all been explained. But the light at the end of the tunnel is often brighter now too. Especially as the end of school and the beginning of Year 13 approach, they can see what they want and, perhaps more importantly, what they don't want. They're beginning to understand who they are and who they want to be. So many forces continue to mould their personality. Social media remains overwhelmingly seductive. So does group-think, although for many its appeal is beginning to shatter. Romantic partners take up space. The lives of their peers, as much as social media, can still drive their decision-making. A clever educator can change views. So can an influencer. And let's not forget the wallpaper of dark ads streaming onto their smartphone. But the light at the end of the tunnel starts to make sense of that. It's as scary as hell. The future. That bright white light. Tarnished by climate change before they reach it. Continuing that journey of discovery. The workforce. TAFE. A trade. University. What might happen? What might not happen? But what is so elevating is how Mum's advice, in particular, is no longer so brashly discarded. Others' advice is valuable too – from teachers and partners, big sisters and brothers to aunts and grandparents and cousins. But having researched ten-year-olds for my book *Ten-ager* and 14-year-olds for *Being 14*, and even daughters and their dads for *Fathers and Daughters*, there is no doubt this cohort can see their parents standing at the end of that tunnel, holding a torch. Who is the person you rely on most?

'I can't forget Mum. She always gives insightful advice.'

'Maybe my mum.'

'They are both funny and clever so we get on just as people as well as a family.'

'Maybe my mum or best friend when it's something I can't tell Mum.'

'Wow, there are a lot of people I rely on or go to for help. I wouldn't be able to choose because each person differs from what they help me with. My little sister. My boyfriend. And my parents I probably rely on the most.'

'I rely on different people for different things. I rely on my mum for help with work, and my friends.'

'I can tell [my parents] everything.'

'I told my parents I was struggling to choose between two subjects and they sat with me while I talked it through. My parents also ask my input before making family decisions.'

'My mum. I feel bad because she pays for everything since my dad won't pay anything and I haven't got a job yet to pay for myself which is why I'm trying to get one.'

'I rely on my parents a lot. But also myself, because at the end of the day, no one else is going to do life for me.'

That last comment shows the maturity that envelops many teenage girls as they move beyond school. Of course, that tunnel remains long for some. Even those actively seeking their parents' advice will routinely dismiss it. Other girls wish they could find the voice to seek their parents' counsel. 'I feel really supported at home – my main problem is whether I can admit to how I feel and ask for support,' one student says. Another says, 'I wish I felt comfortable enough to ask them to take me to a therapist but I just can't.' Or this: 'It would make me feel guilty to ask for more support.' Others don't want to – not because they don't value it, but because they feel they will be judged or not properly heard. 'Please listen and hear what I am trying my best to say,' one says. 'My mother loves me but is so judgemental,' another says. Or this: 'My mother advocates me speaking up to her but when I do, she says I'm a child or completely invalidates my feelings.' That, in itself, shows the importance of parents continuing to turn the dial on the open conversations we might not have had with our own parents; the importance of not just listening, but hearing what our teens need us to hear. That's because, at this age, we can perhaps learn as much from our teens as they can learn from us. Their passion. Their ability to prosecute their case. Their commitment. Their multi-skilling. They can find their way out of that tunnel earlier and more easily with a good parental Sherpa, but that's helped by parents' commitment to understanding this generation and what makes it tick. And perhaps from our own introspection – an attribute our daughters have in droves. What advice would we give ourselves if we were back walking into Year 11 or 12 or 13 – those years of senior school or that scary year when some of us found jobs, while others went nursing or to TAFE, or to university? I asked all those I interviewed for this book – school principals and teachers, psychologists and authors, parenting experts and school counsellors – that question. What advice would you give yourself if you were back at that age? And what advice would they offer to this cohort of girls?

'You've got so much to offer the world and it is different to what the other 16-year-old girls are offering,' says psychologist Amanda Abel. 'You don't need to be the same. It's okay to be different. You don't have to fit a mould.' 'They are enough,' says Dr Toni Meath, principal of Melbourne Girls Grammar School. 'Whatever is in your mind and in your heart, you've got this. You are enough. And there are people around you to walk with you, to support you and to ask for help. Put your hand up. Being brave means asking for help.' Someone told Dr Meath that when she was a young teacher. 'It allowed me to be my authentic self.' That message – you are enough – gives girls the permission to be themselves. To eschew perfection and live life. 'You are more than your school marks,' educator and author Dannielle Miller says. It is advice she'd give to herself. And to every other 16-year-old in the world. Psychologist Laura Lee says she'd tell herself, back at 16, that she had the tools she needed to cope with whatever came next. Whatever life's ups and downs were. She wants every 16-year-old to know that, and also to be in on another secret: 'Often girls at that age think older women have a lot of the answers, but we don't really. A lot of us just make it up as we go along!'

'You're so much stronger, more capable and clever than you give yourself credit for,' says Victorian educator Kellie Lyneham. 'Trust yourself,' says psychologist Majella Dennis. 'There's an incredible amount of skill that goes into that.' Sydney school principal Paulina Skerman says she'd give herself that same message. 'Don't underestimate what you can achieve. I never imagined the life I'm living for myself. I came from a very different place. Take every opportunity and don't underestimate your capacity, and everything will be okay. Trust yourself and do it. Just do it.' Olympian Libby Trickett wants to tell 17-year-olds the advice she'd give herself if she were 17: 'Be patient. Be kind to yourself. And get out of your comfort zone.'

'Pick subjects that you like,' says principal Andrew Pierpoint. And have a tough and honest Q&A session with yourself. Do you want to go to university? If not, get work placement and work experience in place. 'It's really horses for courses. It's what you like, what you're good at and where you want to go,' he says.

Brisbane principal Dr Andrew Cousins says, 'Have the courage to do what you love – there's always a way to get there.' Gold Coast principal Susan Dalton wants 16-year-olds to 'read more than I did'. 'I read for compliance as a teenager rather than for enjoyment. In my adult years, I have learnt the power and joy of reading.' She wishes her father were alive to hear that; he'd be 'stoked', she says.

Professor Mark Scott, University of Sydney Vice-Chancellor, says he'd give every 18-year-old walking into the university the same advice. 'I would say dive in and take advantage of all the opportunities that exist – not just around classes, but clubs, societies, communities of interest. Go out of your way, even out of your comfort zone, to meet different people who went to different schools or have come from different parts of the city or around the country,' he says. He knows that is hard for some freshers.

'Try not to be shy. You'll find your people. You'll find your tribe and they will often be the most important friendships and connections you make in your life.' And you know he's talking as much about himself as he is giving advice to those on his campus. Sydney GP Dr Danielle McMullen says the same. She went to the University of New South Wales as a 17-year-old to study medicine. 'Make sure you throw yourself into it and don't just lock yourself in a room studying all the time,' she says. 'Learn what you need to know, but it's really important that you also get involved in the social side of university.'

Digital wellbeing expert and author Dr Kristy Goodwin's advice is around technology, as you would expect. And she knows it sounds simple, but her advice is to control the technology and not let it control you. 'I often talk about containing the technology and not being a slave to the screen. What can you put in place so you use it in a way that is empowering and makes you feel good?' Not blanket bans – but so the user remains in the driver's seat. That requires downtime to think. The advice offered by Kids Helpline counsellor Josie Tucker requires that time too. 'You get to decide who you are in this world, and you get to decide who you want to surround yourself with and who you want to be in your relationships. Really taking the time to think about who you would like to be and who you would like around you and how you would like to communicate and participate in the world is a really valuable way to spend your time,' she says. We are told so often what we 'should' be doing that we can forget to consider our own voices. She doesn't want our daughters to do that. Melbourne educator Deborrah Francis, who comes from a very traditional Indian family background, echoes that. 'In the Indian culture, not so much today but back when I was growing up, if you were a female you needed to learn to cook, you needed to be seen and not heard. And it took university for me to find my voice and to learn my strengths.'

Adelaide school principal Dr Nicole Archard wants 16-year-olds to understand that life is long. 'I think when you're 16, you really think life is over by the time you're 21. Your idea of a life time-frame lacks perspective. And you need to focus more on enjoying that time of not having the hang ups that you put on yourself when you're 16. Give up the hang ups because when you're older they're going to be so insignificant, they're going to be so meaningless to your life.' The small stuff won't matter. The marks won't matter. In fact, Dr Archard can't remember what her ATAR-equivalent score might have been. 'It's not meaningful to me now.' That message is beautiful. But it's a hard one for girls who are hell-bent on deciding their lives to take in. Do you tell them that, I ask? 'Over and over until I'm blue in the face,' Dr Archard says. 'The woman who you're going to become – that's what's important. Think about what sort of woman you want to be in the future and just focus on what you need to do to be that person. That's not about an ATAR. What kind of person do you want to be?'

Dr Jodi Richardson says that if she could travel back and give herself advice at 16, she'd talk about anxiety. 'I would say: Do you know why you feel like this, Jodi? You have what's called anxiety and lots of people understand it. It's something that happens because your brain has detected a threat and you have a brain that's a bit sensitive to threats. Some other people don't react in the way you do. And did you know there is so much that you can do about understanding it and managing it? This is not something that has to get in the way of you living a really fantastic life,' she says. Almost all our teen girls need to hear that. Toni Riordan, from Brisbane, says she remembers the age of 16 as being 'a time of challenges'. Comparison became a constant and often unwelcome visitor. 'Am I as good as the other person beside me? Should I be experiencing these problems and things at home and with friends?' Now it is more difficult. While many girls are more open with their parents, they might still struggle to seek advice on some issues. 'So, as much as we talk about student protection officers and guidance counsellors and psychologists and all those sorts of things, there's still a lot of stuff that young girls try to work out between themselves,' she says. Women are almost 'socialised' to try to be perfect, and teens need to 'run their own race and look out for one another'.

The author of *Eat Pray Love*, Elizabeth Gilbert, says the world is filled with two types of people: jackhammers and hummingbirds. Author Rebecca Sparrow says she wants every 16-year-old to know that story. Some students, like her nephew, are jackhammers. Since they were toddlers, they knew what they wanted to do. They were focused on a single goal. Her nephew wanted to be a pilot. 'He's a jackhammer. Pilot. Pilot. Pilot. Pilot.' 'But other people like me are hummingbirds and we follow our curiosity and go from this thing to the next thing. Life is a zigzag. It's not a straight line. There's a great quote: "I don't want to live the length of my life. I also want to live the breadth of it",' she says. She wishes she knew about jackhammers and hummingbirds back in Year 11. 'A lot of times you go sideways. There's no right or wrong way. Jackhammers are great and hummingbirds are great.' Her other tip for girls is for them to build their social skills muscles because 'nothing beats seeing people in person'. That's an antidote to the awful loneliness that is filling the days of some teenagers.

Putting your hand up, seeking advice and knowing you have backstops featured heavily in the advice adult educators would give themselves. Melbourne educator Linda Douglas would tell herself to stop worrying so much. 'Stop living your life in your head before it's happened. And stop worrying about things before they happen. Because I know at that age, I tied myself into a knot of anxiety before things had even eventuated,' she says. And lean on those who are trying to help you. She wishes she'd done that more too. Sunshine Coast educator Anna Owen says everything will fall into place if important relationships are nurtured. 'Learn to communicate. Learn to listen. Learn to empathise.' 'Be curious. Have someone who you trust that you can ask questions of,' psychiatrist Dr Steve Stathis says. 'Preferably your parents, but if not, find someone else who's a bit older and wiser than you.'

Guiding a 16-, 17- or 18-year-old is not easy. 'I'm going to suggest that one of the hardest tasks of parenthood occurs around this period,' Dr Justin Coulson says. 'There is a literal grieving process that most parents will go through as their little girl becomes a grown-up woman. And there's really nothing you can do to prepare for it.' He says we see them growing, knowing that one day they'll leave the nest. 'And then that day arrives and you just weep.' It is happy and sad, exhilarating and crushing, he says. 'Seeing her have to navigate life and make her mistakes and try to figure it all out on her own – it's so hard to watch.'

Wisdom runs two ways, and the aim in *L Platers* has been to give teens a voice that will help their parents be better guides. So what advice would they give to us – their parents and educators – that might help them find that bright light at the end of the tunnel? Their answers are raw and honest and cut to the heart of the struggles they've raised in preceding chapters. In almost 1000 answers, it's hard to choose a couple of dozen.

'*Let us be teenagers. We're going to do the wrong thing. It's life. You did it. So just trust us.*'

'*Don't smother us. Allow us to have a break from normal school. We need to reset sometimes.*'

'*Give us a little bit of latitude and we might even surprise you.*'

'*Please be willing to look at something from a different perspective.*'

'*Listen to our needs. Listen to our ideas and what is troubling us – that will help us. Don't just assume. And listen to a wide variety of people. Listen to young people.*'

'*Don't base my worth on education.*'

'*Tell me you're proud.*'

'*Don't get mad if I have different opinions from you.*'

'*Take my mental health more seriously.*'

'*Listen. Don't try to fix it.*'

'*Tell me it will be okay, please.*'

'*Don't teach kids that failure is a bad thing. If there's anything I've learnt through high school, stuffing up and making mistakes, and not getting the mark you wanted on an exam or missing out on a team, has taught me a lot.*'

'Don't view TAFE or traineeships as something for dumb students. I'm an ATAR student and I've picked up a traineeship and I just love it. My parents are saying why are you doing this; you're wasting your brain.'

'Stop putting me in the middle of your divorce.'

'Just listen more, without getting angry or having something to say that invalidates my feelings and emotions.'

'If you are disappointed in me over a mark, know that I'm more disappointed in myself.'

'At times we find it difficult to discuss things that we don't think are right within a relationship (red flags) because we are embarrassed or nervous or scared of being judged.'

'Listening and hearing are different things. If we say we need more help, that might mean independence – but that's not what they are hearing.'

'Give us more exposure to the real world; we are so sheltered. We are so focused on Year 12. We're told Year 12 is the destination. Now we are here – and it's where are we going now? I kept looking to Year 12. So what do I do? Where do I go from here?'

'Learn patience. I'm not really sure what I want to do in the future. I suggest a lot of things about what I want to do and I'm told I need to decide now, otherwise I'll miss out. So I'm confused. What do I pick?'

'We're going to stuff up. Life can be messy.'

'Kids aren't built to be perfect. When we're younger and as we're maturing and going through high school, there are all these expectations on us to be successful in sport, to be academically successful, to be happy, to have a good social life, to look perfect all the time, have a tidy room, but the reality is that we're not going to have that breadth across the board.'

They're L platers, looking for adults to help them on the open road to adulthood.

Endnotes

Chapter 3: The corona-coaster

1. Charlie Mackesy (2019), *The Boy, the Mole, the Fox and the Horse*, Ebury Press, London, no page numbers.

Chapter 5: Friends and family

1. Brené Brown (2021), *Atlas of the Heart*, Ebury Press, London, p. 157.

Chapter 6: Unsocial media

1. Jamie Ducharme (2018), 'People are getting plastic surgery to look like Snapchat filters, doctors warn', *Time*, 5 August, <https://time.com/5357262/snapchat-plastic-surgery>.
2. The Insights Family is a market research company that focuses on children, parents, and families. See: <https://theinsightsfamily.com>.
3. Jacinda Santora (2022), *Key influencer marketing statistics you need to know for 2022*, Influencer Marketing Hub, <https://influencermarketinghub.com/influencer-marketing-statistics>.
4. Jeremy Knibbs (2018), 'Brexting: Smartphone addiction and babies', *Wild Health*, 7 August, <https://wildhealth.net.au/all-humans-have-three-lives-public-private-and-secret-gabriel-garcia-marques-privacy-has-come-out-of-the-shadows-and-into-the-mainstream-in-australia-the-level-of-repo>.
5. The 'still-face' experiment was developed in the 1970s by developmental psychologist Edward Tronick. In the experiment, mothers sat with their babies but remained expressionless, not reacting to the babies at all, and the babies' reactions were studied. The experiment found the babies became agitated, but then withdrew and turned away from their mothers.

Chapter 10: Going places

1. Queensland Government (2022), *Protect your P-plater*, StreetSmarts, <https://streetsmarts.initiatives.qld.gov.au/parents/protect-your-p-plater>.

Chapter 11: The gender agenda

1. This statistic draws on a 2017 study of 1000 Australian young people and their parents, as explained by Dr Stathis in a keynote speech to a paediatric conference in April 2019. See: Don't Forget the Bubbles (2019), *Gender identity – what does it mean to be male or female?*, online video, 19 April, YouTube, <https://www.youtube.com/watch/?v=qPWTSCn8uwU>.

Chapter 12: Consent and what we all need to learn

1. Chanel Contos's website *Teach.Us.Consent.™* includes thousands of stories, and the petition for change. See: <https://www.teachusconsent.com>.
2. Australian Institute of Health and Welfare (2020), *Sexual Assault in Australia*, cat. no. FDV 5, Australian Institute of Health and Welfare, Canberra, p. 1, <https://www.aihw.gov.au/getmedia/0375553f-0395-46cc-9574-d54c74fa601a/aihw-fdv-5.pdf.aspx?inline=true>.
3. Hill, Lyons, Jones, McGowan, Carman, Parsons, Power and Bourne (2021) cited in Helen Connolly, Commissioner for Children and Young People, South Australia (2021), *Sexual Health and Education in South Australia: What young people need to know for sexual health and safety*, report project no. 22, Commissioner for Children and Young People, Adelaide, p. 18 <https://www.ccyp.com.au/wp-content/uploads/2022/03/Sex-Education-in-South-Australia.pdf>.
4. Diana Warren and Neha Swami (2019), 'Teenagers and sex' in *The Longitudinal Study of Australian Children Annual Statistical Report 2018*, Australian Institute of Family Studies, p. 51, <https://growingupinaustralia.gov.au/sites/default/files/publication-documents/lsac-asr-2018-chap5-teenagers-and-sex_0.pdf>.
5. Connolly (2021), *Sexual Health and Education in South Australia*, p. 6.
6. Christopher Fisher, Andrea Waling, Lucille Kerr, Rosalind Bellamy, Paulina Ezer, Gosia Mikolajczak, Graham Brown, Marina Carman and Jayne Lucke (2019), *6th National Survey of Australian Secondary Students and Sexual Health 2018*, ARCSHS series no. 113, Australian Research Centre in Sex, Health and Society, La Trobe University, Melbourne, p. 37, <https://www.latrobe.edu.au/__data/assets/pdf_file/0004/1031899/National-Survey-of-Secondary-Students-and-Sexual-Health-2018.pdf>.

Chapter 13: Party scenes

1. Nicola Guerin and Victoria White (2018), *ASSAD 2017 Statistics & Trends: Australian secondary students' use of tobacco, alcohol, over-the-counter drugs, and illicit substances*, Cancer Council Victoria, Melbourne, p. 49, <https://www.health.gov.au/sites/default/files/secondary-school-students-use-of-tobacco-alcohol-and-other-drugs-in-2017.pdf>.
2. Australian Institute of Health and Welfare (2020), *National Drug Strategy Household Survey 2019*, Drug Statistics series no. 32, cat. no. PHE 270,

Australian Institute of Health and Welfare, Canberra, p. x, <https://www.aihw.gov.au/getmedia/3564474e-f7ad-461c-b918-7f8de03d1294/aihw-phe-270-NDSHS-2019.pdf.aspx?inline=true>.

3. Guerin and White (2018), p. 31.
4. Resilient Youth Australia (2021), *Student Resilience Survey: Cross-sectional report*, Resilient Youth Australia, Melbourne, <https://resilientyouth.org/survey>.
5. Queensland Health (2019), *The known harms of e-cigarettes and vaping*, Queensland Government, <https://www.health.qld.gov.au/news-events/news/known-harms-of-e-cigarettes-vaping-smoking>.
6. New South Wales Health (n.d.), *Are electronic cigarettes and e-liquids safe?*, New South Wales Government fact sheet, p. 1, <https://www.health.nsw.gov.au/tobacco/Factsheets/e-cigs-are-they-safe.pdf>.

Chapter 14: Finding balance

1. Sleep Health Foundation and Australasian Sleep Association (2020), *Transforming the Sleep Health of Australians: Pre budget submission 2020–21*, Sleep Health Foundation and Australasian Sleep Association, Sydney, p. 3, <https://treasury.gov.au/sites/default/files/2020-09/115786_SLEEP_HEALTH_FOUNDATION_AND_AUSTRALIASIAN_SLEEP_ASSOCIATION_-_SUBMISSION_2.pdf>.
2. Ibid.
3. Ibid.
4. Eric Suni (2022), *Teens and sleep*, American Sleep Foundation, <https://www.sleepfoundation.org/teens-and-sleep>.
5. Casimira Melican and Grace Mountford (2017), *Why we've introduced a menstrual policy and you should too*, Victorian Women's Trust, <https://www.vwt.org.au/blog-menstrual-policy/>.
6. Helen Connolly, Commissioner for Children and Young People, South Australia (2021), *Menstruation Matters*, project report no. 21, Commissioner for Children and Young People, Adelaide, p. 11, <https://www.ccyp.com.au/wp-content/uploads/2022/03/Menstruation-Matters.pdf>.
7. Ibid.

Chapter 17: Navigating campus life

1. UQ News (2021), *The real struggles for 'first-in-family' university students*, media release, University of Queensland, 16 December, <https://www.uq.edu.au/news/article/2021/12/real-struggles-%E2%80%9Cfirst-family%E2%80%9D-university-students>.
2. Wendy Heywood, Paul Myers, Anastasia Powell, Gillian Meikle, Diana Nguyen (2022), *National Student Safety Survey: Report on the prevalence of sexual harassment and sexual assault among university students in 2021*, The Social Research Centre, Melbourne, pp. 1, 2, 3, <https://www.universitiesaustralia.edu.au/wp-content/uploads/2022/03/2021-NSSS-National-Report.pdf>.

References

Applebaum, A (2021), 'The new puritans', *The Atlantic*, 31 August, <https://www.theatlantic.com/magazine/archive/2021/10/new-puritans-mob-justice-canceled/619818>.

Australian Institute of Health and Welfare (2020), *National Drug Strategy Household Survey 2019*, Drug Statistics series no. 32, cat. no. PHE 270, Australian Institute of Health and Welfare, Canberra, <https://www.aihw.gov.au/getmedia/3564474e-f7ad-461c-b918-7f8de03d1294/aihw-phe-270-NDSHS-2019.pdf.aspx?inline=true>.

Australian Institute of Health and Welfare (2020), *Sexual Assault in Australia*, cat. no. FDV 5, Australian Institute of Health and Welfare, Canberra, <https://www.aihw.gov.au/getmedia/0375553f-0395-46cc-9574-d54c74fa601a/aihw-fdv-5.pdf.aspx?inline=true>.

Australian Medical Association (2021), *Confronting the nicotine vaping pandemic*, 30 September, <https://www.ama.com.au/ama-rounds/1-october-2021/articles/confronting-nicotine-vaping-pandemic>.

Brown, B (2015), *Rising Strong*, Ebury Press, London.

Brown, B (2021), *Atlas of the Heart*, Penguin Random House, London.

Button, J (2021), '"They cancelled me as a human": What nearly killed Logie winner Hugh Sheridan', *Sydney Morning Herald Good Weekend*, 20 November <https://www.smh.com.au/national/they-cancelled-me-as-a-human-what-nearly-killed-logie-winner-hugh-sheridan-20211027-p593ls.html>.

Cohen, J (2021), 'The perfectionism trap', *The Economist*, 10 August, <https://www.economist.com/1843/2021/08/10/the-perfectionism-trap>.

Connolly, H, Commissioner for Children and Young People, South Australia (2021), *Menstruation Matters*, project report no. 21, Commissioner for Children and Young People, Adelaide, <https://www.ccyp.com.au/wp-content/uploads/2022/03/Menstruation-Matters.pdf>.

REFERENCES

Connolly, H, Commissioner for Children and Young People, South Australia (2021), *Sexual Health and Education in South Australia: What young people need to know for sexual health and safety*, project report no. 22, Commissioner for Children and Young People, Adelaide, <https://www.ccyp.com.au/wp-content/uploads/2022/03/Sex-Education-in-South-Australia.pdf>.

Corrigan, K (2021), 'How to let go of your irreplaceable, unstoppable daughter', *The New York Times*, 5 September, <https://www.nytimes.com/2021/09/05/opinion/parenting-college-empty-nest-pandemic.html>.

Coulson, J (2020), *Miss-connection*, HarperCollins, Sydney.

Don't Forget the Bubbles (2019), *Gender identity – what does it mean to be male or female?*, online video, 19 April, YouTube, <https://www.youtube.com/watch/?v=qPWTSCn8uwU>.

Ducharme, J (2018), 'People are getting plastic surgery to look like Snapchat filters, doctors warn', *Time*, 5 August, <https://time.com/5357262/snapchat-plastic-surgery>.

Dunn, P (2021), *The Limited Edition Leader*, Rethink Press, United Kingdom.

The Economist (2021), 'The pandemic will spur the worldwide growth in private tutoring', 7 October, <https://www.economist.com/international/the-pandemic-will-spur-the-worldwide-growth-of-private-tutoring/21805216>.

Everymind (2021), *Guidelines on Reporting and Portrayal of Eating Disorders: A Mindframe resource for communicators*, Everymind, Newcastle, <https://butterfly.org.au/wp-content/uploads/2021/09/Mindframe-Media-Guidelines_Eating-Disorders_2021.pdf>.

Fisher, C, Waling, A, Kerr, L, Bellamy, R, Ezer, P, Mikolajczak, G, Brown, G, Carman, M, and Lucke, J (2019), *6th National Survey of Australian Secondary Students and Sexual Health 2018*, ARCSHS series no. 113, Australian Research Centre in Sex, Health and Society, La Trobe University, Melbourne, <https://www.latrobe.edu.au/__data/assets/pdf_file/0004/1031899/National-Survey-of-Secondary-Students-and-Sexual-Health-2018.pdf>.

Fitzsimmons, TW, Yates, MS and Callan, V (2018), *Hands Up for Gender Equality: A major study into confidence and career intentions of adolescent girls and boys*, AIBE Centre for Gender Equality in the Workplace, University of Queensland, Brisbane, <https://bel.uq.edu.au/files/28153/Hands_up_for_Gender_Equality.pdf>.

Guerin, N and White, V (2018), *ASSAD 2017 Statistics & Trends: Australian secondary students' use of tobacco, alcohol, over-the-counter drugs, and illicit substances*, Cancer Council Victoria, Melbourne, <https://www.health.gov.au/sites/default/files/secondary-school-students-use-of-tobacco-alcohol-and-other-drugs-in-2017.pdf>.

Hattie, J (2021), 'An ode to expertise: What have we learnt from COVID and how can we apply our learning?', paper presented at the Victorian Education State Principals Conference, August.

Heywood, W, Myers, P, Powell, A, Meikle, G, and Nguyen, D (2022), *National Student Safety Survey: Report on the prevalence of sexual harassment and sexual assault among university students in 2021*, The Social Research Centre, Melbourne <https://www.universitiesaustralia.edu.au/wp-content/uploads/2022/03/2021-NSSS-National-Report.pdf>.

King, M (2017), *Being 14*, Hachette Australia, Sydney.

King, M (2018), *Fathers and Daughters*, Hachette Australia, Sydney.

King, M (2021), *Ten-ager*, Hachette Australia, Sydney.

Knibbs, J (2018), 'Brexting: Smartphone addiction and babies', *Wild Health*, 7 August, <https://wildhealth.net.au/all-humans-have-three-lives-public-private-and-secret-gabriel-garcia-marques-privacy-has-come-out-of-the-shadows-and-into-the-mainstream-in-australia-the-level-of-repo>.

Mackesy, C (2019), *The Boy, the Mole, the Fox and the Horse*, Ebury Press, London.

McCrindle, M and Fell, A (2021), *Generation Alpha*, Hachette Australia, Sydney.

Melican, C and Mountford, G (2017), *Why we've introduced a menstrual policy and you should too*, Victorian Women's Trust, <https://www.vwt.org.au/blog-menstrual-policy/>.

Mitchell, M (2019), *Everyday Resilience*, Big Sky Publishing, Sydney.

Moller, H, Ivers, R, Cullen, P, Rogers, K, Boufous, S, Patton, G and Senserrick, T (2021), 'Risky youth to risky adults: Sustained increased risk of crash in the DRIVE study 13 years on', *Preventive Medicine*, vol. 153, <https://www.sciencedirect.com/science/article/pii/S0091743521003558>.

New South Wales Health (n.d.), *Are electronic cigarettes and e-liquids safe?*, New South Wales Government fact sheet, <https://www.health.nsw.gov.au/tobacco/Factsheets/e-cigs-are-they-safe.pdf>.

Orenstein, P (2016), *Girls & Sex*, HarperCollins, New York.

Paul, K (2021), '"She opens the app and gets bombarded": Parents on Instagram, teens and eating disorders', *The Guardian*, 13 October, <https://www.theguardian.com/technology/2021/oct/12/instagram-eating-disorders-teen-girls-parents>.

Queensland Government (2022), *Protect your P-plater*, StreetSmarts, <https://streetsmarts.initiatives.qld.gov.au/parents/protect-your-p-plater>.

Queensland Health (2019), *The known harms of e-cigarettes and vaping*, Queensland Government, <https://www.health.qld.gov.au/news-events/news/known-harms-of-e-cigarettes-vaping-smoking>.

Quick Parrish, A (2014), 'Advice to high school graduates: You are not special', *The Atlantic*, 8 May, <https://www.theatlantic.com/education/archive/2014/05/advice-to-the-graduates-you-are-not-special/361463>.

Resilient Youth Australia (2021), *Student Resilience Survey: Cross-sectional report*, Resilient Youth Australia, Melbourne, <https://resilientyouth.org/survey>.

Santora, J (2022), *Key influencer marketing statistics you need to know for 2022*, Influencer Marketing Hub, <https://influencermarketinghub.com/influencer-marketing-statistics>.

Savage, G (2021), 'Want to improve our education system? Stop seeking advice from far-off gurus and encourage expertise in schools', *The Conversation*, 21 September, <https://theconversation.com/want-to-improve-our-education-system-stop-seeking-advice-from-far-off-gurus-and-encourage-expertise-in-schools-165320>.

Sharp, G (2021), *Changing the chatter on body image with the help of a chatbot called KIT*, Lens, Monash University, 2 July, <https://lens.monash.edu/@medicine-health/2021/07/02/1383462/changing-the-chatter-on-body-image-with-the-help-of-a-chatbot-called-kit>.

Sleep Health Foundation and Australasian Sleep Association (2020), *Transforming the Sleep Health of Australians: Pre budget submission 2020–21*, Sleep Health Foundation and Australasian Sleep Association, Sydney, <https://treasury.gov.

au/sites/default/files/2020-09/115786_SLEEP_HEALTH_FOUNDATION_
AND_AUSTRALIASIAN_SLEEP_ASSOCIATION_-_SUBMISSION_2.pdf>.

Stetka, B (2017), 'Extended adolescence: When 25 is the new 18', *Scientific American*, 19 September, <https://www.scientificamerican.com/article/extended-adolescence-when-25-is-the-new-181>.

Stynes, Y and Kang, M (2020), *Welcome to Consent!*, Hardie Grant Books, Melbourne.

Suni, E (2022), *Teens and sleep*, American Sleep Foundation, <https://www.sleepfoundation.org/teens-and-sleep>.

Teach.Us.Consent.™ (2021), <https://www.teachusconsent.com>.

Telfer, MM, Tollit, MA, Pace, CC and Pang, KC (2020), *Australian Standards of Care and Treatment Guidelines for Trans and Gender Diverse Children and Adolescents*, version 1.3, Royal Children's Hospital, Melbourne, <https://www.rch.org.au/uploadedFiles/Main/Content/adolescent-medicine/australian-standards-of-care-and-treatment-guidelines-for-trans-and-gender-diverse-children-and-adolescents.pdf>.

Terhaag, S and Rioseco, P (2021), 'COVID-19 has led to a sharp increase in depression and anxiety', *The Economist*, 11 October, <https://www.economist.com/graphic-detail/2021/10/11/covid-19-has-led-to-a-sharp-increase-in-depression-and-anxiety>.

Terhaag, S and Rioseco, P (2021), *Self-injury among adolescents*, Growing Up in Australia Snapshot Series, issue 4, Australian Institute of Family Studies, Melbourne, <https://growingupinaustralia.gov.au/research-findings/snapshots/self-injury-among-adolescents>.

Tiller, E, Fildes, J, Hall, S, Hicking, V, Greenland, N, Liyanarachchi, D, and Di Nicola, K (2020), *Youth Survey Report 2020*, Mission Australia, Sydney.

Turnbull, D (2021), 'Let's talk about who we are online – because that is who we are', *Sydney Morning Herald*, 10 October, <https://www.smh.com.au/politics/federal/let-s-talk-about-who-we-are-online-because-that-is-who-we-are-20211008-p58yfy.html>.

UQ News (2021), *The real struggles for 'first-in-family' university students*, media release, University of Queensland, 16 December, <https://www.uq.edu.au/news/article/2021/12/real-struggles-%E2%80%9Cfirst-family%E2%80%9D-university-students>.

Warren, D and Swami, N (2019), 'Teenagers and sex' in *The Longitudinal Study of Australian Children Annual Statistical Report 2018*, Australian Institute of Family Studies, pp. 47–56, <https://growingupinaustralia.gov.au/sites/default/files/publication-documents/lsac-asr-2018-chap5-teenagers-and-sex_0.pdf>.

Wehbe, J, McKeon, S, Dempsey, D, McConnell, T, Monardo, G, Hodge, J, Glass, M, Jensen, J (2021), *18 & Lost? So Were We*, Doohat Labs, Sydney.

Acknowledgements

This book is owed to all our teen daughters as they travel the road to adulthood. To the almost 1000 teens who answered my questions, thank you. I promised to tell your stories and I hope I have not let you down. Thanks for your openness, your lack of judgement of each other and the passion you wear on your sleeves. Thanks for the time you spent helping me; I hope I'm returning the favour.

To our educators, I remain in awe. Your schedules are now filled with so much more than a curriculum. But it's your care for our teens and your ability to think strategically that stand out – and I wish you had a greater role in the policies and platforms that underpin the national education system. To those school principals, leaders and teachers who spent time answering my questions, thanks for doing that – and for what you do every single day. The same thanks goes to our health professionals – and I met so many wonderful GPs and psychologists and counsellors during this project. Their aim, unanimously, is to help our girls become awesome, content adults. Thanks goes to

Robyn Holland, who helped me access relevant psychological expertise, and Loren Bridge and Teva Smith from the Alliance of Girls' Schools Australasia.

To everyone who volunteered their time – from economists to social demographers, researchers, academics and worried parents – thank you. I hope this helps answer the original email from a concerned parent that prompted the research.

The team at Hachette play the role of parents during the birth of a book: cajoling and encouraging, providing guidance and certainly discipline to some of my long stories! Thanks to the publisher who keeps encouraging me to write books, Vanessa Radnidge, editor Rebecca Allen, who sets a new bar in patience, Susan Jarvis, proofreader Meaghan Amor and Melissa Wilson. To PR supremo Emily Lighezzolo, who I have not yet seen without a smile – we need more smiles in the world, Emily, and it's hard not to feel yours. To those who read my manuscript and provided advice, especially Majella Dwan, I appreciate your time and comments.

Finally to my family. My hubby David, an old newspaper editor, kept me focused on what was new in the research – what I could tell you that you might not know. That was invaluable advice. My two teen girls, while not in this book, certainly provided advice on everything from the colour of the cover to the best pathway to explaining those issues so crucial to their generation. *L Platers* is immeasurably better for your support.

Index

Abel, Amanda 15, 32, 37, 106, 119, 129,
    145, 146, 332–3
'academic anxiety' 138
'academic buoyancy' 138, 139–40
adolescence
    anxiety 127
    body image 157
    brain 18
    confidence drop 126, 174
    gender dysphoria 210
    identity, discovery of 206, 209, 217
    social degradation 310
    tunnel analogy 328–9
adrenaline 266
adulthood 189, 318, 320, 323
    perception 189
    'practicing' 19
    transition, eating disorders and 155
    university college as stepping stone 318
    voice 73
    Year 13 as start 320
adulting 18–19, 189, 191, 197
advertisements, online 108–11
alcohol see drugs and alcohol
Amnesty International 67
anorexia nervosa 153, 154, 155
anxiety 124, 142, 143, 153, 162, 176, 217,
    337
    'academic' 138

advice 140–1
alcohol and 244
ATAR 24, 25, 132
avoidance and 135, 187
climate change 63
comparison 4
complexity 126
COVID-19 10, 46, 49, 58, 125–7
dam analogy 124, 136
driver's licence 186
exercise, impact of 265–6
gender differences 138–40
genetics 126
helpful activities 137
'name it and tame it' 137
normalising 125, 141
perfectionism and 133–5, 143
physiological response 128–9
post-school 89, 293–4, 306, 324
school and 126, 129–30, 133–4, 138,
    282
sensitive personality 187–8
sleep deprivation 258, 263, 265
social connection, lack of 89
social media and 101, 127–8
'uncertain control' 138–9
unpredictability as driver 265
validation 136–7
'worry' and 131, 338

Arbuckle, Christie 158
Archard, Dr Nicole 49–50, 66, 126,
    137–8, 168–9, 171, 175–6, 257–8,
    336–7
Attention Deficit Hyperactivity Disorder
    (ADHD) 25, 31–2, 324
Australasian Sleep Association 258
Australian Secondary Students' Alcohol
    and Drug Survey 242–3
Australian Tertiary Admission Rank
    (ATAR)
  anxiety and 18, 24, 25, 132
  burnout 317
  career choice 302–3
  concerns 26, 34–5
  focus 24–5
  gender differences 21–2
  life-determiner 4
  scaling algorithm 22
  significance 20–1
  success and 169, 279, 284
  university admission 22, 34–5
autonomy 193
  bodily see bodily autonomy

Being 14 6, 330
Bell, Dr Amanda 301, 302, 312, 320–1,
    322–3, 325–6
belonging 12, 14, 42, 56, 78, 82, 90, 283,
    301, 326
binge-drinking 159
Blackwood, Beth 76
bodily autonomy 221
body image 6, 15–16, 90, 101, 116, 142
  eating disorders and 152, 153, 154
  'function over form' 157
  heart of issues 102
  positive 156, 157
  social media and 107, 112, 114, 146
  vulnerable age 329
boundaries
  relationships and 117–18, 235–6
  testing 209, 212, 245, 253
boys
  ADHD diagnosis 31
  alcohol use 242, 243
  anxiety 126, 138–40
  career and education, understanding of
    280
  dating violence 235
  expectations 237
  gender-diverse 209
  neurological development 236–7

online harassment 101, 227
  sexual assault 230
  success, perceptions of 280
  tertiary education 292
'boys will be boys' 226, 236–7
'brexting' 123
Brisbane Girls Grammar School 12
Brown, Brené 82
bulimia 153, 154
bullying 44–5, 81, 146, 221
  online see cyberbullying
burnout 317
Butterfly Foundation 154, 156

Canberra Girls Grammar School
  The House program 74–5
'cancel culture' 76–9
capacity, building 166, 172
careers
  ATAR ranking as basis 302–3
  choice 281, 302–3, 306
  COVID-19, impact of 55
  focus on 282
  friendship skills, role of 88
  identity and 275
  maths and science 26
  parental expectation 276, 293–4, 303
  pathways 18, 26, 106
  success, perceptions of 280–2
Carey Baptist Grammar School
    (Melbourne) 14, 130, 268
character development 325
charity, principle of 77
choice 80–2
  academic subject options 2, 27, 32
  careers 280–1, 306
  feminism and 221–2
  friends', criticism of 174
  friendships and 81–5
  paradox of 18
  post-school 318–19
  school uniforms 214
  tertiary education 131, 301, 302, 306–7
circadian rhythms 258–9
Clarke, Hannah 234
Clayfield College (Brisbane) 14, 24
coercive control 188, 196, 222, 233–4, 235
Commissioner for Children and Young
    People 231
communication
  art of 67
  open 91, 97–8
  'serve and return' interaction 98

comparison 3, 4, 5, 6, 14, 17, 88, 293, 337
  social media and 101, 113, 114, 127–8
confidence
  detractions 168
  employment and 166–7
  experience ad 169
  factors generating 167
  genetic blueprint 174
  growth 180–1
  leadership, correlation with 177–8
  learning to drive 187
  mistakes, role of 169, 177, 197
  parental 97, 192
  realistic assessment 173
  role of parents 175–7
  'saving' child and 176
  schools and 175, 315
  teenager perceptions 171–3
  'tiny voice', encouraging 174
  university students 324
connection 1
  COVID-19, impact of 29, 42, 45–6, 54,
    56, 57, 58–9, 319
  lack of 89, 319–20
  parents 16, 90–3, 97–8
  real people, with 123, 319
  school 25
  social issues and interests 71–2
  social media and 17, 123, 319
  'still-face' mother–infant experiments
    123
  university 319
Consent and Sex podcast 230
Consent Labs 232, 233
contentment 276
Contos, Chanel 63, 223, 224–5, 232
Corinda State High School (Brisbane) 13,
  315–16
cortisol 266
cosmetic surgery 102–3
cotton-wool parents 175
Coulson, Dr Justin 4–5, 97–8, 236–7, 238,
  304–5, 339
  Miss-connection 97
courage 64, 334
Cousins, Dr Andrew 14, 24, 88, 97, 297,
  334
COVID-19 9–12, 19, 28–30, 33
  alcohol consumption 252
  anxiety 126–7, 135–6
  creativity 56
  'disconnect' 45–6
  education, impact on 51–6, 130–1

employment, impact on 43–4, 49, 299
independent learning 29, 52, 53, 200–1
legacy 59–60
mental health challenge 44–5, 49, 58–9,
  130–1, 150, 322
parental involvement 56–7
related terminology 50
rites of passage 19, 42, 321
social life, impact on 9, 19, 41–3, 45–7,
  57–8, 310–11
uncertainty 48–9, 286–8, 311
university life 309–12, 314, 320, 321–2
video gaming 106
cyberbullying 101–2

Dalton, Susan 33–4, 38, 55–6, 193, 334
'dark ads' 109, 329
dating violence 235
debt 320
  good versus bad 191
  HECS 320
  household, changes to 288–9
Dempsey, Byron 17–18, 35, 191, 230, 278,
  297–8, 305, 308
Dennis, Majella 124, 206, 207, 213, 214,
  217, 235, 281, 317, 333
depression 107, 142, 143, 152, 153, 155,
  162, 258, 324
  see also mental illness
difference, acceptance of 6–7, 169
Dillon, Paul 29–30, 241–2, 246, 252, 254
direction 14
'disengagement rate' 30
disordered eating see eating disorders
diversity 2, 7, 77
  gender see gender diversity
Dober, Carly 29, 64, 70–1, 103, 113, 187,
  217, 219, 321
dopamine 113, 115
Douglas, Linda 5, 48–9, 53, 78–9, 138,
  200–1, 338–9
DownAgers 19
downtime 335
drive, learning to 182–9
Driven Young podcast 17, 35, 191, 230,
  278, 297
Drug and Alcohol Research and Training
  Australia (DATA) 241
drugs and alcohol 162, 241–5
  advice for parents 252–3
  alcohol energy drinks 243
  binge-drinking 159, 240
  COVID-19, consumption during 252

illicit drug use 245–6
metabolism, gender differences 240, 241
parental attitudes 244–5, 251–2, 253
prescription medication, interaction with 254
sexual assault and 223
Drum, The 69–70

eating disorders 25, 90, 143, 146
age of onset 154, 329
cause 154–5
communal responsibility 158–9
disordered eating 153–6, 269
varieties 153–4
warning signs 158
e-cigarettes 248, 250–1
see also vaping
ecstasy (E) 246–7
education
secondary *see* school
tertiary *see* TAFE; university
elastic band theory 170
'emotional brain' 122
emotional regulation 161
employment
see also careers
casual jobs 166
customer abuse 164–5
gender composition 285, 289, 307
opportunities 289–90
outlook 285–6
skill shortages 303–4
success and 281–2, 284
university students 320
empowerment 65–6, 68, 74, 121, 223
endorphins 159–60
engagement 45, 71, 75
parental 95, 97, 176
Enlighten Education 15
expectations
comparison and 282
cultural and social 171, 304
family 23
friends 115
gender differences 236–7
'inflation' 292
lowering 257
parental 284, 292–3, 297, 302–5, 307
perfectionism and 127, 133
self 9, 146, 147, 171
workload 33

Facebook 108, 117
failure 178–9, 180, 340
fairness 199–200
Fanning, Ellen 69–70
Fathers and Daughters 330
feminism 221
fight or flight response 266
financial literacy 191–2, 308
financial security 278
Fitzsimmons, Dr Terry 166–7, 173, 177–8, 179–80, 280, 281
Forbes, Jody 12–13, 86, 99, 114, 200, 235–6
Francis, Deborrah 6–7, 14, 50, 60, 89, 170, 206, 310, 336
friendships 9, 10, 11, 16, 33, 39, 78, 257
analysis 86–7
choice and 81–5
'coexisting' 85, 93
COVID-19, impact of 85, 89
discerning 87
drama 81
'groups' 86
healthy and unhealthy 235
maturity 82
myth 87–8
networking 88
social media and 87, 89–90, 115–16, 146–7
transactional 83, 87
university 88–9, 322
FRIES acronym 224

gamma-aminobutyric acid (GABA) 266
gap year 298–301
gender diversity 208, 209, 215, 216, 219, 228, 231
gender dysmorphia 217–18
gender dysphoria 203, 207, 208–9, 210
gender fluidity 67, 205, 219
gender identity 9, 16, 203–6, 216
advice to parents 217–19
school uniforms and 203, 212–14
sex distinguished 204
single-sex schools 203, 205, 215, 216
gender identity disorder 207
gender-neutral parenting 177
gender spectrum 212
generalist generation 1, 8
Generation Alpha 2
Generation Z 2, 76
generational chasm 5–6
Gilbert, Elizabeth 338

Golding, Penny 17, 33, 42, 45, 59, 60, 159, 161, 252, 284, 286, 299
'good girl' syndrome 236–7
Goodwin, Dr Kristy 104–5, 121–2, 335
group think 329

harassment, online 115, 227, 323
Health At Every Size (HAES) principle 271
HECS fees 320
helicopter parents 175, 190, 200
Higgins, Brittany 51, 63, 144, 232
housing affordability 19, 63, 70, 71, 288

idealism 287
identity 1–2, 38–9, 147, 169
  defining 8
  development 86
  formation 15, 154
  gender see gender identity
  post-school 307, 322
imposter syndrome 9, 179–80
inclusion 2, 77, 228
independence
  casual jobs 166
  driving analogy 188–9
  leaving home 200
  parents, from 189–92, 322–3, 341
independent learning 29, 52, 53, 200–1, 312
influence 8, 65, 68, 87, 90, 107
influencers 1, 76, 110, 113, 116, 120, 329
Instagram 17, 87, 105, 108–9, 111, 117, 170–1, 190, 224, 257, 261
instant gratification 89–90, 118
iron deficiency 272–3
isolation 142, 146
  COVID-19 10, 12, 42, 44, 47, 50, 58, 320, 322
  university students 89, 311, 319, 320, 322, 323

jackhammer/hummingbird analogy 338
Jamieson, Helen 13, 97, 316

'Karen' 165
Kearney, Flo 319, 324
Kids Helpline 17, 45, 71, 94, 145, 146, 161, 199, 310–11, 316, 319–20, 335
Kiepe, Kim 3, 66–7, 72, 73, 75, 178–9
KIT chatbot 157

labour market 285–6
  see also careers; employment

lawnmower parents 175
leadership
  confidence and 177–8, 179
  development 167–8
  opportunity 290
  roles 167–8
  self 302
  success and 280
Lee, Laura 15–16, 87, 112, 147, 170, 203, 212–13, 271, 282–3, 284, 333
leverage 65
LGBTQIA+ people 39, 202–3, 228–9
  see also transgender people
life experience 325
life skills 35–6, 325
Life360 194, 195, 196
Loreto College Marryatville (Adelaide) 49, 168
Loveday, Melissa 302, 305–6, 313
Lyneham, Kellie 14, 130, 268, 333

Mander, Dr David 30
Marcroft, Sally 56
Martin, Professor Andrew 31–2, 138, 139–41
McCrindle, Mark 1, 2, 12, 18–19, 41, 42, 43–4, 65, 253–4, 287, 303–4, 325
Mackesy, Charlie
  The Boy, the Mole, the Fox and the Horse 54–5
McLean, Susan 101, 230, 233
McMullen, Dr Danielle 31, 143–4, 155, 158, 198–9, 250, 251, 254–5, 269, 270, 320, 335
Meath, Dr Toni 50–1, 54, 268, 333
media literacy programs 113
Medicare 199, 200
melatonin 261
Melbourne Girls Grammar School 50, 333
menstrual leave 272
mental health
  breadth of 145
  challenges 142–5, 147, 153, 329
  COVID-19 and 42, 44–5, 49, 58–9, 130, 150
  gender dysphoria 210
  gender identity and 217–19
  professional assistance 151–2, 218–19
  role of schools 150
  sleep and 122, 258–9
  social media, impact of 119, 146
  university students 317–18, 324

mental illness
  acceptance 149–50
  anxiety *see* anxiety
  diagnosis 31, 145
  emergence 33, 145
  multi-factorial causes 146
  parental responses 135–6, 150–1
  transition periods, coincidence with 154, 155, 160
mentors 3–4, 72, 92
methylenedioxymethamphetamine (MDMA) 246–7
Miami State High School (Gold Coast) 33, 38, 55, 193
Miller, Dannielle 15, 77–8, 87, 222, 229, 235, 239, 262, 270, 303, 333
'mindful moments' 118–19
mindfulness 138, 157
Mitchell, Michelle 92, 150, 159, 173–5, 192
  Everyday Resilience 92, 173
Modern Parent, The 113, 273
Monro, Reverend Dr Anita 180–1, 317, 319, 324, 325
Moreton Bay College (Brisbane) 25, 34, 269
  Keep Learning wellbeing framework 269
motivation 59, 138, 268
  COVID-19, impact of 10, 28–9, 46, 47, 51–2, 57, 59, 267, 273, 274
Mouawad, Georgette 28, 321, 323, 324
Mount Alvernia College (Brisbane) 302
muck-up day 42
Mullins, Saxon 234

National Student Safety Survey 323
neuroplasticity 60
night owls 261
non-binary identity 203, 205, 212, 216, 219, 231
nuance 13, 264

Oglethorpe, Martine 113, 116–21, 273–4
opinions
  expression and validation 69–70
  opposing 77–8
  self-censorship 77
orthorexia nervosa 153–4
over-scheduling 37
Owen, Anna 74–5, 77, 299, 318, 339

panic attacks 129, 142, 151
parents
  advice 328, 330–1, 337, 342
  alcohol, attitudes towards 244–5, 251–2, 253
  attention 99
  building confidence, role in 175–6
  challenges 95–7
  competition between 284
  confidence of 97, 192
  detachment from 93
  divorce 93–4
  education, involvement in 56–7, 95–7
  engagement 95, 97, 176
  expectations 284, 292–3, 297, 302–5, 307
  fathers, engagement of 95
  feelings, containment of 99
  grieving process 339
  healthy eating behaviour, modelling 270, 271
  independence from 189–92, 322–3, 341
  mental health challenges, response to 135–6, 150–1
  positive attributes 97
  problem solving 16
  reconnection 98
  relationship between 238–9
  relationship with 16, 90–3, 145, 199–200, 218, 317, 322–3, 328, 330–2, 337
  schools and 37–8, 193
  separation 93–5
  'serve and return' interaction 98
  sexual relationships, education about 237
  success, perceptions of 275–8, 284, 297, 305
  tracking apps 194–6
  'unhinging from' 174
parties 254
pastoral care 313
peer pressure 242
perfection 4, 5, 13, 170, 337
perfectionism 6, 132–5, 143, 257–8, 265
period pain 271–2
period products 272
Peter, Matthew 65, 285–90
physical activity 123, 137, 257, 265, 266, 268, 269, 271, 273
Pierpoint, Andrew 34, 37, 144–5, 150, 262, 267–7, 334
popularity 169

pornography 102, 226–7, 231
puberty blocking 210–11, 216
public debate 70
purpose 7, 14, 36, 42, 161
Pymble Ladies' College (Sydney) 300, 315

racism 7, 76
resilience 13, 44, 54, 75, 139, 169, 176,
    178, 321, 325
Resilient Youth Australia 248
Richardson, Dr Jodi 127–8, 131, 135, 137,
    141, 265, 266, 337
Riordan, Toni 10, 45, 54, 56, 64, 207, 236,
    337
rites of passage
    COVID-19, impact of 42, 321
    driving 183
role models 2
    choice 3, 72–3
    drugs and alcohol 251–2
    healthy eating 156, 270
    parents 97, 156, 251–2, 270, 284
    power 72
Rowlands, Danni 154, 156–7
Ruyton Girls' School (Melbourne) 5

SA Commissioner for Youth and Young
    People 272
'safe place' 254–5
Sanders, Brent 230
Santa Sabina College (Sydney) 53
school 17, 20–1, 22–3, 26–8
    anxiety 129–30, 133–4, 138
    confidence, building 175
    eating disorder prevention 156
    expectations 284, 292–3, 297, 302–5,
        307
    'hand-holding' 313, 316
    parental involvement 56–7, 95–7
    post-secondary planning 291–2, 301–2
    single-sex, gender identity and 203, 205,
        215, 216
    sleep, interaction with 261–3
    STEM pathway 20, 27–8, 282
    structure 316–17, 319
    subject selection 2, 20, 22–8, 32, 34–5,
        95, 176, 183, 281–2, 284, 296, 306,
        334
    support 96, 316–18
    uniforms 203, 212–14
    university compared 309, 311–14
    'unlearning' 308
    workload 33, 36–7, 56, 129, 144

school refusal 25, 135, 153, 213
Schoolies 292
Scott, Professor Mark 320, 326, 327,
    334–5
self-acceptance 5, 74
self-assuredness 170, 180
self-censorship 77
self-concept 168
self-doubt 9, 217, 283
self-efficacy 169, 178, 297
self-esteem 116, 145, 146, 157
self-harm 155, 159–161, 218, 329
self-judgement 6, 74, 101, 282, 283
self-talk 13
sense of self 6, 71, 147, 161, 168, 325
sensitivity 187
sex
    gender identity distinguished 204
sex education 227–9, 231
    contemporary content, need for 231
    criticism of delivery 220–1, 229
    'dumbed down' 222
    inclusivity, eschewing 228
    overhaul 224–5
sexual assault 50, 77, 234, 238
    boys' perceptions 230
    Contos petition 224–5
    feminism, importance of 221
    parental relationships and 238
    personal accounts 225–8
    pressure 222–3
    statistics 225, 323
    support 233
    Tame experience 232
    university campus 323
sexual health 231
sexual relationships
    assault 50–1
    coercion 238
    consent 50, 63, 66, 73, 77, 221–4,
        228–35, 239, 308
    FRIES acronym 224
    healthy and unhealthy 231, 233, 235,
        238
    parental education 237–8
    pressures 229–31
    roles and responsibilities 228–9, 236–7
    statistics 237
    'stealthing' 221, 224
shame 75, 77, 218, 225
'sharenting' 123
Sharp, Dr Gemma 153, 155, 157
Shaw, Julie 300

Sheerazi, Noor 183, 187–8
Siegel, Dr Daniel 137
Skerman, Paulina 53, 60, 114, 116, 117, 333–4
skill markers, focus on 325
sleep 257, 258
    exercise and 265
    factors affecting 260–1
    hygiene 258, 262–3
    importance 263
    poor, impact of 258
    quantity 259–60
    school timetable, interaction with 261–3
    screens and 122–3, 258–9, 263
Sleep Health Foundation 258
slut-shaming 225
smartphones 2, 4, 103, 121
    average daily use 8
    choice and 80
    connections, replacement of 273
    'dark ads' 329
    displacement of needs 122–3
    influence 81
    instant gratification and 118
    omnipresence 117
    relationship with 103–4
    sleep and 121, 258
Snapchat 105, 117, 257, 261
    dysmorphia 103
    surgery 4, 103
social capital 179
social development 325
social issues
    activism 67–8
    campaigns 67
    'cancel culture' and 76–7
    charity support 76
    climate change 8, 50, 55, 61, 62, 63, 64, 65, 71
    expression of opinion 68–70
social justice 73–4, 207
social media 13, 68, 78
    advertisements 108–10, 329
    algorithms 108, 115
    benefits 120
    body image and 102–3, 109–10, 112, 116, 146
    comparison through 114, 127
    confidence, relationship with 168
    critical analysis 192, 264
    dating 310
    'digital traces' 108
    displacement of needs 122

formal dress pages 100–2
friendships and 87, 89–90
'girl next door' models 113
impact 107–8, 114–15, 118–19, 146
instant gratification and 118
marketing 114, 116
models 113
online generation 319
parenting and 123
perfectionism and 134
pervasive nature 144
relationship with 105–7, 111, 329
seduction 329
sleep and 265
social activism 64, 66
thoughtful use 77, 119, 122
untruths 117
usage 17, 103–9, 116, 119–22
social skills 338
societal inequality 229
'soft skills 35, 177, 302, 315
Somerville House (Brisbane) 3, 67, 319
Sparrow, Rebecca 44, 78, 87–8, 89, 91, 99, 307, 312, 338
sport 38, 267
    benefits 167, 187, 266–9
    gender identity and 203, 214, 216
    perfectionism 134, 265
St Aidan's Anglican Girls' School (Brisbane) 10, 56, 64
St Margaret's Berwick Grammar (Melbourne) 7, 14
Stahl, Garth 317–18
Stathis, Dr Stephen 204–5, 207–112, 215–17, 339
'stealthing' 221, 224
Stewart, Janet 25, 34, 89, 269
'struggle for power' 199
student agency 53–4, 201
Student Resilience Survey Cross-Sectional Report 248
student voice 53–4, 75, 201
success
    academic 21, 24, 169, 279, 283–4
    expectation 284
    factors 169, 179
    internal motivation 160
    leadership versus career-oriented 280
    material 276
    parent versus teen perceptions 8, 275–8, 284, 297, 305
    right to 65
    traditional relevance 278

suicide 147, 217–18
Suicide Six 27–8

t (testosterone) parties 211
TAFE 284, 294, 302, 316, 341
Tame, Grace 51, 63, 79, 144, 232
Teach.Us.Consent.™ platform 224
team sports 167
technology
  career opportunities 289–90, 304
  consent and 233
  control over 263, 335
  detox 104
  downside 287
  phones see smartphones
  reliance on 273
Ten-ager 134, 235, 330
tertiary education 295
  university see university
'third gender' 212
TikTok 1, 105, 107, 117
time management 9, 17, 32, 38, 143, 256,
  257, 308, 317
time poverty 264, 269
tobacco smoking 251, 252
tracking apps 194–6
transgender people 208, 212, 216–18, 219,
  228, 231, 323
travel 167
Trickett, Libby 162–3, 334
trust 195, 197, 198, 333, 334
Tucker, Josie 45, 71–2, 145–7, 161,
  199–200, 310–11, 319–20, 335–6

Uber Eats 269
university
  admission pathways 35, 293
  advice 334–5
  attributes for success 324–5
  colleges 318–19
  COVID-19, impact of 309–12, 314,
   321–2
  delivery 326–7
  dropout rate 304
  engagement challenges 326–7
  expectation 292–3, 297, 303–4
  first family member 317–18
  focus 297, 304–5

  friendships 88–9, 322
  mental health issues 317–18, 323–4
  parental relationship 322–3
  rural students 325
  sexual assault 323
  social aspect, changes in 320, 326
  structure 309, 311–15, 317, 319
University of Sydney 326

values 276
van der Nagel, Dr Emily 108–9, 110–111
vaping
  danger 249
  ingredients 250–1
  opinions 247
  peer pressure 242
  regulation 249–50
  statistics 248–9
victim blaming 221
Victorian Women's Trust 272
video games 106, 168
voice
  challenging 73
  change, encouraging 74
  dismissing 68, 71, 331–2
  finding 53, 62–6, 72, 175
  listening to 68–71, 78, 332, 340
  validating 68, 79

Wan, Angie 232–3
'whole' person 256
Wimmera Development Association 56
'wired and tired' 122–3
wisdom 339
work–life balance 257, 264–5, 273, 276, 282
Wyse, Nikki 301, 315

Year 13 12, 301
  anxiety 324
  COVID-19, impact on 29, 41, 43, 309,
   316
  friendship changes 86
  key developmental stage 320
  new beginning 322
Young, Nicole 17, 101, 135, 169, 229–30,
  263, 322
YouTube 105, 174, 261
Yu, Dr Joyce 232